Dubosc & Landowski

Environmental Architecture

Introduction by
Jacopo della Fontana

Photographers Credits

Jacky Charrier
Stephane Couturier (Archi Press)
Guy Depollier
Herve Hughes
Patrick Manez & Anne Favret (Archi Press)
Jean Marie Monthiers
Pino Mussi
Dahliette Sucheyre

Editorial Director USA
Pierantonio Giacoppo

Chief Editor of Collection
Maurizio Vitta

Publishing Coordinator
Franca Rottola

Graphic Design
Paola Polastri

Editing
Martyn J. Anderson

Colour-separation
Litofilms Italia, Bergamo

Printing
Poligrafiche Bolis, Bergamo

First published February 1998

ISBN 88-7838-034-2

Contents

5 Structure and Architecture *by Jacopo della Fontana*
9 Works
10 Le Castel Eiffel Housing Complex
14 Saturne III Housing Complex
20 Marcel Dassault Housing Complex
24 Kronos Housing Complex
28 Sollac Research Center
32 National School of Statistics and Economic Affairs
36 Departmental Assembly
40 Pasteur Gymnasium
44 Town Hall
50 D'Auguesseau Housing Complex
54 Architecture Atelier
60 Amitié Housing Complex
64 West Side Complex
68 Le Vénérie Housing Complex
72 Space Museum
76 Gérard Philippe Elementary School
80 Proposal for a Church
84 Synagogue
88 Parc des Taillées Housing Complex
92 Academy of Music
98 Projects in Progress
106 List of works
108 Biographies

Structure and Architecture

by Jacopo della Fontana

*Celui qui veille modestement quelques moutons
sous les etoiles,
s'il prend conscience de son rôle,
se retrouve plus que serviteur:
il est une sentinelle et,
chaque sentinelle est responsable de tout
l'empire.*

Antoine de Saint-Exupéry

The history of architecture has been written in the form of a succession of ideas in a sort of historical continuum, it has also been interpreted as a series of sudden breaks with tradition or, alternatively, as a form of technological determinism in which building innovation go along what has already been experimented with in industry or, more specifically, in economics and science. Whatever your point of view, whether you view it as an innovating within continuity, propositive break with well established practices, or process of technological research, all three aspects are found in the work of the "Dubosc & Landowski Architecture and Style Workshop". Nevertheless, we need to point out a few things about each of these separate approaches.

Glancing briefly through the pages that follow, it is immediately obvious that these two French architects have dedicated their careers to creating their own special meta-project, renewing and elaborating upon this sense of continuity through the opportunities provided by peculiar features of site locations and by the clients for whom they work. All this is clearly part of a deliberate process, as opposed to the "usual unfolding" of current building procedures, and, most significantly, the experimentation it involves, ultimately rests on a great "love" for "meccano" structures.

As a psychologist could explain more accurately, in any love affair our romantic feelings do not really depend upon the eye or aesthetic considerations, it is actually the mind and its mad bounds forward in pursuit of new and unexplored frontiers that triggers off and sustains our interest in another person.

Similarly, Dubosc & Landowski have searched for, experimented on and radically revised a construction method hinging primarily around metal scaffolding and a system of beams and columns. The technique also draws on a box-structure coating technique and on light, efficient building structures carefully gauged to the constantly changing demands of their users. Originally focused on housing projects, their experimentation has now widened its horizons to encompass architecture in general, touching on both public buildings and the services sector and constantly backed up by the great desire of these two workmates to make a cultural impact on the institutions, academic environment, and business sector in general. Both actually teach in and are members of scientific institutions in the building sector. Right from the very first projects that attracted attention to their work, like for instance the "Castel Eiffel" housing complex in Dijon, certain key features were already evident. Firstly, the deliberate attempt to free the site plan and functional layout from any structural constraints or restrictions. The building-system's main structure supports all the other elements - from the partitions to the roof - but it does not serve any other additional purposes in their designs. At most, it takes on a communicative-aesthetic role designed to highlight its peculiar function in the overall design. Functions are kept separate and materials are chosen for their contribution to the building's overall flexibility and lightness. The site plan of the "Castel Eiffel" housing complex stands out for its structural simplicity and efficiency.

The spatial complexity of its section, divided over two or three levels for each apartment, actually adds to the pleasure of living in this complex. Even though one of the two facades is more "urban" and closed over the roadway, and the other is more "private", opening up through glass windows onto a small garden backing onto a wide valley, they both express the same stylistic freedom expressed in the structural design of the zinc-coated tubular metal columns marking the structural pattern on top of the outside skin.

It was Le Corbusier who opened up the way to separating self-contained structures from the main facade by setting back the supporting columns of his Maison

Domino from its main facade; he then taught how to enrich the spatial experience of inhabitable cells with so-called double-height living rooms. Nevertheless, most of his work hinged around the use of reinforced concrete, sanctioning its supremacy over metal structures through his later projects in particular. The use of steel (and both iron and cast iron before that) as a building material has never been very popular, perhaps because it was "the first artificial material in the history of Architecture" (W. Benjamin) or because it was first discovered and exploited to its full potential by people who did not adhere to the reigning mentality in the late XIXth century. It was, of course, all right to use it as a back-up hidden behind huge facades or for engineering purposes in the construction of industrial buildings or temporary structures, but that was all; later, in the early XXth century, it was even camouflaged behind a naturalistic stylistic idiom (liberty) in stark contrast to its own "artificial" nature.

France initially played an important part, second only to Anglo-Saxon countries, in the development of iron constructions. We need only remember men like Labruste, Eiffel, Dutert, Contamin, Baltard and Guimard.

France went on to play an even more important role in its replacement by a rival material, reinforced concrete, thanks to such famous names as Coignet, Monier, Hennebique, Perret, Garnier and, of course, Le Corbusier.

Without wishing to take sides in favour of one material or other, it seems obvious that each entails a totally conflicting approach to architecture. The kind of lack of mass and, hence, apparent solidity required to counteract criticism (by nineteenth-century opponents of iron) of the legacy of Vitruvius ("firmitas") is easily provided by concrete structures. But just how sustainable is the environmental impact caused by a material which cannot be recycled into new constructions after the original casting process? Considering that we live in an increasingly densely populated and hectic world, even building operations now need to be as meticulously engineered as possible, making the best possible use of new technology and focusing on extensive research; risks and delays in projects due to external factors will have to be confined to a minimum.

The construction of concrete works of architecture poses, for instance, a series of problems related to weather conditions, such as drying times and their repercussions on structural standards (recent research shows that this is the main cause of collapsing structures); building times and operations are also responsible for semi-paralysing entire neighbourhoods. On the other hand, iron pays the price of the technological backwardness of the business world in general; although this was originally due to the devastating situation after the war, which called for cheap labour involving no real expertise, this is no longer an acceptable explanation for the current state of inertia.

Dubosc & Landowski are right in calling for a global approach on the part of the whole of the building industry, so as to experiment on all the various alternatives now available and, at the same time, to carry out research along new lines. All their own work is gauged to practical (rather than futuristic) experimentation into the latest theoretical concepts and newly emerging technology.

The metal structure chosen for constructing the "Marcel Dassault" housing complex in Boulogne Billancourt was the real key to the success of a major construction project quite literally wedged into a built environment covering 100% of the building plot.

The project drew on a system involving the almost total absence of building materials at the site, thanks basically to the use of materials and components designed to be assembled and finished without any mixing or modifying of materials prior to construction work. This technique in no way jeopardises the environmental insertion of a work of architecture that remains at the cutting edge on both a conceptual and stylistic level.

The sheet metal used for the facade cladding, suitably insulated on the inside, is designed to interact with the surrounding urban context: it was decided to use primary colours, plus white, to make the building stand out and, at the same time, to highlight its structural features. The choice of the colour scheme is also one of hit solution upon the project designed for the Gauchy Town-hall; it only apparently plays second fiddle to the building's overall structural design. The bronze patina over all the metal components (it was Mies who first used it) provides the local community with its own authoritative and rather stately landmark. The slightly sloping site suggested projecting the city council chamber outwards facing the gothic basilique of St. Quentin, rather like a ship's bow, accentuating its separation from the ground by a very sculptural rather than structural support, whose red-coloured forms break decisively with the overall unity of the design.

Of course, tradition and rupture are part and parcel of Dubosc and Landowski's repertoire, so a number of their projects are deliberately reactive to the corruption of the existing environment; not just for the sake of it but in a carefully controlled manner "justified" by either the basic design theme or, more frequently, the characteristic features both of an unique beauty or complexity of the surrounding context.

The "Saturn III" complex in Givors certainly does not pass unnoticed on the surrounding skyline, due to both its long, bright red-coloured roof and the austerity of the towers marking the front facing the valley. These two disruptive features call for a dialectically effective reading of the site location. In their project to modernise and restructure the Paris Music Conservatory, our two architects actually dared to remove its typical mansard-roof which, together with the classical Parisian stone cladding, used to sew the building into the city's nineteenth-century architecture, to replace it with their own trademark: a vaulted roof. Although this substitution was not actually necessary - they could have simply raised the old top-floor structures to provide more room - it was a most effective way of underlining the renovating and restoring of a building that really had become obsolete.

This recurring feature of almost all their roof designs was actually turning into a sort of abstract conceptual constant in their quest for a stylistic signature. The recent project for the Parc des Taillées in Saint Martin d'Heres broke with this language, simultaneously signalling the possibility of using a dry interactive composite system for practically the all building. This technique proved that it was actually possible to do without cast materials (even those used for floors), thereby drastically reducing the weight of the floors themselves and reducing construction time by half. Dubosc and Landowski think that: "Use of current and available industrial products for specific solutions to specific problems comes naturally. To heat or sound insulate to mechanically resist lateral shocks, to be air proof to be weather resistant... there exist beautiful products of industry exactly adapted, the combination of which will produce effects beyond the simple addition of each unitary quality. This combination allows to create new flors, new facades, new side walls... If the public enemy number one of a construction site is water, there exists in our eyes another that is no less harmful and that is weight: the beauty of things is confined in the 'pounce of the cat', the exact effort for an exact result. The more precise a construction the more we may control its weight, and its price... because weight is expensive".

The desire to open up different stylistic horizons from those they first began working on is another recurring conceptual feature in their choice of structural layouts and materials. The idea of perpetualness is now being replaced by new concepts such as mobility, adaptability, and openness to change. The use of metal structures, in conjunction with "dry" materials only (notably, plaster and glass wool) and mechanical assembly procedures (often deliberately drawing on bolted rather than welded joints), also derives from these factors and may even be compared to a sort of "mission" for these two architects. A way of working which, in the wake of Pierre Chareau and Jean Prouvé's exciting designs, needed to be injected with fresh life.

This is the real leitmotif motif of their most recent projects. We are not talking about cutting edge scientific research, but experimentation and meticulous control over the organisational-construction aspects of building work. The materials and technology are potentially already available: they just need to be put to the right use, persuading the building industry of their true potential and utility. In this respect, architects, who had gradually lost control over the centre of gravity of all the forces involved in the construction of a building, could draw on these new techniques to recover their role at the hub of the overall design and construction process.

This includes the design of the facade, terraces and roof. The facade is also a very technical element. It insures different functions: mechanical resistance to lateral shocks either external or internal, fireproofing, air proofing, waterproofing, thermal insulation, sound insulation, and humidity regulation.

The response of these functions may be the following: one "skin" stops air, the following water. Two widths of crossed wool, a moisture barrier and one or more plasterboards complete the composite. Two frames bear the different elements and permit two independent fire checks. The ruin of one frame does not imply that of the second. However, one should not be tempted to consider their architecture as "structural" or just "high-tech": they consider the constructive aspect as the most important, but they defend themselves saying that they are not technicians, they are architects. And as architects they are worried about style and architectural composition. In fact, each of their projects is not only designed to cater for specific innovative construction needs, but shows peculiar aesthetic-formal preferences too.

The following text by Eric Dubosc provides useful insight into the way the two architects intend to use the Technical Developments as the "engine" of what they believe beeing the new contemporary architecture, the "Architecture of Environment".

"The new concept of environmental architecture supplies buildings with their own means of evolution, or even dissolution, so at any moment in their existence they may evolve in harmony with their 'sphere'. Again, it must be stressed that this concept brutally counters the 'eternal' idea that Architecture anchors Man in history, and signals his domination (as splendid as it may be) over the territory, over nature.

Environmental architecture, as opposed to the perfect Classical architecture of the 17th and 18th centuries, has the primary ambition of passing without leaving a trace, in the image of the explorer who rejoiced on returning to an isolated site, that there was no trace whatsoever of his previous passage.

In other words, it implies another philosophy, another way of existing in the 'Cosmos' according to the expression of Le Corbusier, but differently from Le Corbusier...

Does this mean that it was necessary to destroy the Crystal Palace or that we should unbolt the Eiffel Tower? A chef d'oeuvre is indifferent to age even if it exists only 'in the space of a morning'.

The techniques used to construct differently are also in harmony with our era: the Homo Sapiens of the year 2000 is less concerned with marking his territory than he is with inserting himself discretely, or with force, but provisionally...!

Similarly, he wishes to work with the tools and techniques, the knowledge of his era. He (mechanically) constructs manufactured products in dry assembly. Building removes itself from heavy and laborious on site fabrication to compose edifices with products of high added value, after profound research: conception, assembly, logistic. 'Industrial' constructio-tight flow, value analysis-rejoins the environmental prescription, the dry procedure is: the material the matter of the Architecture of the Environment".

Works

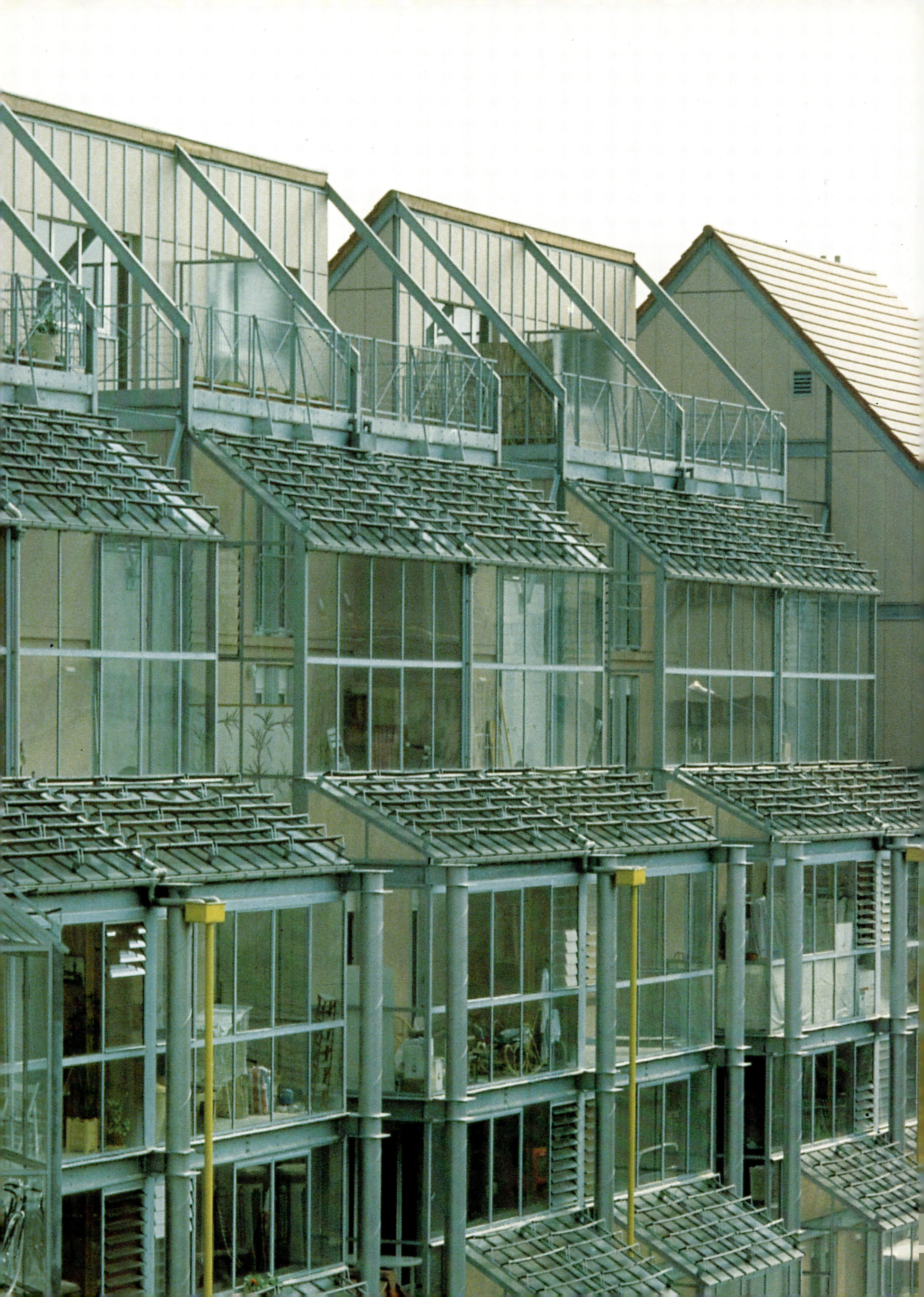

Le Castel Eiffel Housing Complex
Dijon, 1987

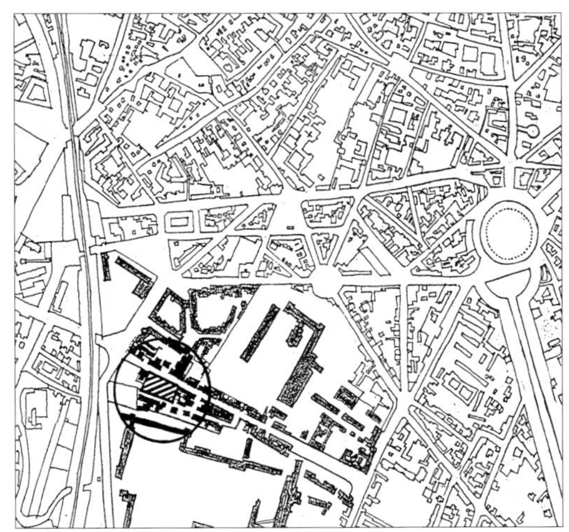

Located along a 35 meter wide avenue on the verge of the historical centre of Dijon, the project was initially intended to be the starting-point of a new urban composition. The avenue was to be changed into a large boulevard with lawns in its central part, structured and patterned by small "hotels", facing the historical centre. The design would also have allowed the high school, which is segregated at the moment, to be kit into the urban fabric. Twenty-seven council flats have been built into the urban scheme. They are divided into four "hotels", jointly named "Le Castel Eiffel", because they are built in the same place as the house where Gustave Eiffel lived when he was a child. The proportions, alignment and rhythm are in scale with the ordering of an avenue. It was the urban impact of the whole and not of just one building to another that was the real objective. The facades along the future avenue, facing old Dijon, are sober, classical in style and highly discrete; pairing themselves with the architectural vocabulary of the courts in the nearby park designed by Le Notre.

The "rear" facades, which run along a little interior street, are composed of a cascade of greenhouses with a delicate framework in galvanised steel.

The use of glass gives the buildings a sense of transparency and strange lightness. These greenhouses, although regulated by the exactitude and precision of their metal sections, create a floating, vibrant space; traps for light and reflection, they lie between the exterior and interior, without really belonging to either; they are the facade and yet their depth is habitable. These apartments may be considered prototypes of contemporary experimentation into structures, habitation, energy saving and maintenance.

A supporting steel structure has been chosen for its precision and speed of assembly: it can be constructed extremely quickly, allowing workmen to prepare its parts in the dry environment of a workshop.

All the flats are triplex apartments, featuring 3.40 meter high living rooms and verandas designed to create a greenhouse effect. The layout of rooms differs from floor to floor.

As far as energy savings are concerned, the badly exposed elevation envelopes are made of high-grade insulating materials with no thermal bridging. Elevation envelopes that are better exposed capture solar energy that accumulates in a thick wall ready to redistributed. The system conforms to HEP (High Energy Performance) standards.

The facades are made of modern materials (glass, galvanised steel, PVC) that require neither rough-casting nor painting.

Cross section, site plan and
main front and, opposite
page, detail of the facade
of the housing complex.

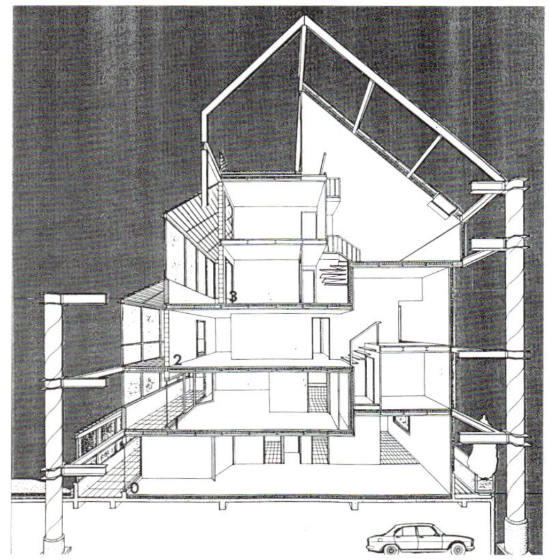

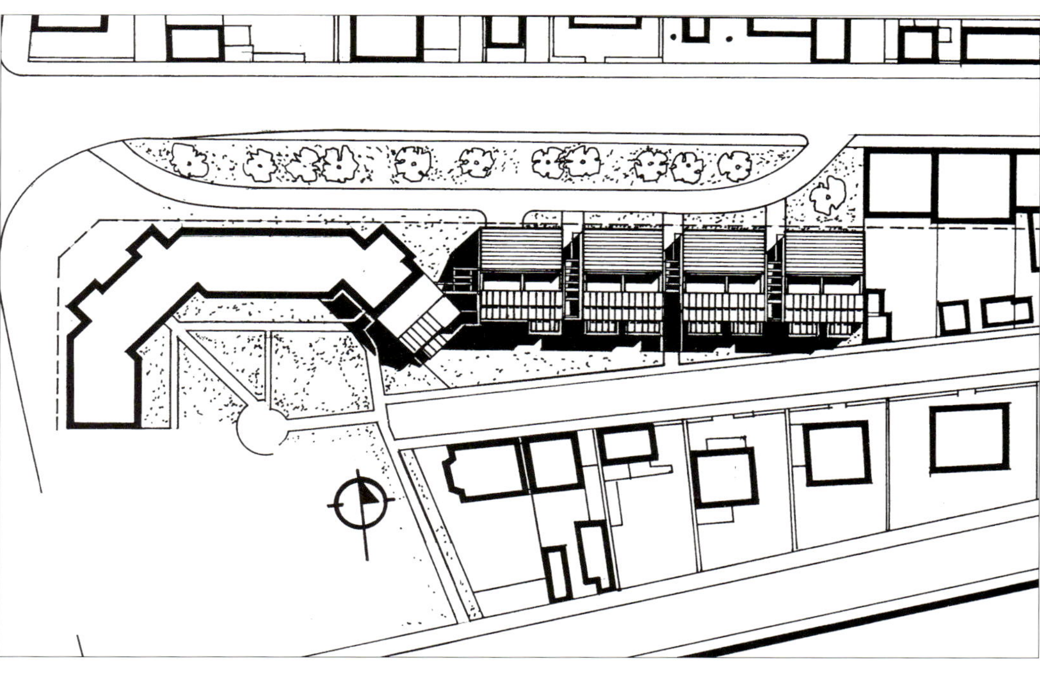

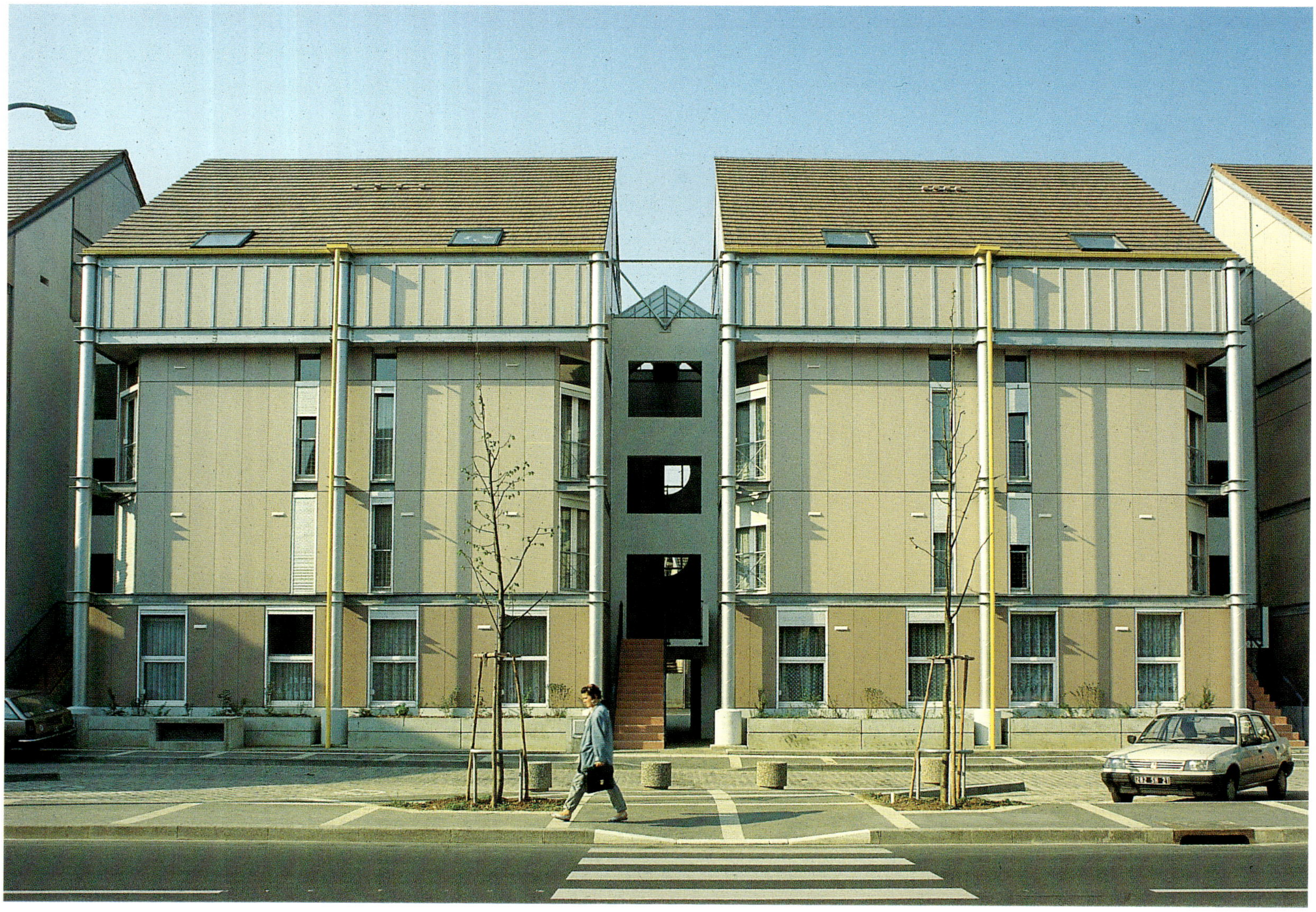

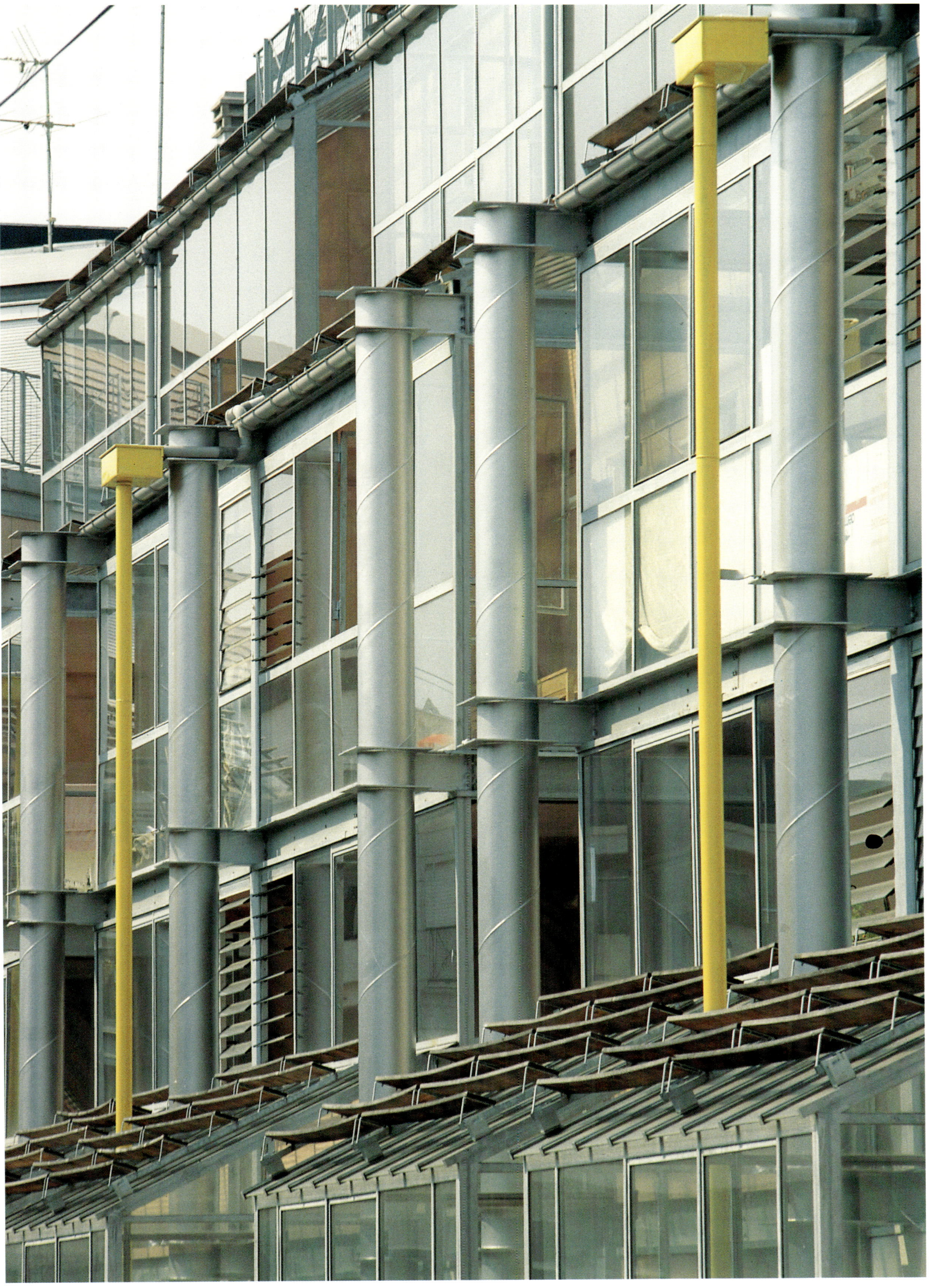

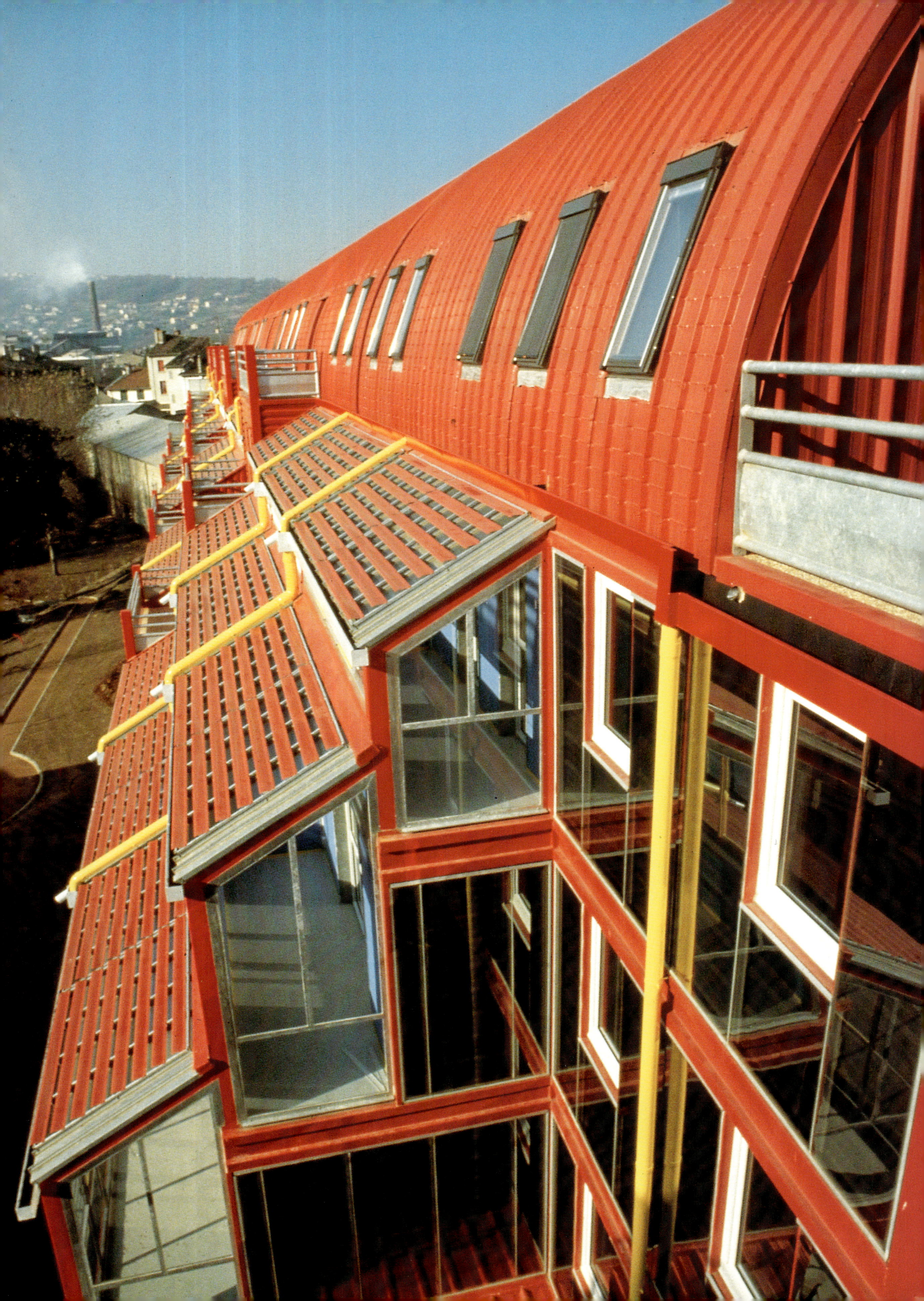

Saturne III
Housing Complex
Givors, 1989

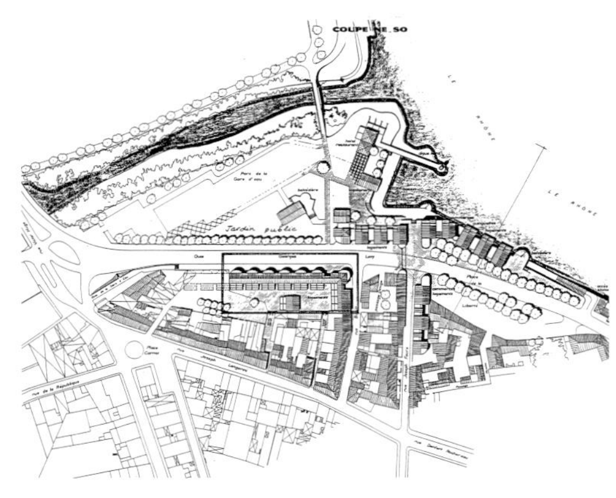

The aesthetic and technical decisions which determined the building's architectural scheme are the result of striking contrasts: an infinite landscape, a densely inhabited old town, a north wall exposed to noise and cold, and a south wall benefiting from the presence of a small inner garden.

The building is constructed over four levels and an attic extension: to the north, it features a redan facade made of semicircular towers, and to the south a cascade of greenhouses and terraces. The circular form of the towers permits the inhabitants to take in both the landscape - towards the Massif Central and its western counterpart facing the River Rhone and Alps. The redans confer a "rampart" character to the building, as well as acting as sound traps.

The roundness of the towers is in perfect accord with the intrinsic qualities of the concrete shell, which acts simultaneously as windbracing for the building. The composite construction system of steel which constitutes the rest of the building is designed for using, as often as possible, industrial products in order to reduce and facilitate assembly at the building site.

The apartments are designed with two basic layouts: either a "classical" site plan, on a single level, with the living room to the north and the kitchen and bedrooms to the south, or a two-level plan with the living room and kitchen to the north in a semi-circular space and the bedrooms looking onto the greenhouses.

The roof, designed like a red stroke, is a real landmark in a dynamic, chaotic environment, shot through with contrasting forces. It traces out a line of tension through Givors' double landscape, as both village and industrial town. The way a semi-cylinder has been placed on a row of vertical semi-cylinders is almost disquieting in its overt abstraction. The towers are carefully constructed to punctuate the linear roof, adding a sense of solemnity, weight and balance to this glowing red semi-cylinder. The facade facing the boulevard, water and city forms the basis of this unbroken stroke of red. Each element of the building draws its meaning from a multiplicity of aesthetic, technical, economic and site-related reasons, all of which are connected to the other elements. The roof swells up in an internal vault and finds its technical expression in the use of the kind of steel structure to which Dubosc and Landowski have devoted their careers and artistic lives for the last seven years.

The straight facades, facing the boulevard, treated like mirrors, permit the towers to continue their curves through reflection; they also provide sound-insulation and, most significantly of all, increase the intensity of light on the front facing north, slightly drawn back compared to the roofline.

The tiered greenhouses offer the apartments an original type of space, increasing energy savings by the way they fit into the metal structure as a whole.

Partial cross section,
and, below the complex
and its urban context.

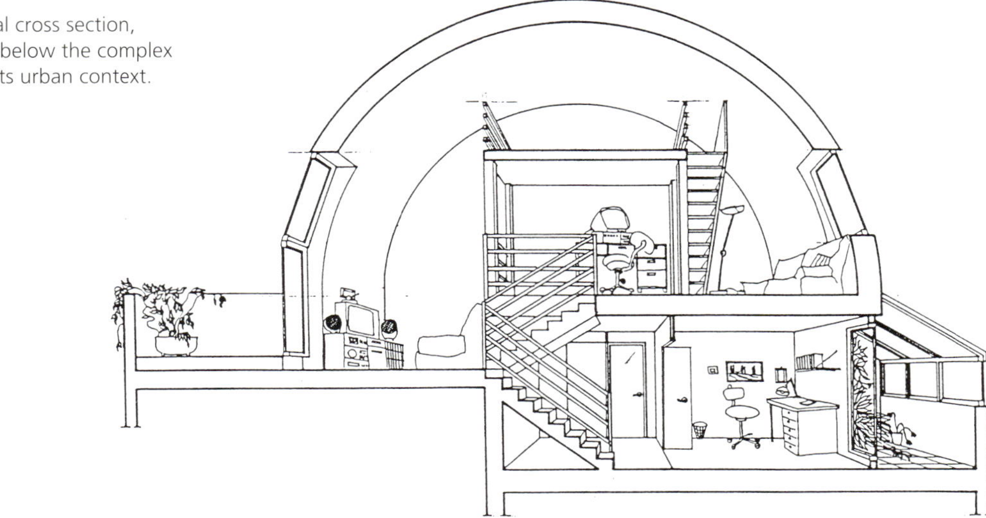

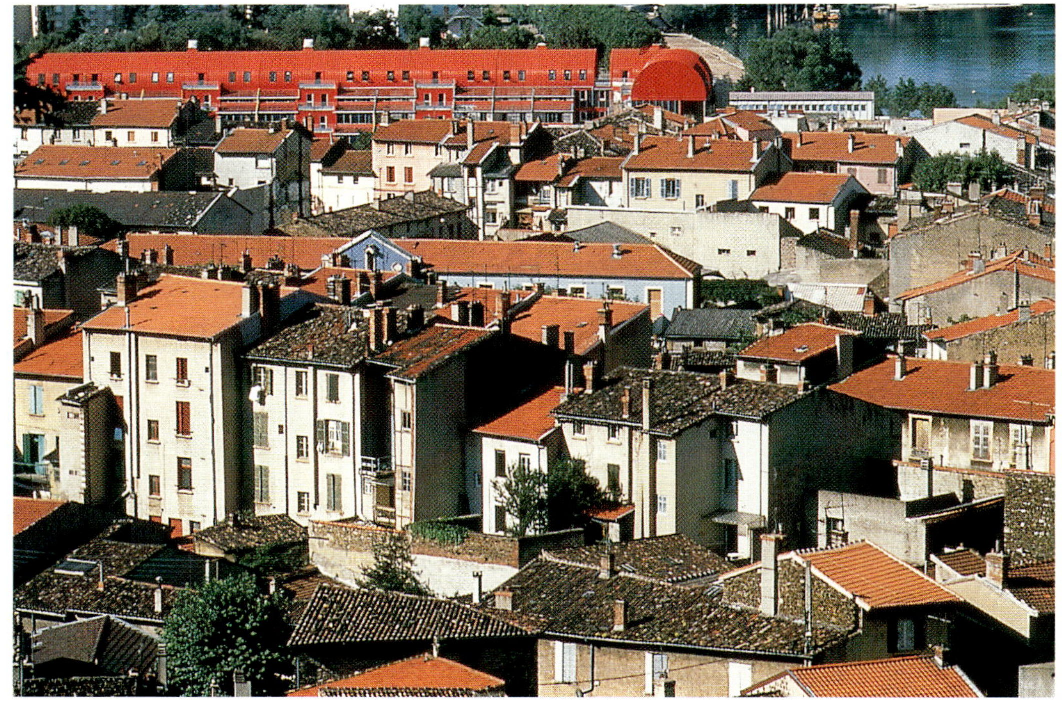

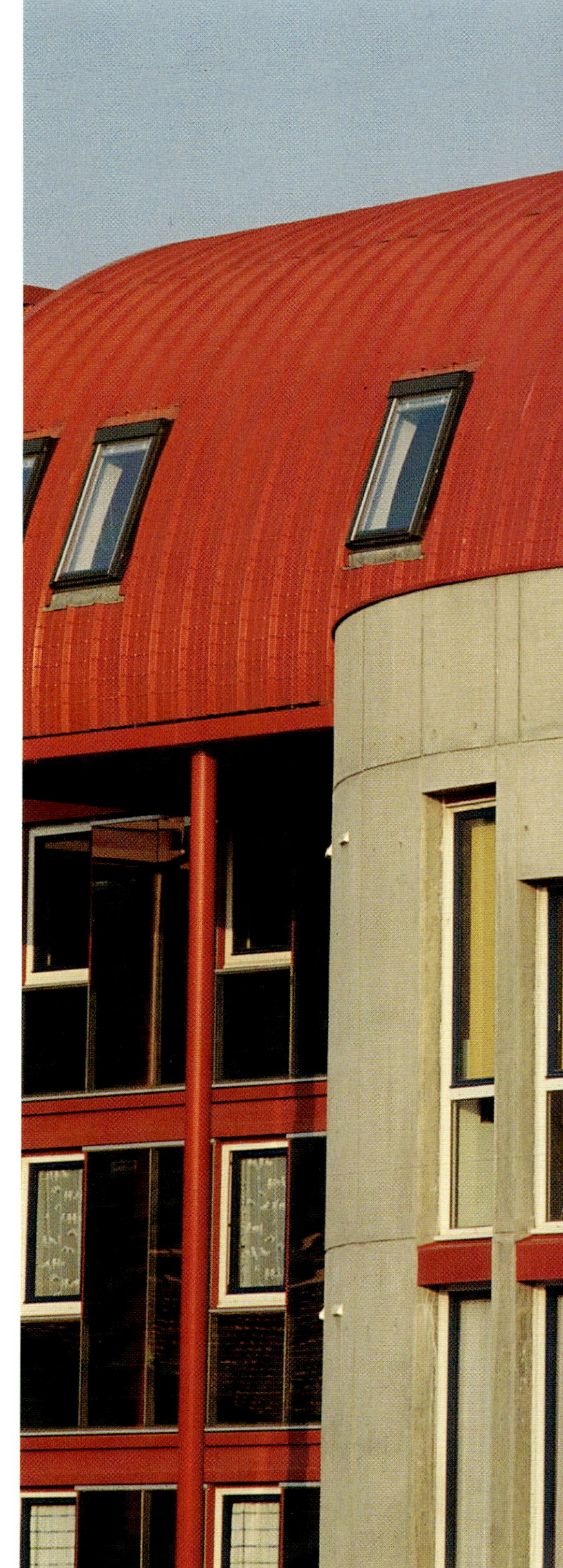

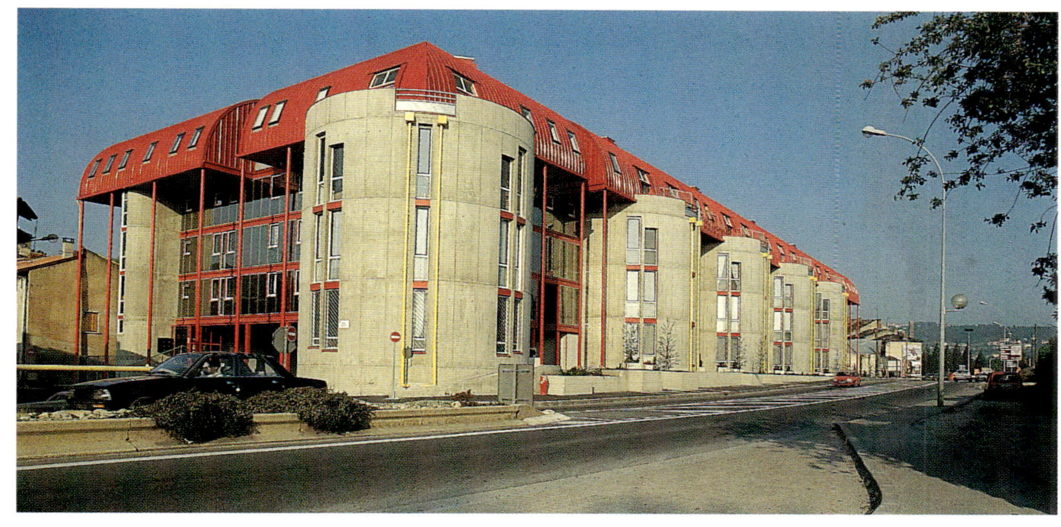

North front, featuring
a series of semi-circular
towers made of
exposed concrete.
Below, detail of the
north-east corner
of the housing complex.

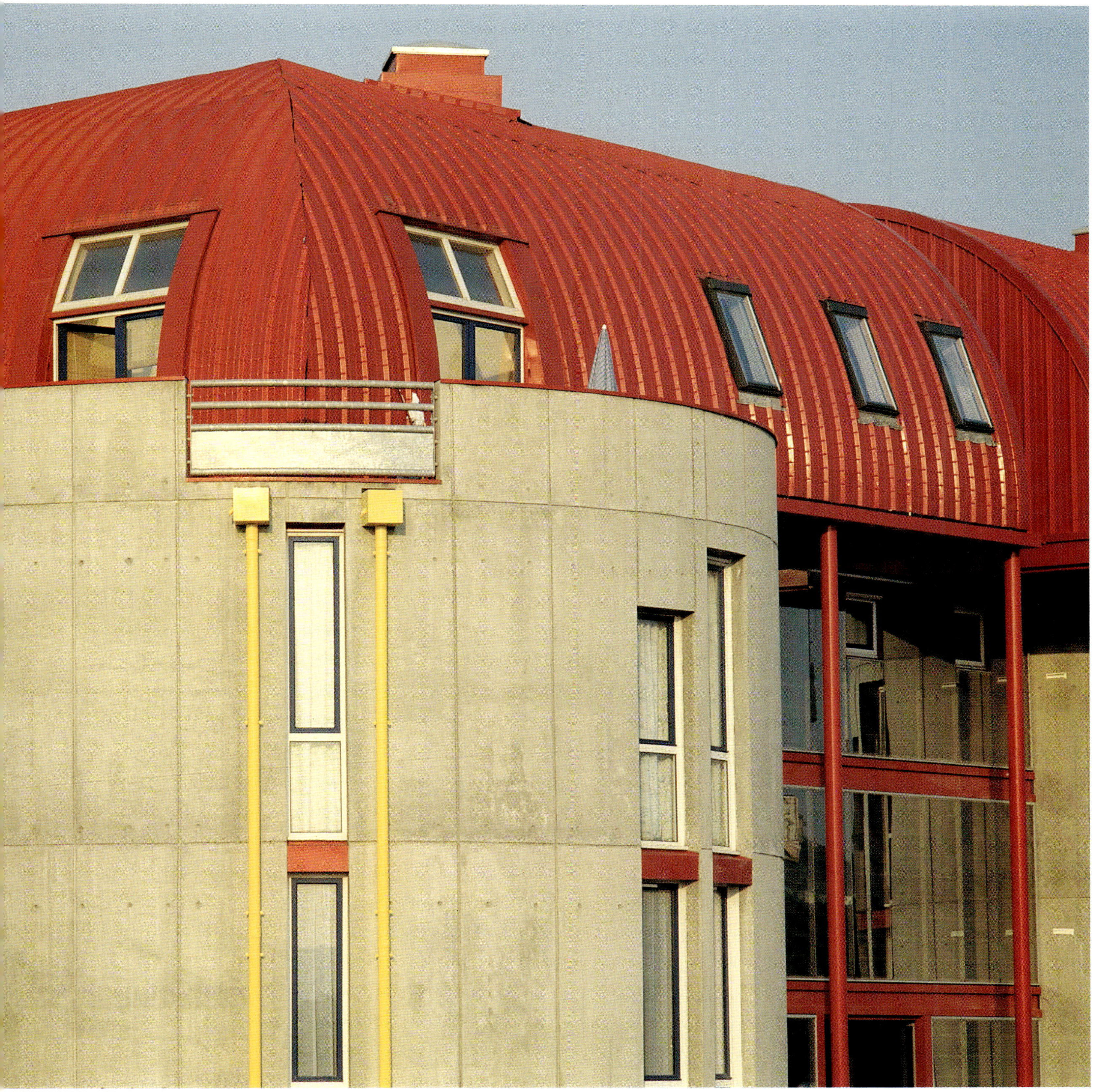

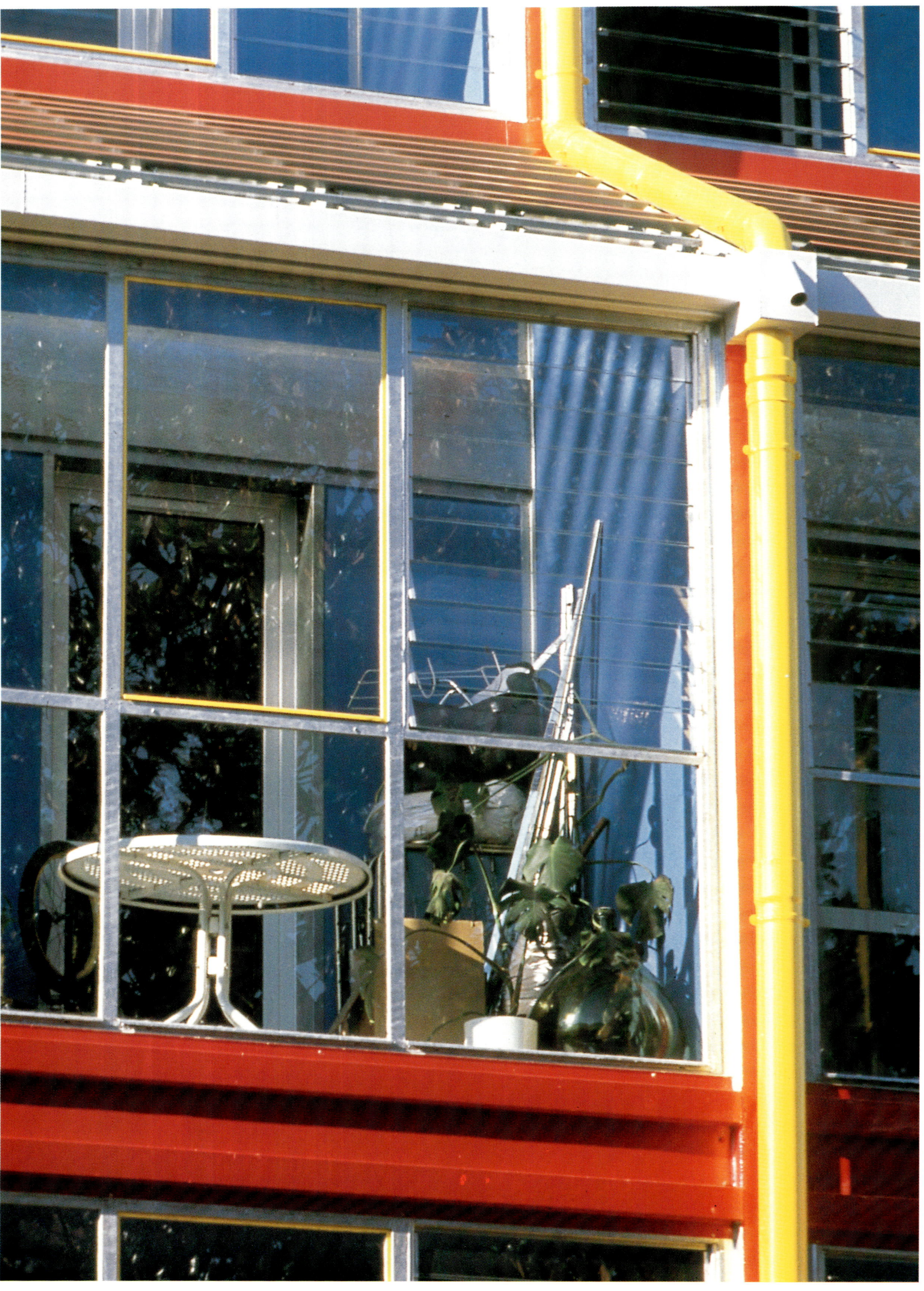

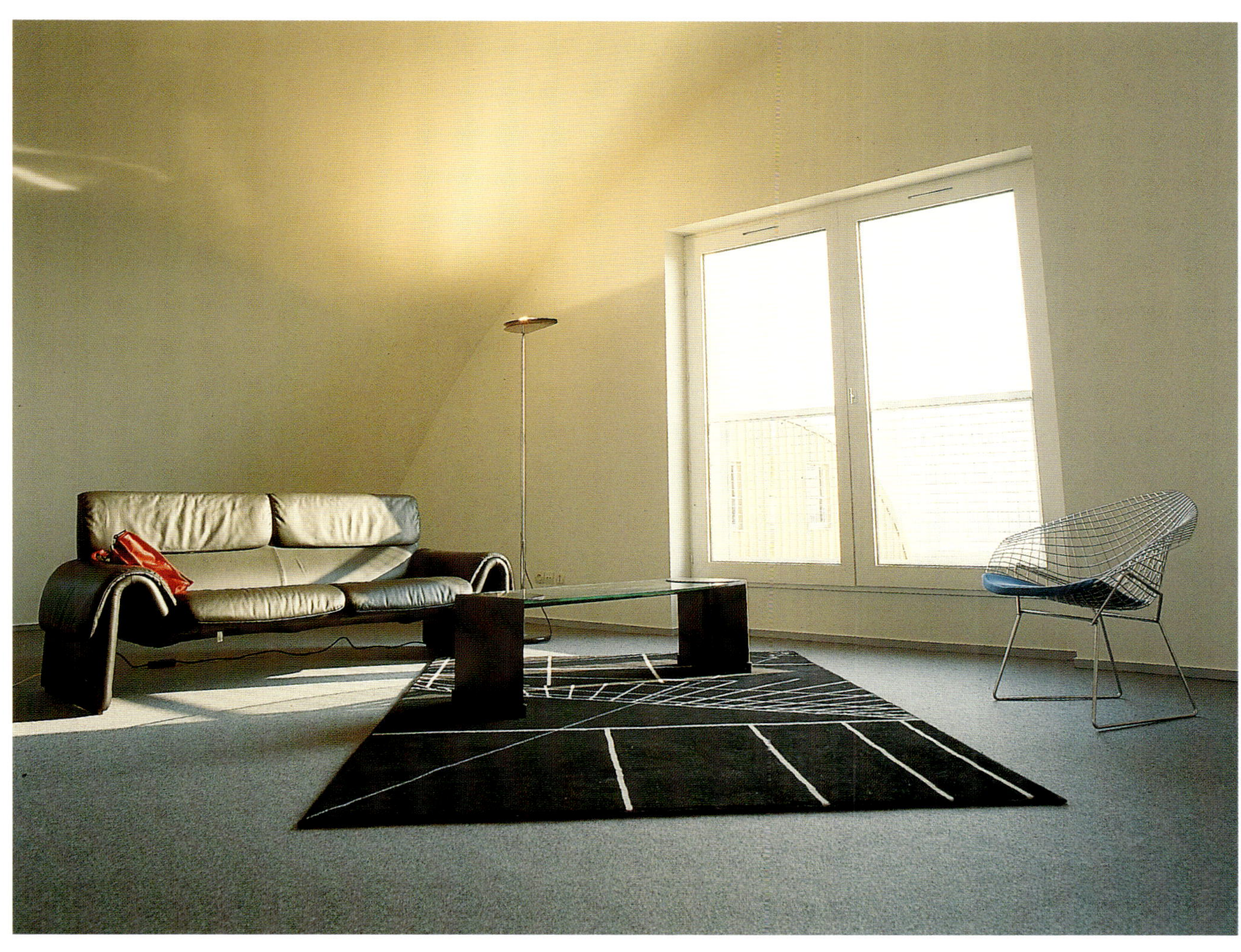

Opposite page, detail of the bow-windows facing the internal courtyard. Left, one typical room, and, below, the internal courtyard.

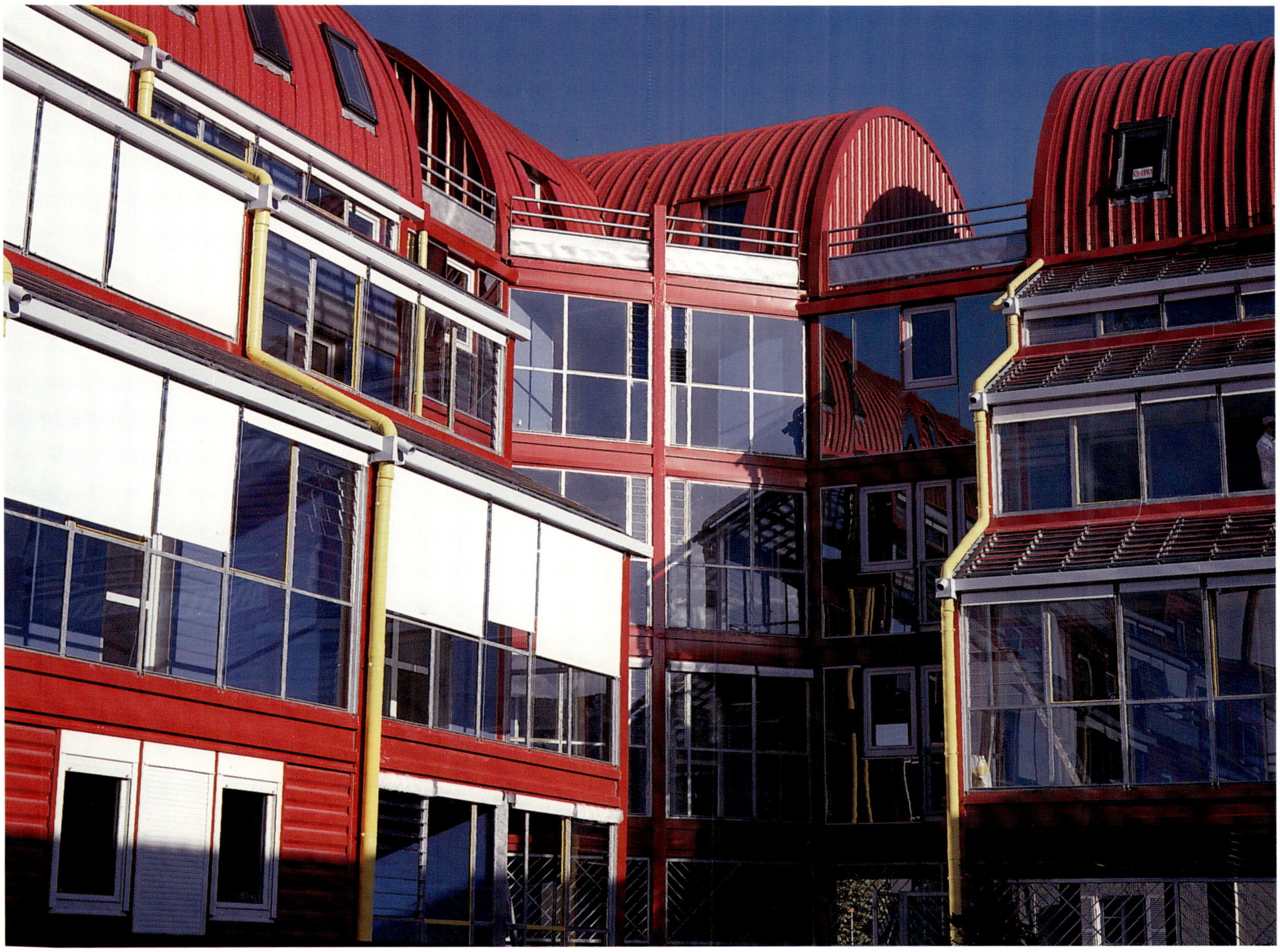

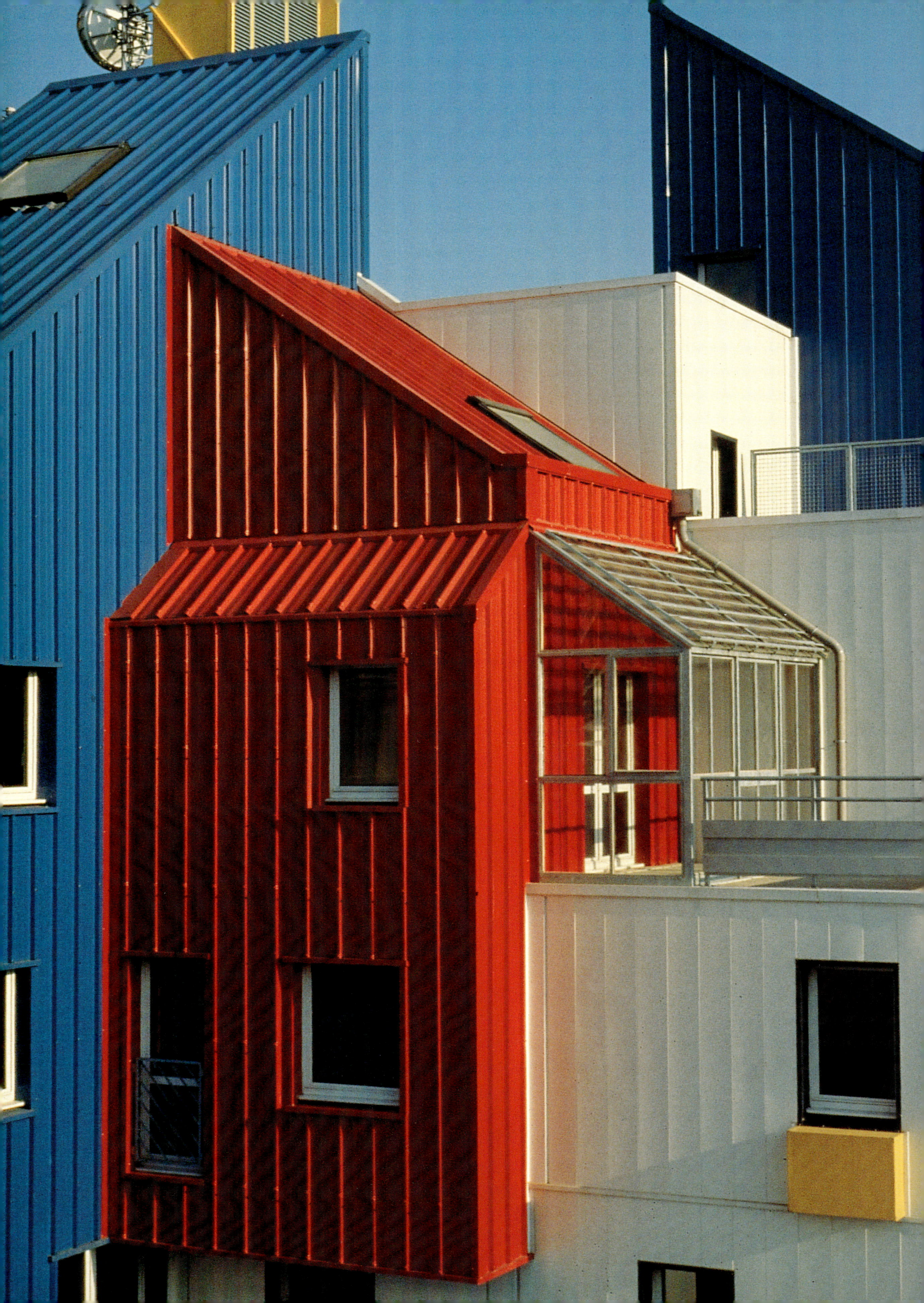

Marcel Dassault Housing Complex
Boulogne-Billancourt, 1990

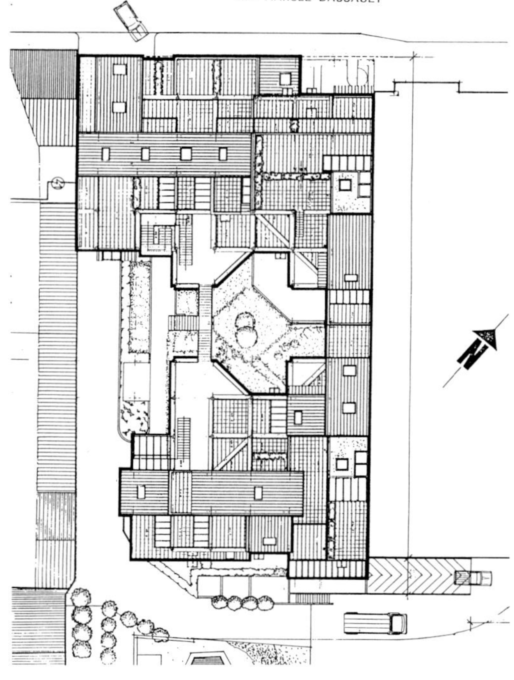

The project specifications set some rather tough design constraints, particularly in relation to the characteristic features of the site location: the building plot is situated inside a densely built urban fabric, which even the construction gear and vehicles had trouble in reaching.

The presence of a line of telephone cables, originating from the nearby exchange, also meant conforming with certain specific height restrictions, while a huge sewage pipe forced the underground levels to be constructed according a carefully gauged layout. The operating programme, and the fact that all the available surface area could be built on, suggested catering for a vast array of closely co-ordinated functions: a nursery for disabled children, offices, a private garage and public car park, storage space for the City Council, and a considerable number of different-size lodgings.

The final decision was to build a kind of hill-shaped complex backing onto the huge blank wall of the telephone exchange, camouflaging it away and branching off from the end through a system of cascading terraces along which the lodgings, usually duplex apartments, are located.

These lodgings are designed like houses piled on top of each other at various levels; each apartment has its own small greenhouse and terrace facing south and west towards the most picturesque landscape. The entrance to the lodgings is often across small ramps of outside stairs that descend and traverse the hillside.

The shades chosen are mainly bright primary colors and white, designed to highlight and brighten up the rather dull, grey atmosphere in the local neighborhood.

The project was designed to be constructed using a traditional system of columns and beams made of either concrete or iron.

The second option was eventually chosen in order to reduce the amount of building materials required and the time it would take to construct the building.

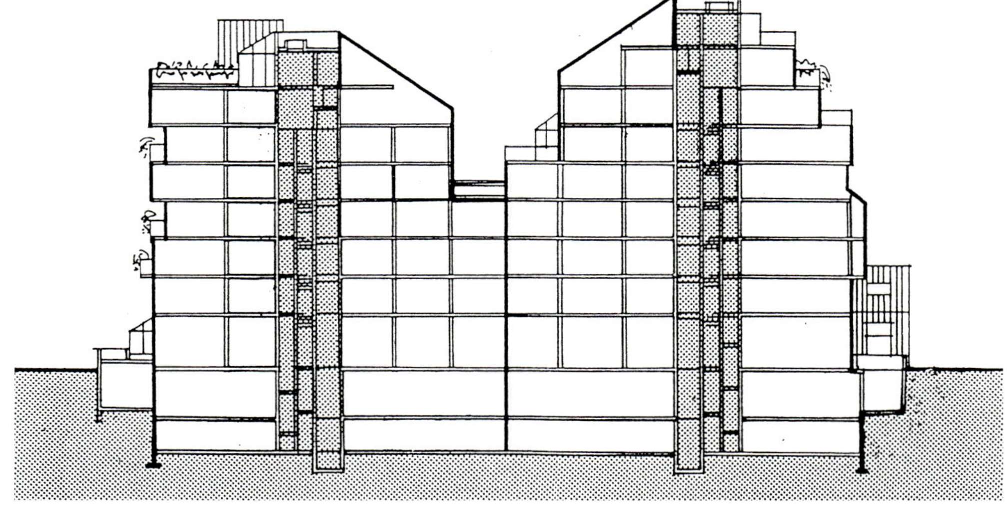
Cross section and view
of the block of flats
in Rue Marcel Dassault
in Boulogne-Billancourt.

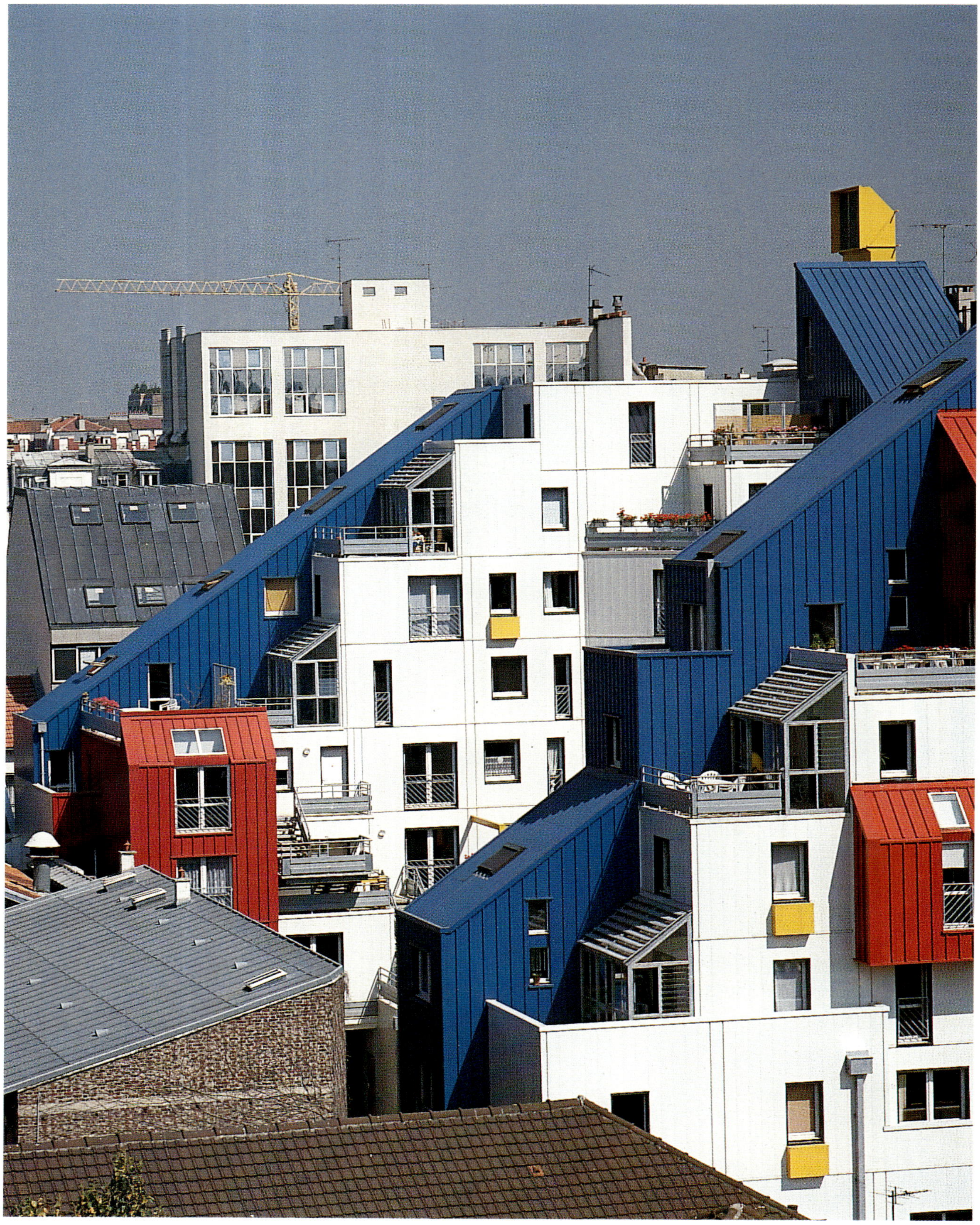

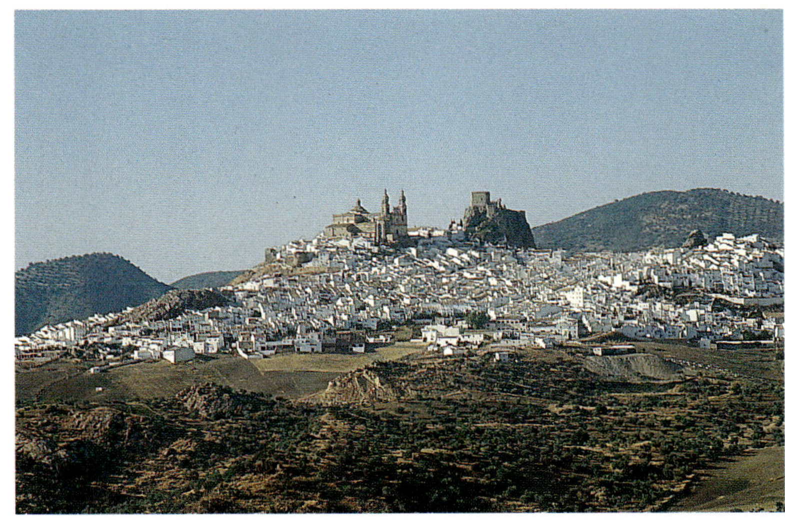

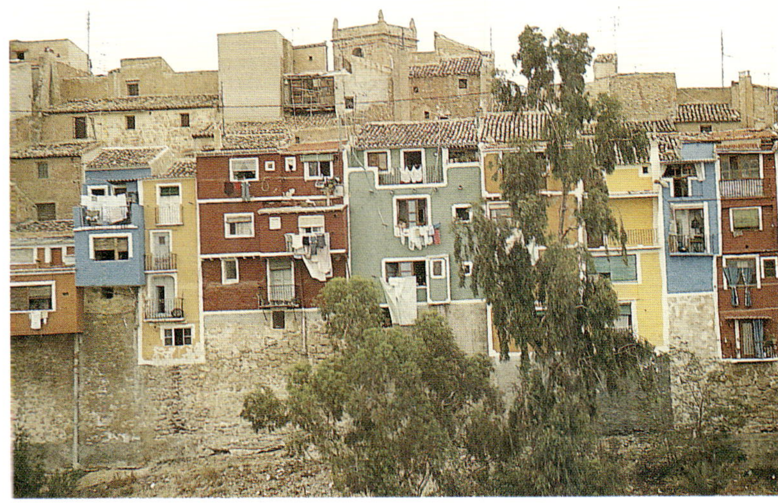

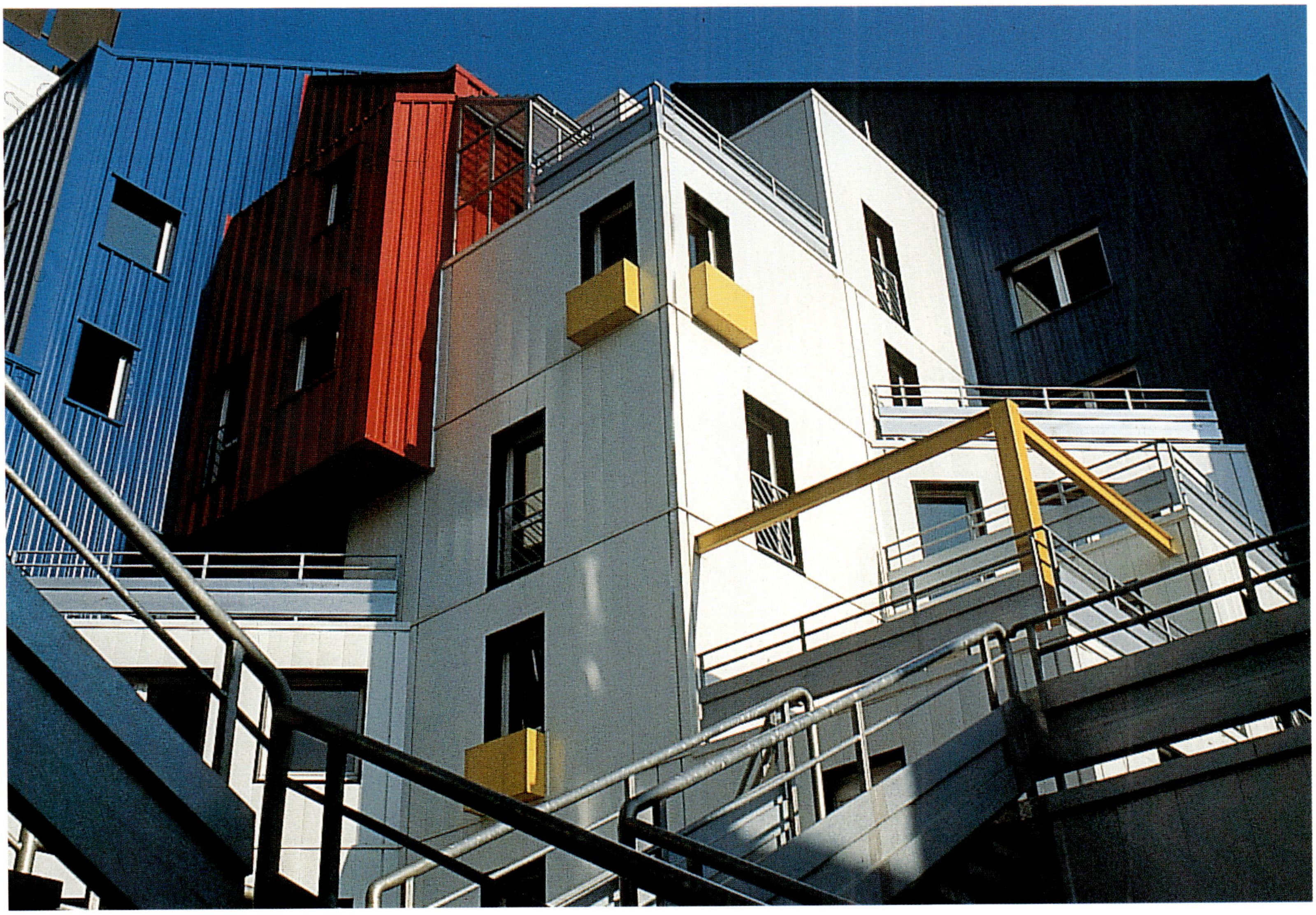

Detail of the facades
clad with metal panels;
top of page views of
a typical mediterranean
town, whose structure
inspired this project.

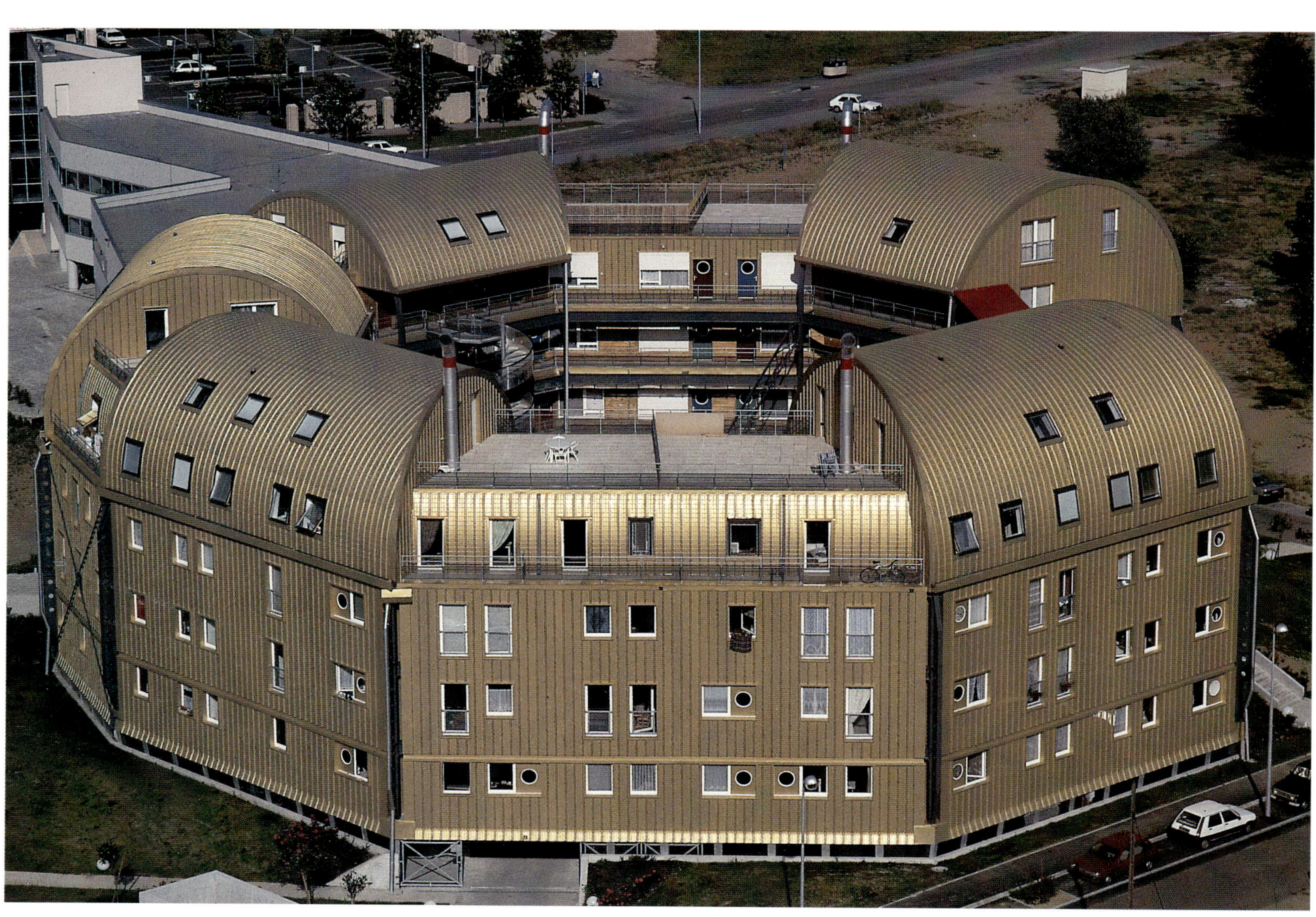

Kronos Housing Complex
Nantes, 1991

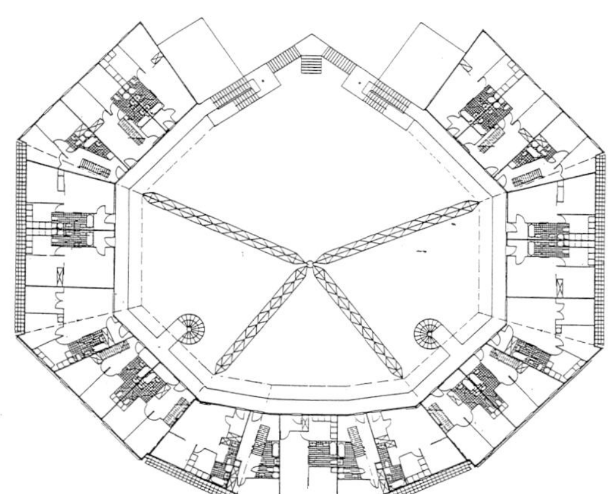

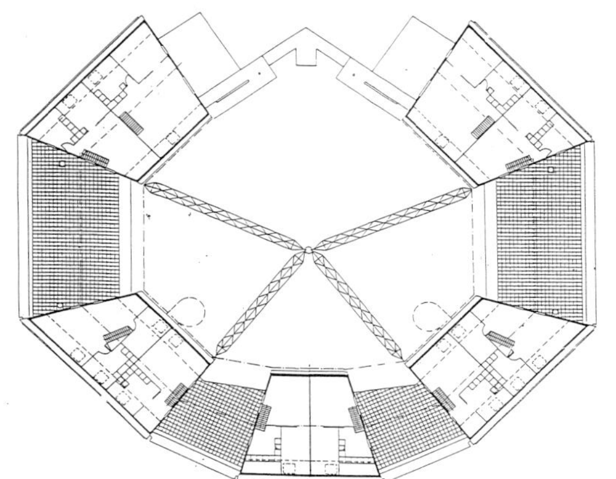

The building seems to have been dropped onto a stray lot in the center of an island surrounded by the River Loire, not far from the estuary in Nantes. Its composition does not rely on the river, nor on its natural or built surroundings.

It is solitary, a landscape in itself, like an oyster smooth on the inside and rough without. It may be compared to a fortress or to those beautiful circular constructions in Southern China, closed on the outside, open within.

The interior is actually a Magnolia garden. A pathway and stairway rising through the central space provide access to the eighty-one apartments. These apartments are distributed around seven sides of the complex's octagonal site plan. To inject even greater life into the building structures, the barrel roof so characteristic of Dubosc and Landowski's designs alternates, from building to building, with a flat roof design. The eighth side, facing south, is a wide window looking onto the communal garden on the inside. Balcony walkways help encourage neighbourly exchanges.

The steel structure has a wide span of 21 meters. This allows for any eventual modifications to the housing units, free of intermediates posts. For the first time, wind bracing is not provided by a concrete stairwell. The structure is designed to be self stable: the door opens up to future developments in completely "dry" construction.

The pre-lacquered steel plate casing is made of gold PVDF and is a sign of great will in these deserted surroundings.

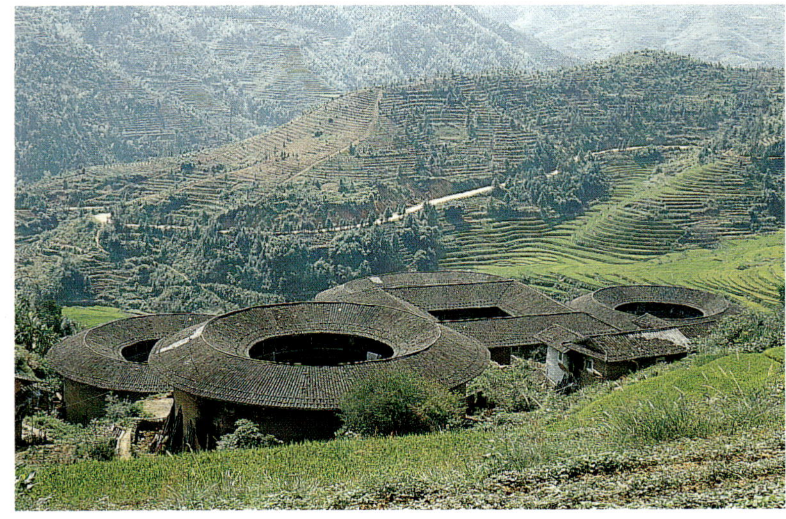

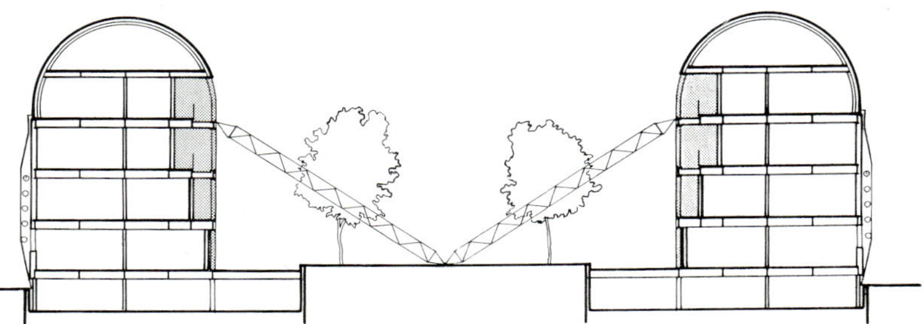

Left, natural and
architectural contex
which inspired this
project. Below, cross
section and the internal
court of the complex.
Opposite, detail of the
internal facade.

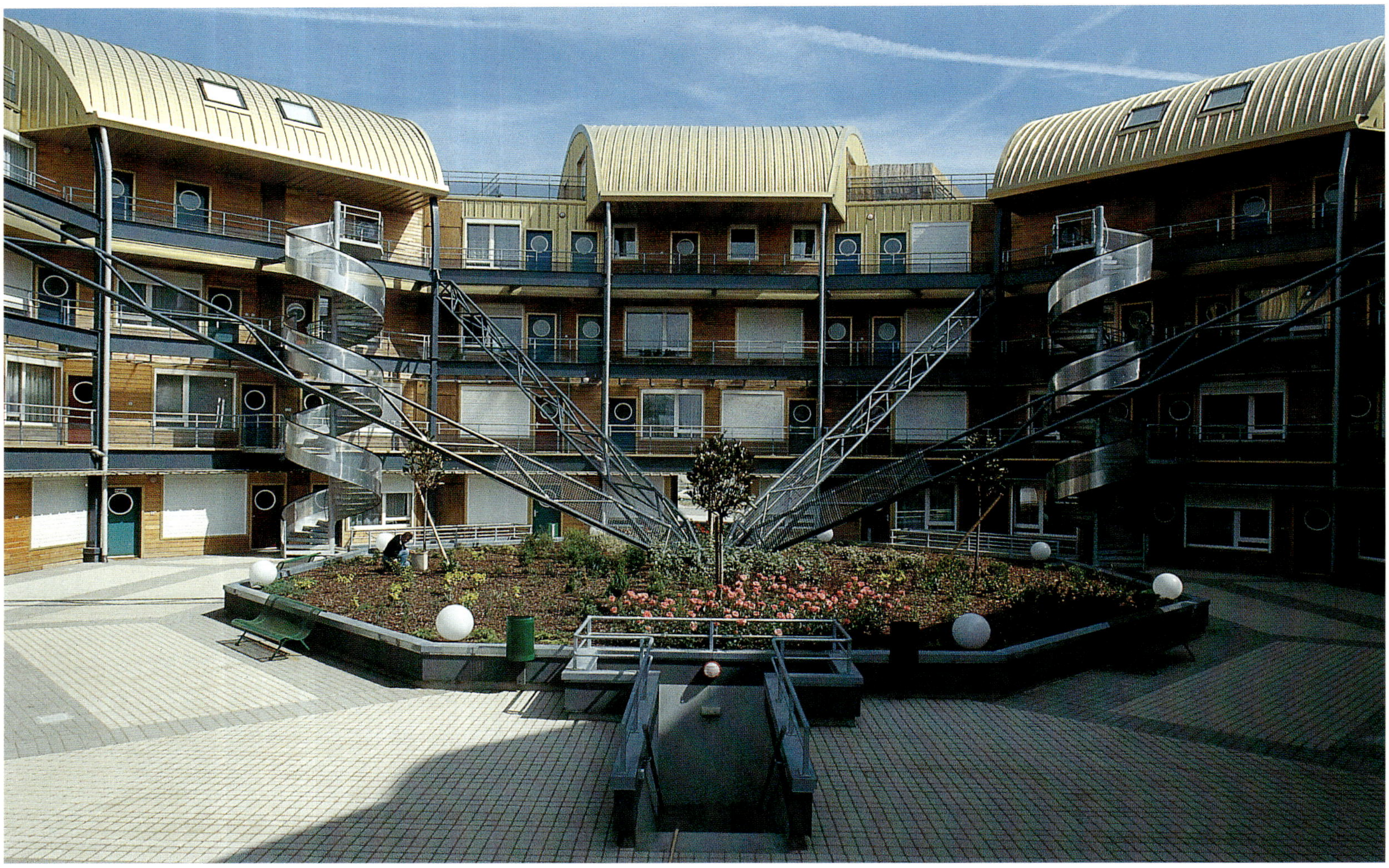

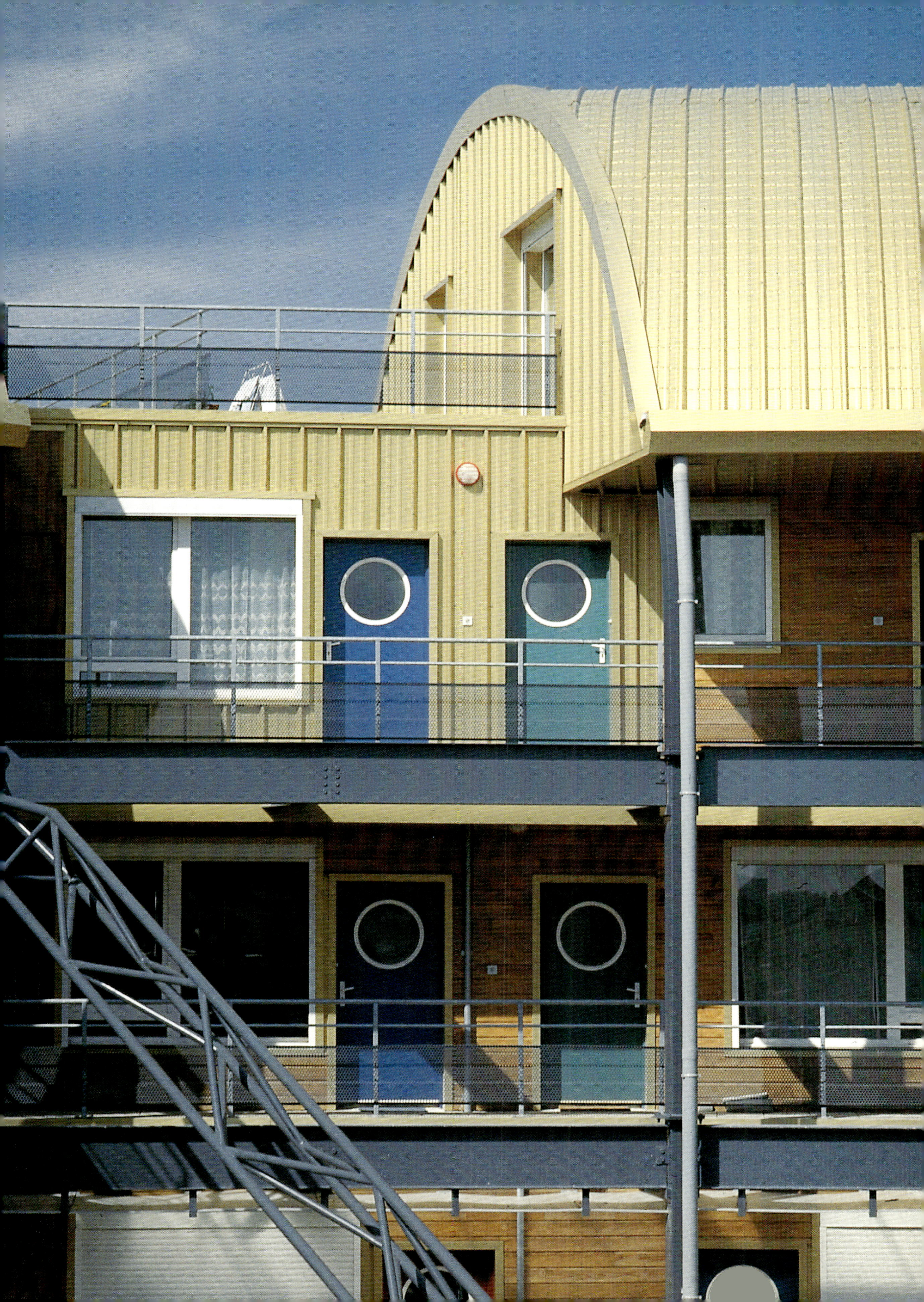

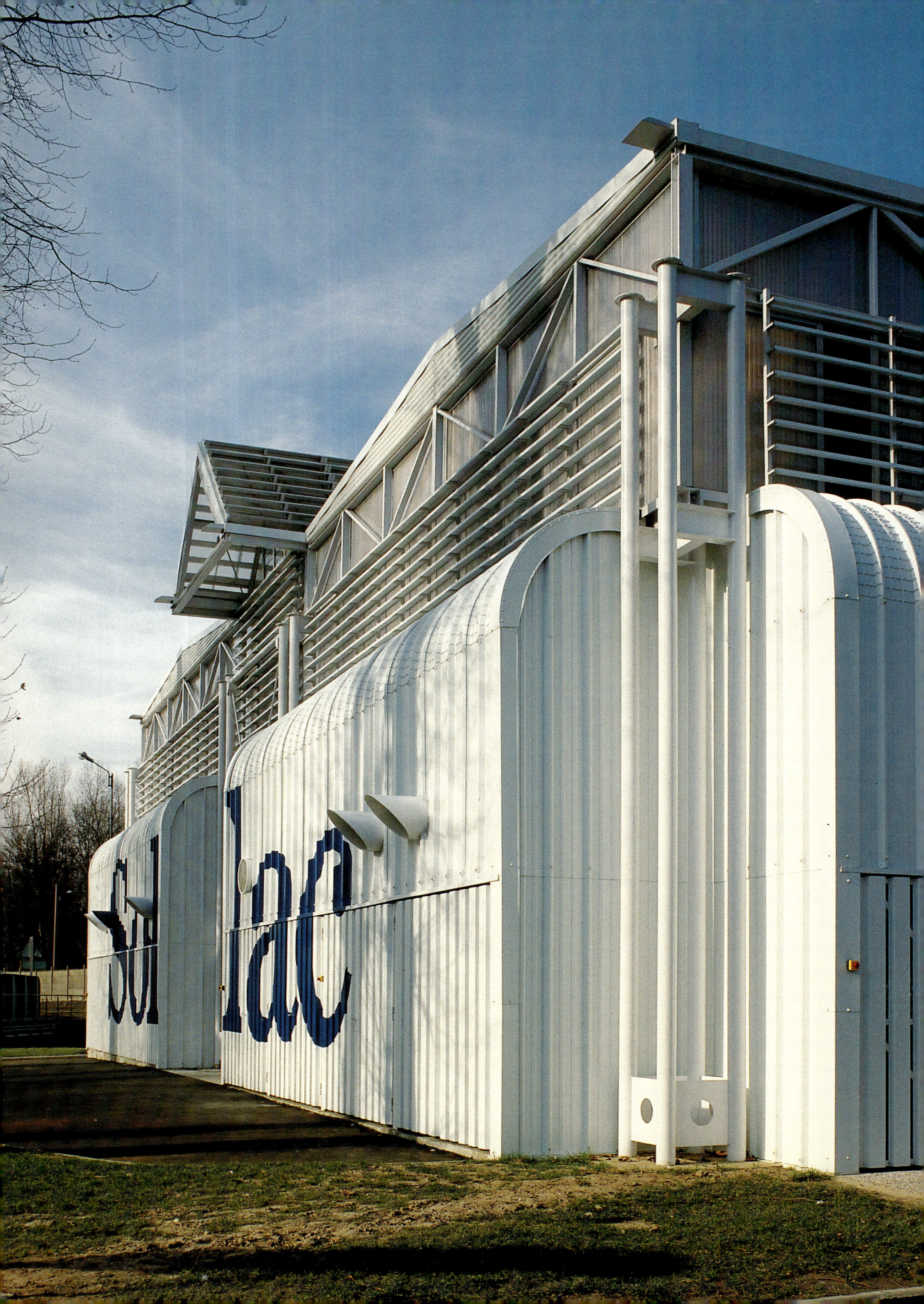
Sollac

Sollac Research Center, Montataire, 1991

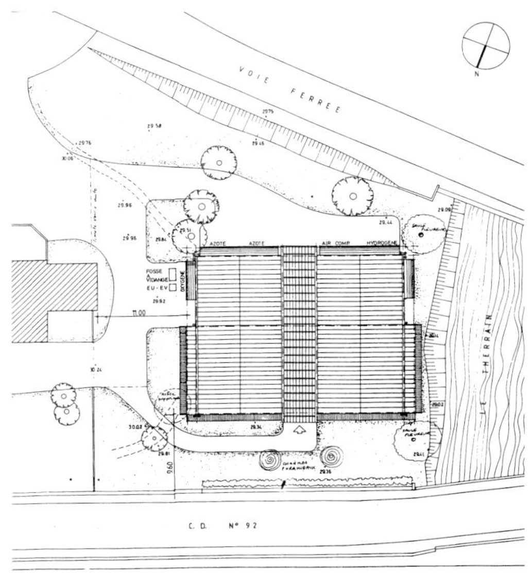

Sollac's board of directors required a building for the extension of their research and development center to be built on their Montataire factory site. Although the building site was small, the project was intended to be evolutionary and to allow for future extensions. The building was to be steel structured and to display a large range of the Sollac cladding products.

Flexibility and evolution dictated the architectural and technical design: the posts are set on an 11 x 11 meter grid leaving floor space free.

Variable ceiling heights are possible in this construction system, allowing multi-purpose use of the offices, small laboratories, and industrial laboratory.

A transparent aisle traverses the building, bringing air and light into the central space and fostering interaction and encounters.

The industrial laboratory is very luminous despite the presence of numerous cells necessary for storing gas. In general, the design privileges the interplay of light within the building; a privilege of steel structured architecture.

Future extension of the building is possible in all four lateral directions as well as vertically over the office floor. Finally, the position of the building was carefully studied to afford views of the castle and church at the summit of Montataire.

Each self-adjusting bearing point is composed of a bouquet of four thin posts (ø 13 centimeters). The running beams permit cantilevering and provide for future extensions.

The floors and roof are composed with steel panelling, the posts are tubular, the beams have PRS (reconstituted welded profiles), truss girders or rolled beams. All the electrical-fluid-mechanical systems are located on the outside of the building in special units inserted in the bottom section of the front elevation. This plays down the rather mechanical nature of the metal structure.

The color white was chosen for the outside of the building for the same reason.

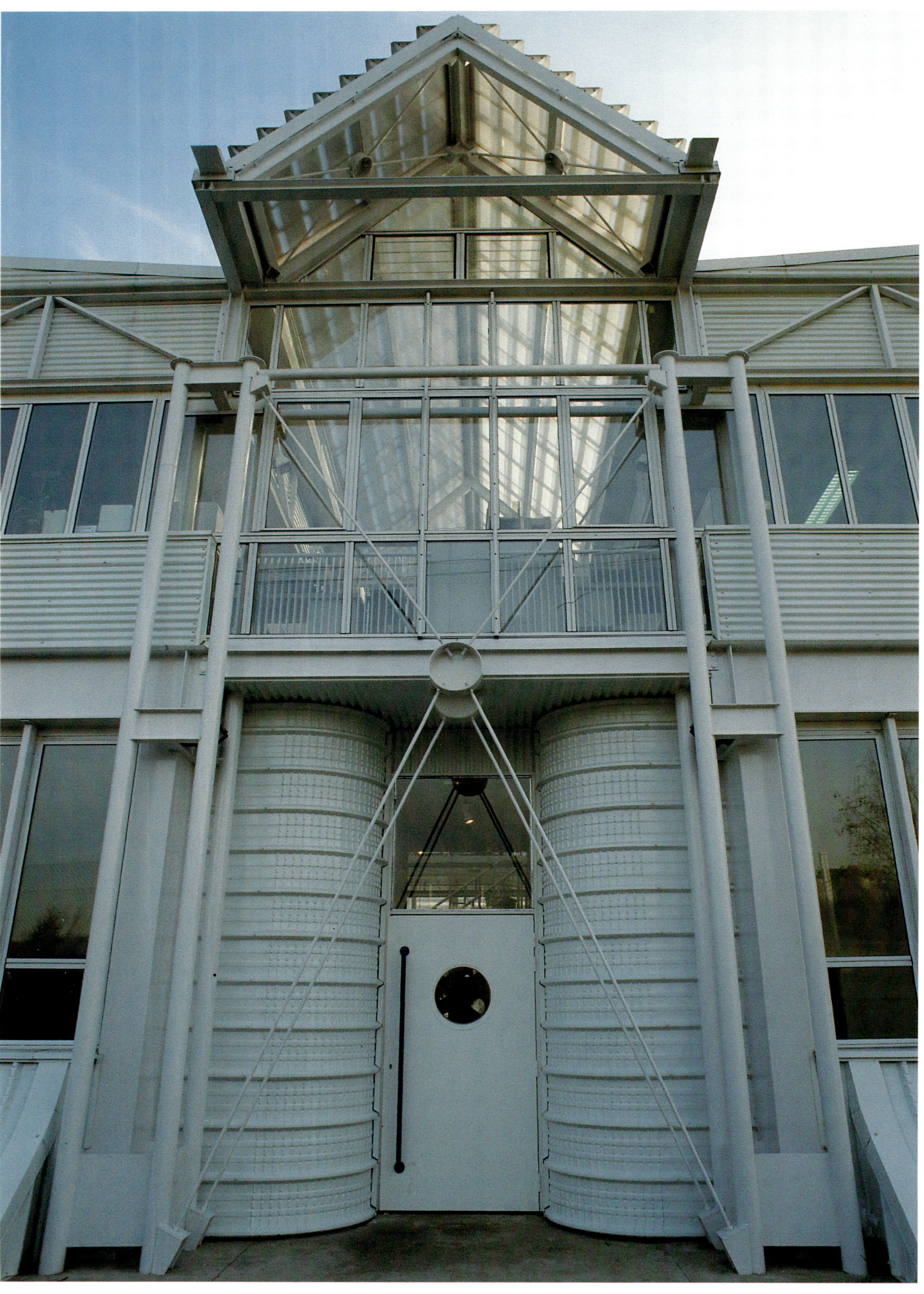

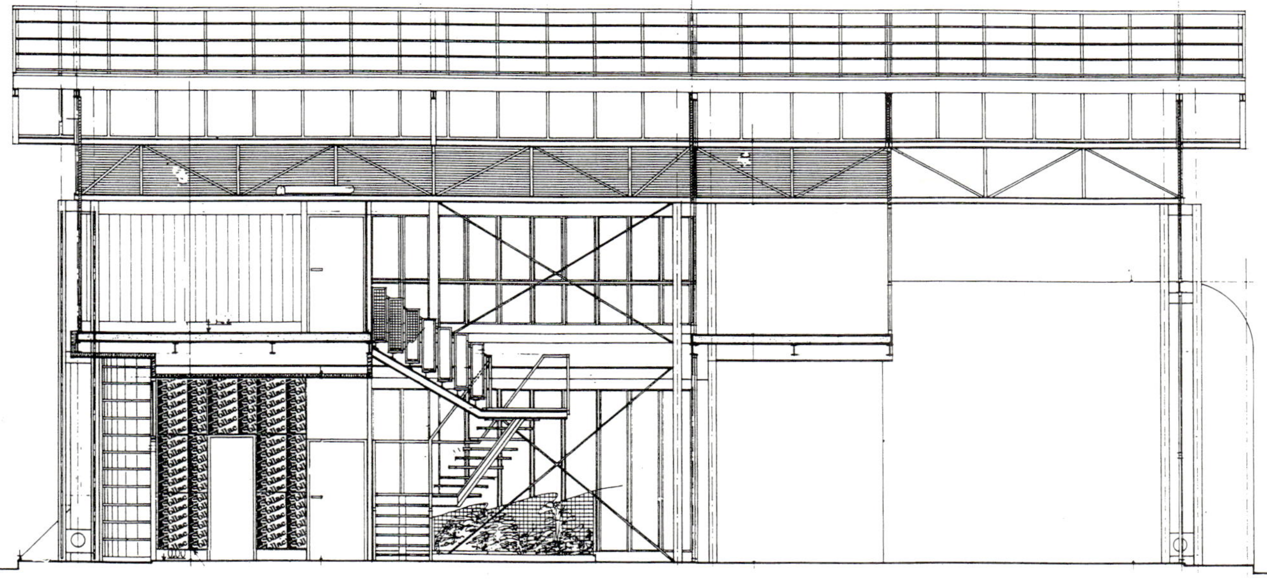

Cross section and, below, interior of Sollac's Research and Development Centre. Opposite page, entrance to the Centre.

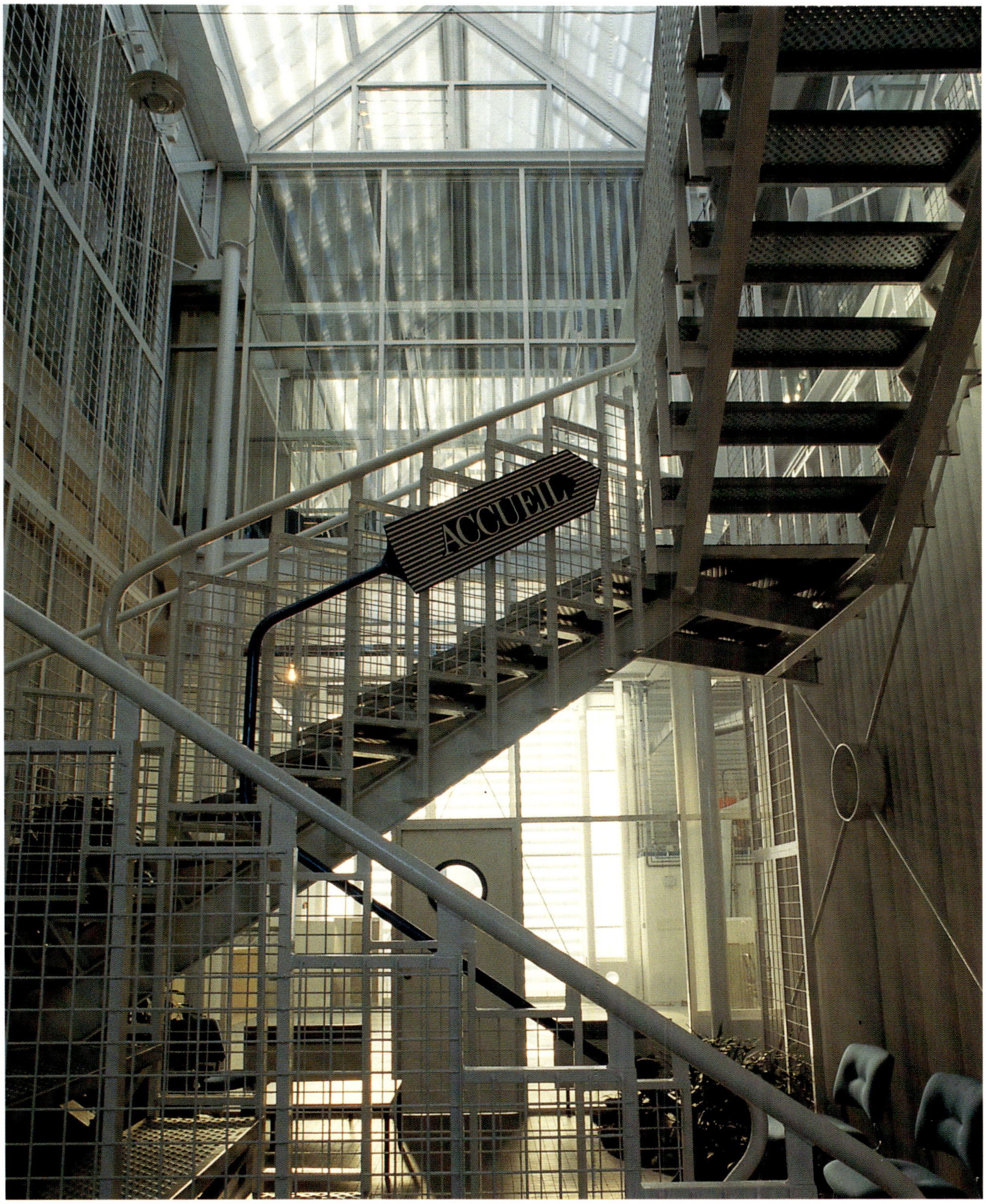

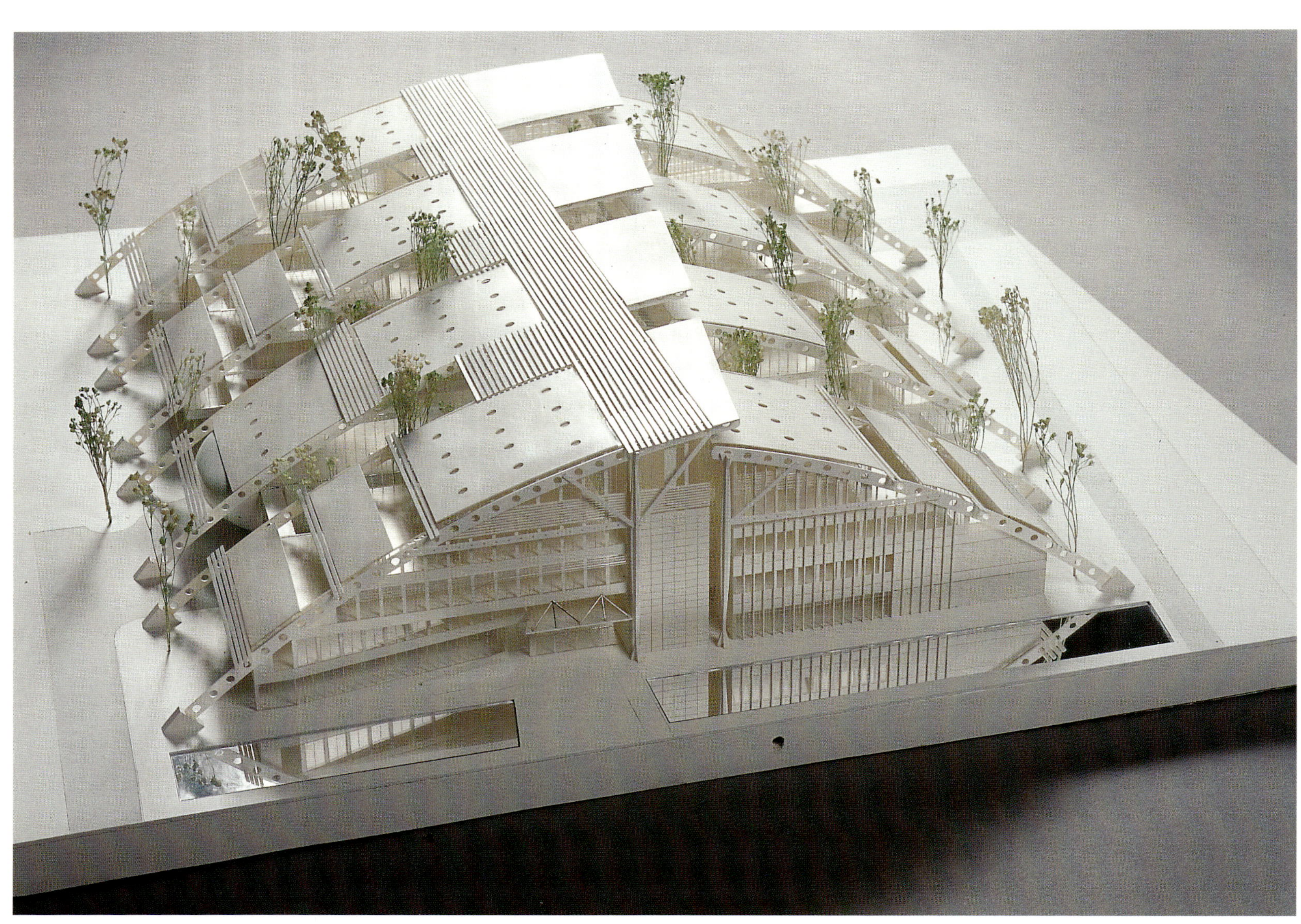

National School of Statistics and Economic Affairs
Marne la Vallée, 1992

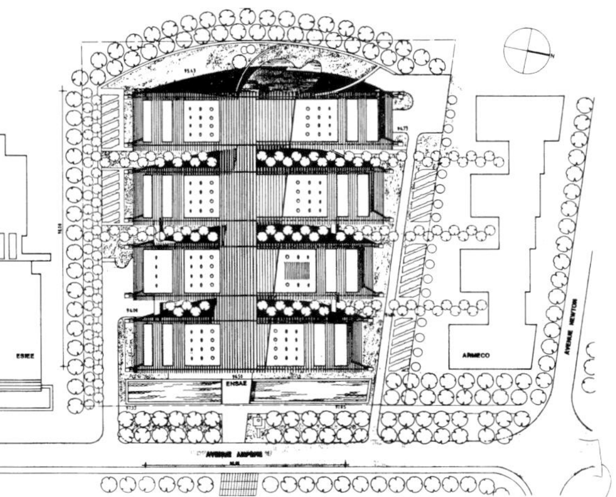

Two major buildings mark the project site, the Bull and the ESIEE buildings. Their formal designs are similar: a powerful curved element contrasts the strong rectilinear force of the main building body.

To the north of the site, the facade of a tall office building is patterned by alternating solids and spaces. The project responds to the site and neighboring buildings drawing on a design that interacts with its surroundings, firstly, by means of its curved shell form in harmony with the entrance to the ESIEE building, and secondly, by "cutting" through this shell to recreate a pattern of spaces and solids similar to our northern neighborhood. Finally, the "shell" element of the project allows the roof to descend towards the ESIEE building avoiding any sudden formal rupture.

The sense of the project was to create a building whose height and mass might "stop" the volume of the avenue and create a visual axis perpendicular to it. It is a tall building (approximately 22 meters) with a nave at the axial point of the composition. The main material used for the structure-envelope sequence of construction is lacquered metal (steel for the structure, aluminium for the envelope). This projects a contemporary image of high technology. The entire building gives onto a large well-lit nave. It is a meeting place, a place of exchange, as well as the focus of pedestrian flow. It is the heart of the school, bordered by the school itself but also by gardens, which flow into the center of the establishment.

The interior organisation of space is designed around eight wings, grafted onto the nave, four to the south, four to the north. Each wing has three levels and a roof space. The height of the building limits vertical flow and gives priority to the horizontal organisation of the school.

The supporting structure is made of steel. The arches of the roof structure are independent of the floor supports, thus the modification of one system does not effect the other. Similarly the framework of the facades supports them independently.

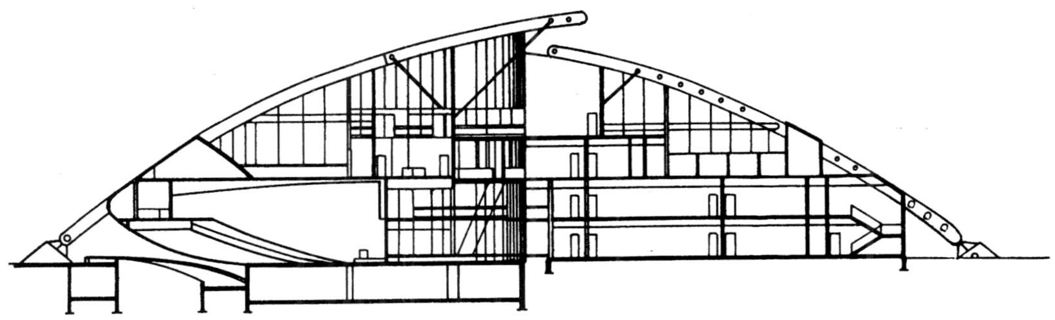

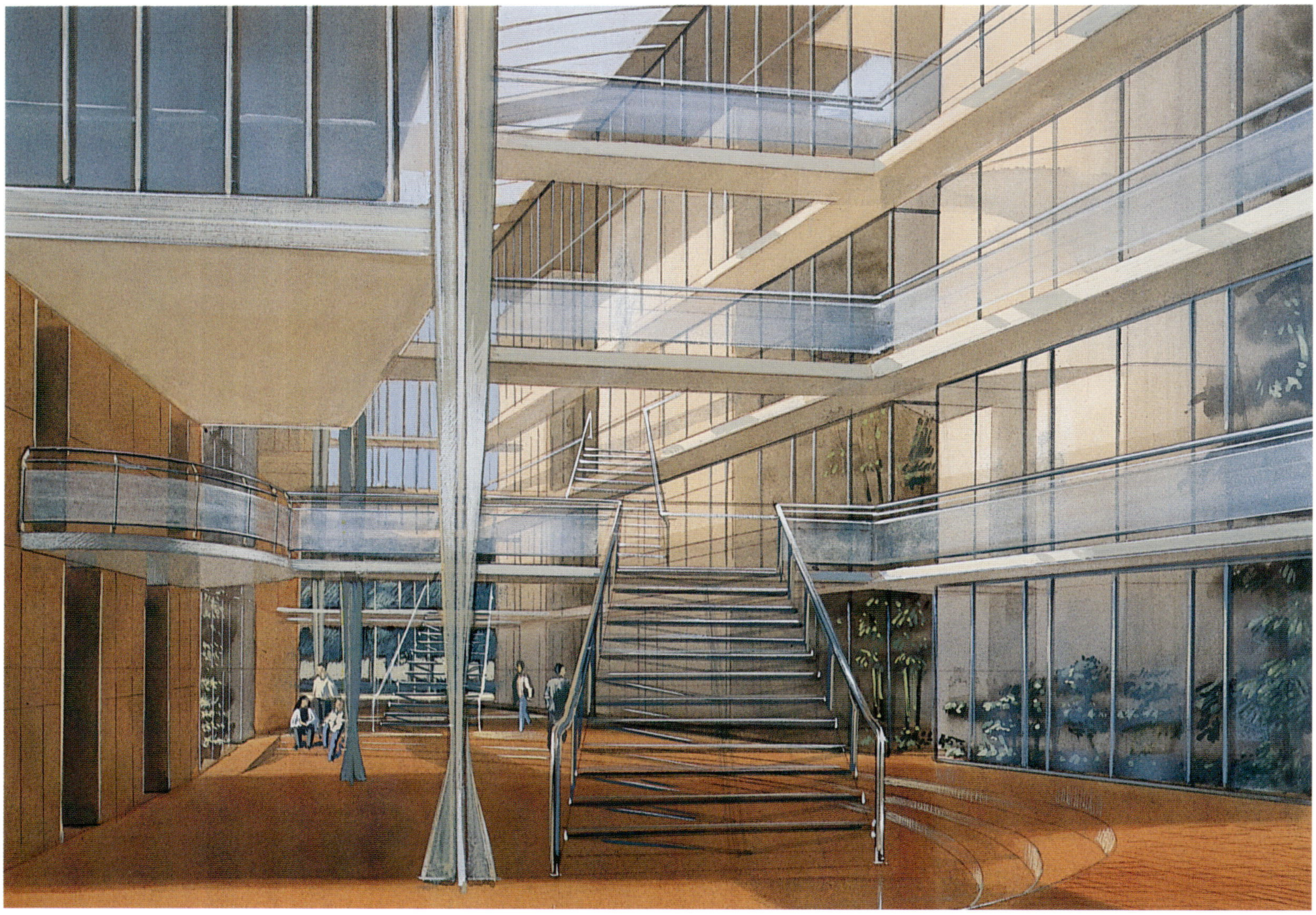

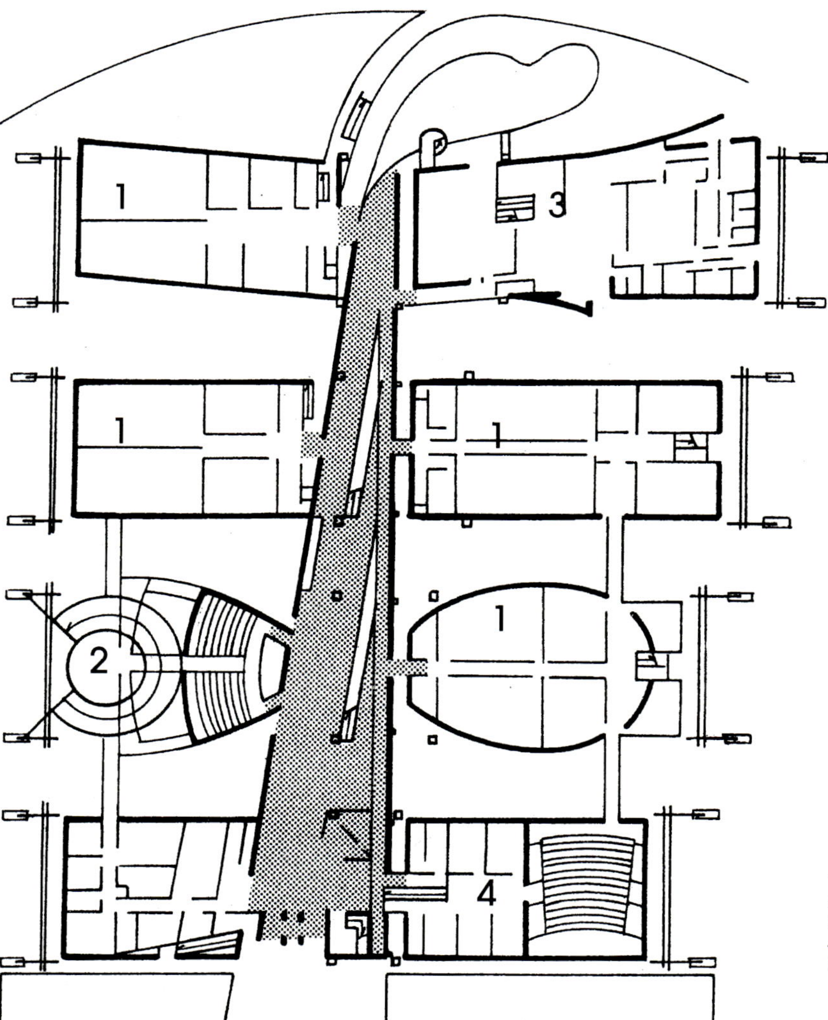

Rendering of the atrium
of the school. Left,
ground floor plan.

1. Classroom
2. Amphitheater
3. Restaurant
4. Rooms
5. Research Center

Side views of the
model. The building
will be constructed
out of a steel structure,
whose roof is
deliberately detached
from the floor supports,
so that construction
elements can be altered
on an independent
basis.

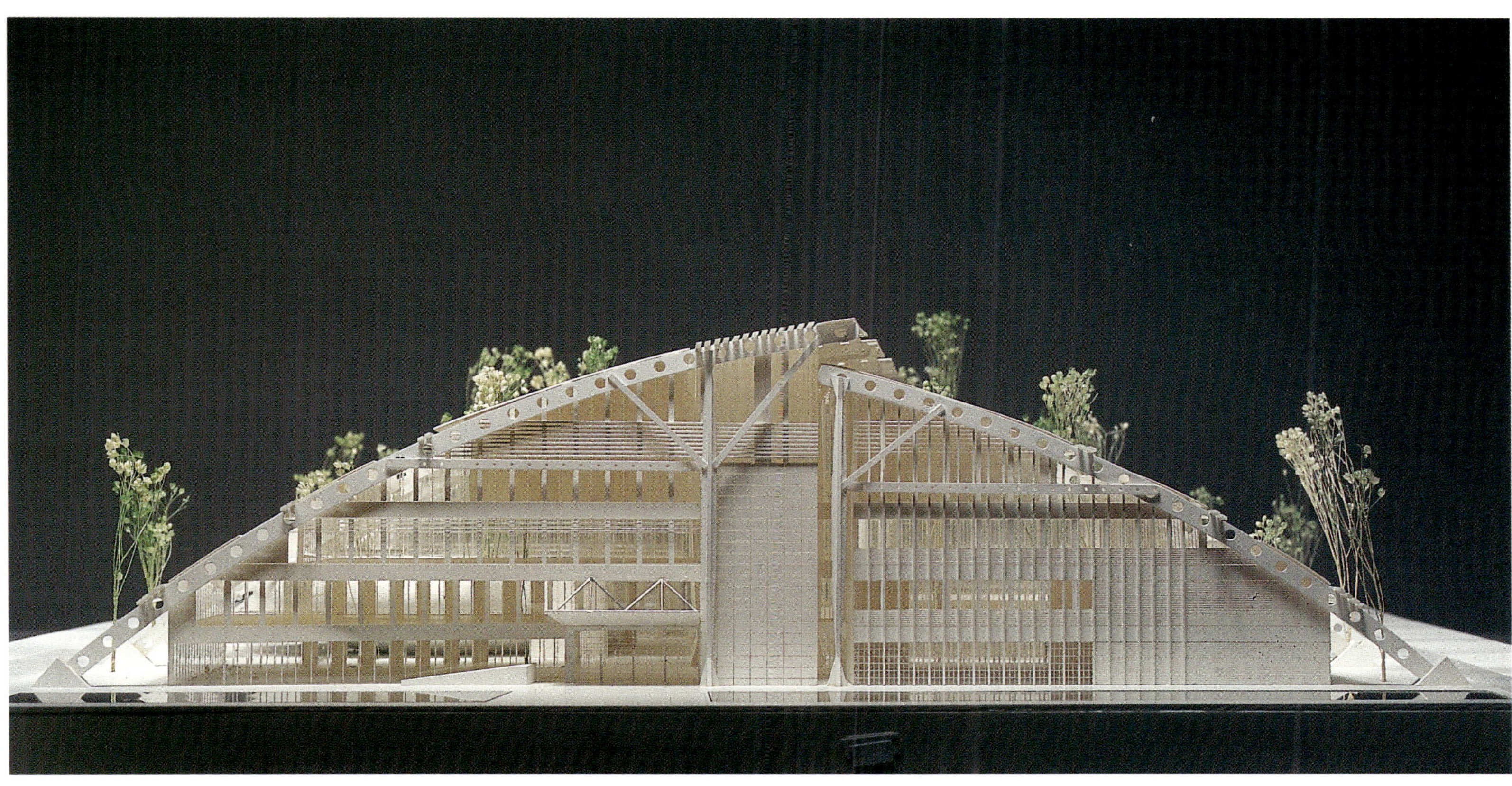

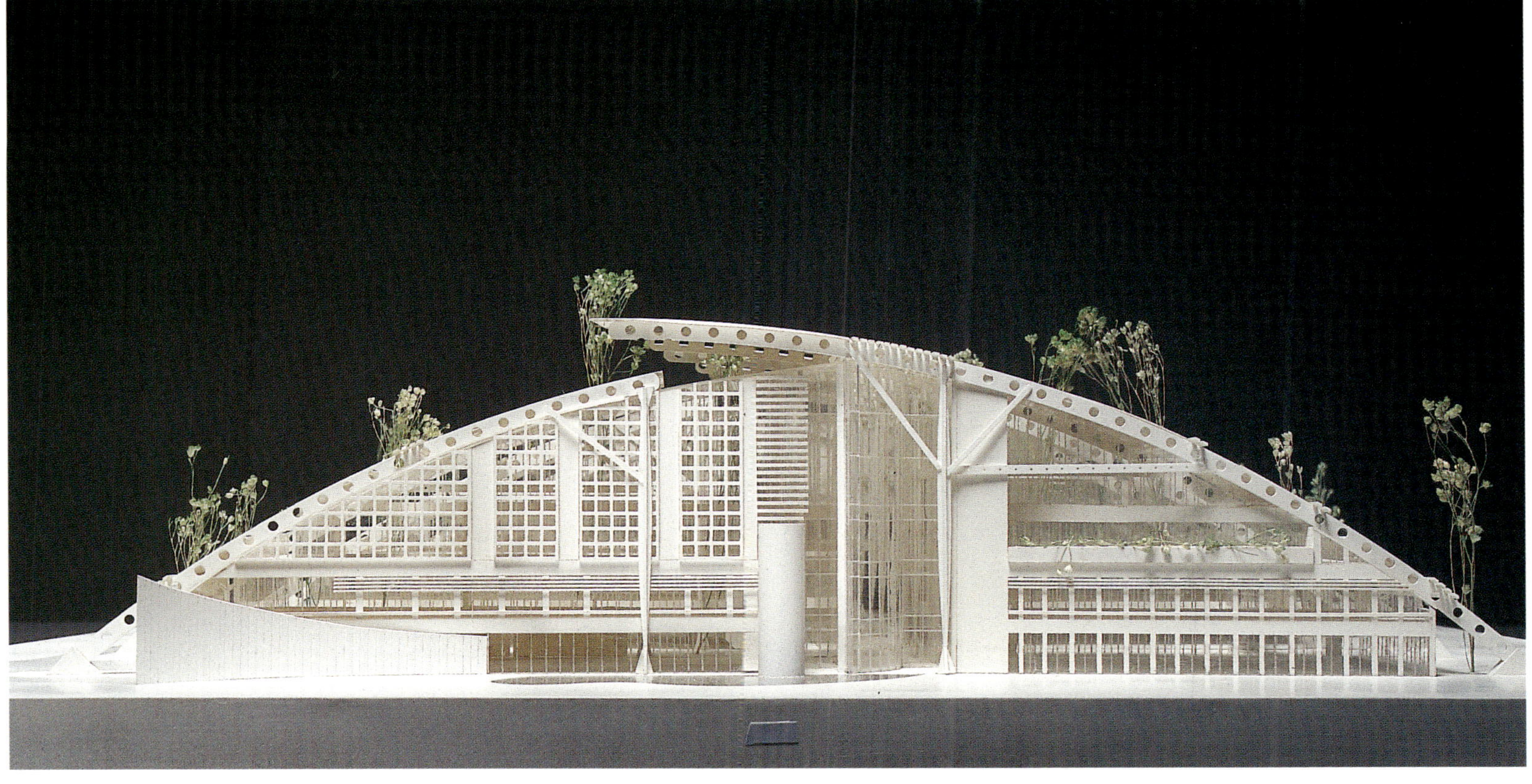

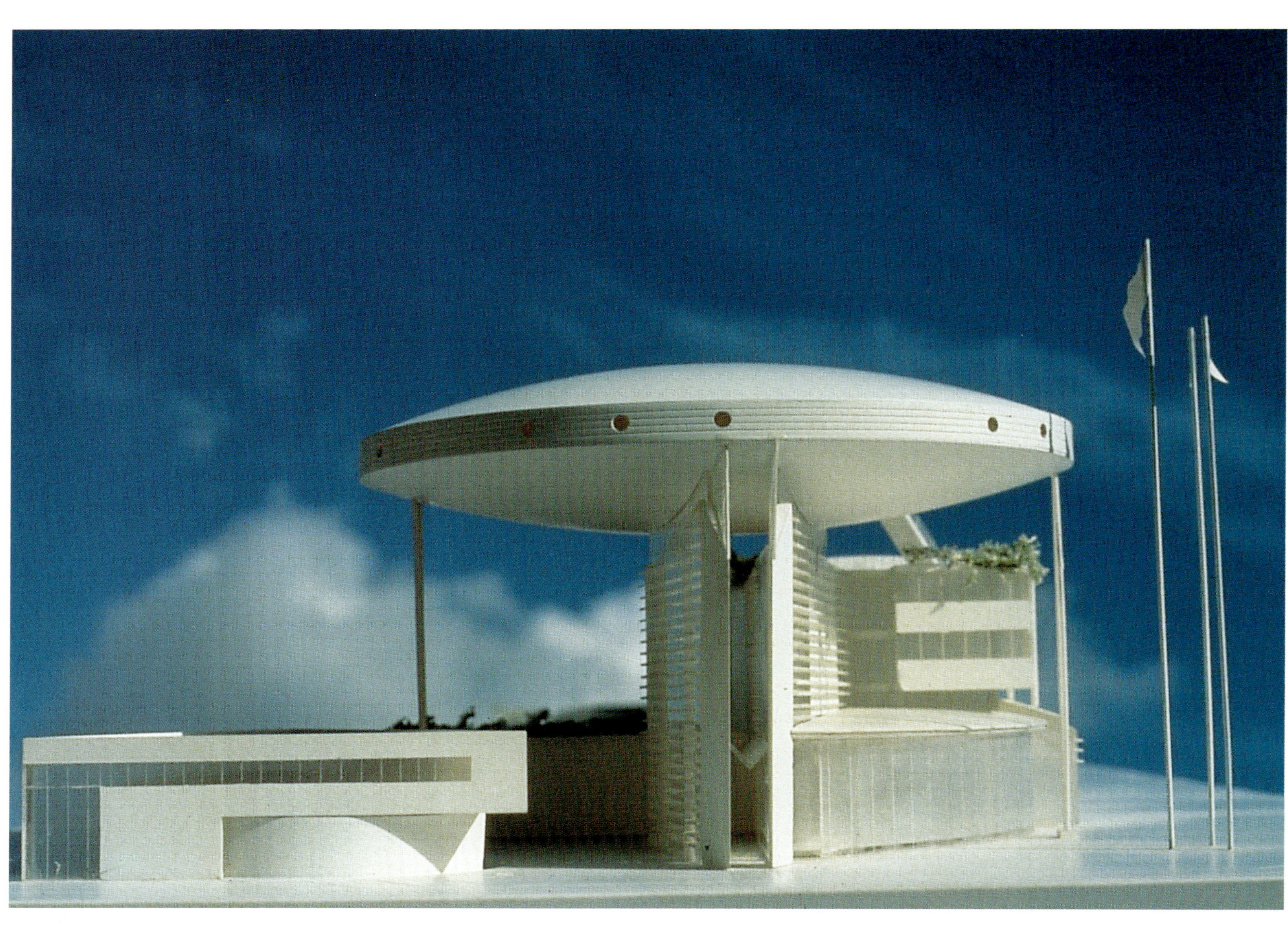

Departmental Assembly
Nanterre, 1992

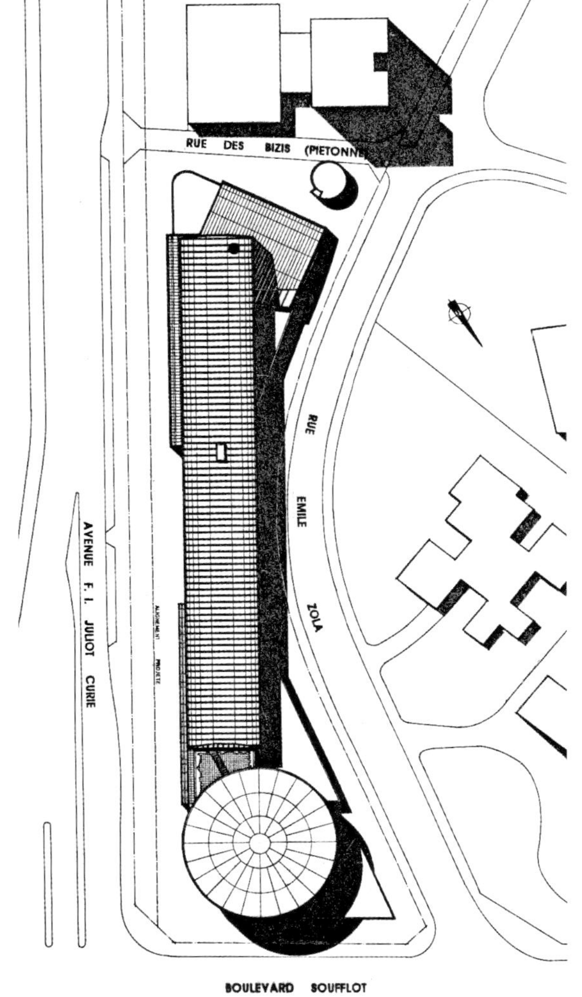

This project for the Conseil Général Hauts de Seine is designed around a circular plan whose tangents respond to the incoherent lines of its diverse urban context.

The idea was also to counterbalance the massive presence of the police headquarters tower, as the only "sign" in the neighborhood.

The project consists of some 11,000 square meters of office space, support areas and social services; it is completed by the large general counsellor's restaurant, a place for debate but also socialising and making decisions. This being the reason for the spectacular flying saucer, very eye-catching, which injects life into the entire structure, like a modern sculpture.

The project was deliberately designed to give the institution a sense of ultra modernity; but, at the same time, there has been an obvious attempt to make the building functions as clearly identifiable as possible.

The interior layout of space on the office side is as free from structural constraints as possible. The long corridor running through them is injected with a series of spatial features designed to break up the monotony.

The dynamic force of the saucer neutralises the wind. It is supported by a bird's cage frame (a technique designed by Colin Chapman, the inventor of Lotus cars). Only a few thin posts are needed to transmit the load to the ground.

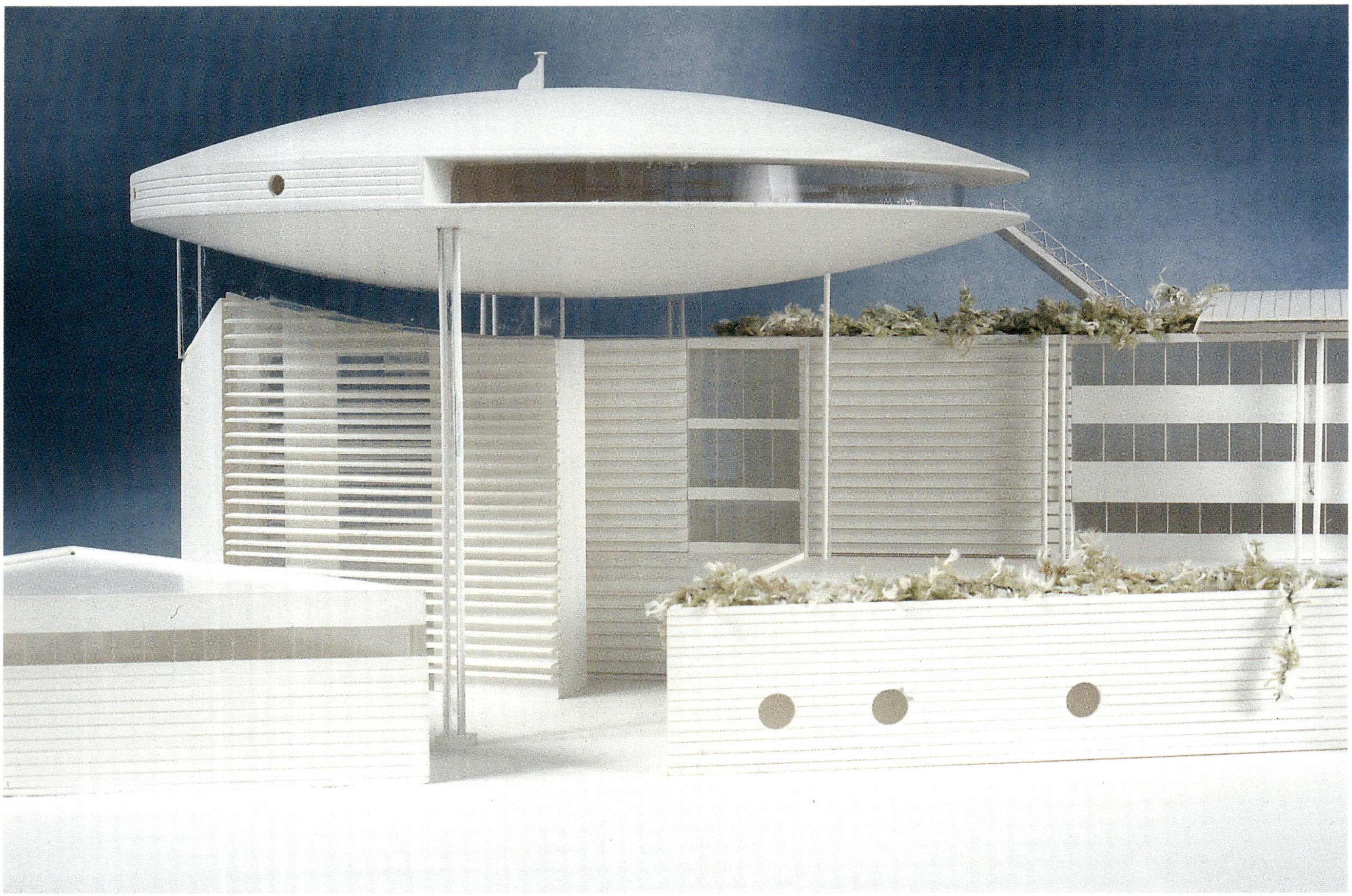

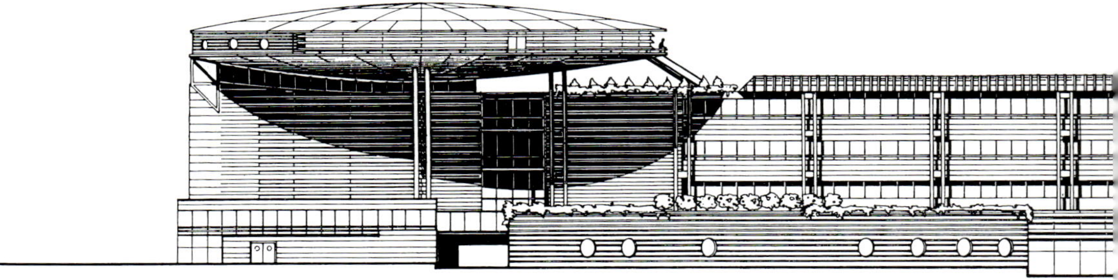

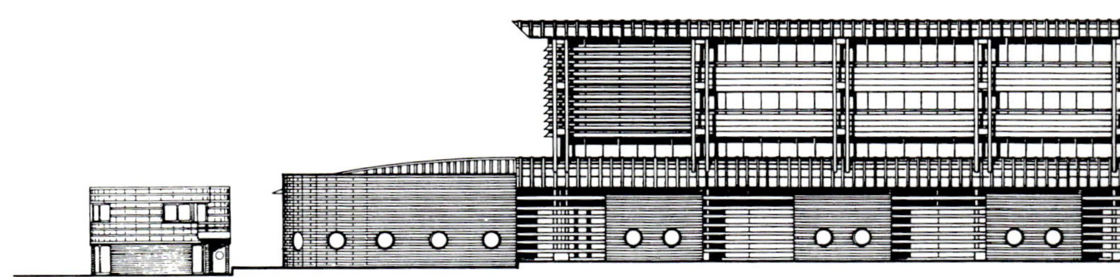

Detail of the model showing the circular structure on the north side of the building housing the council chamber. Right, west elevation and, bottom, east elevation.

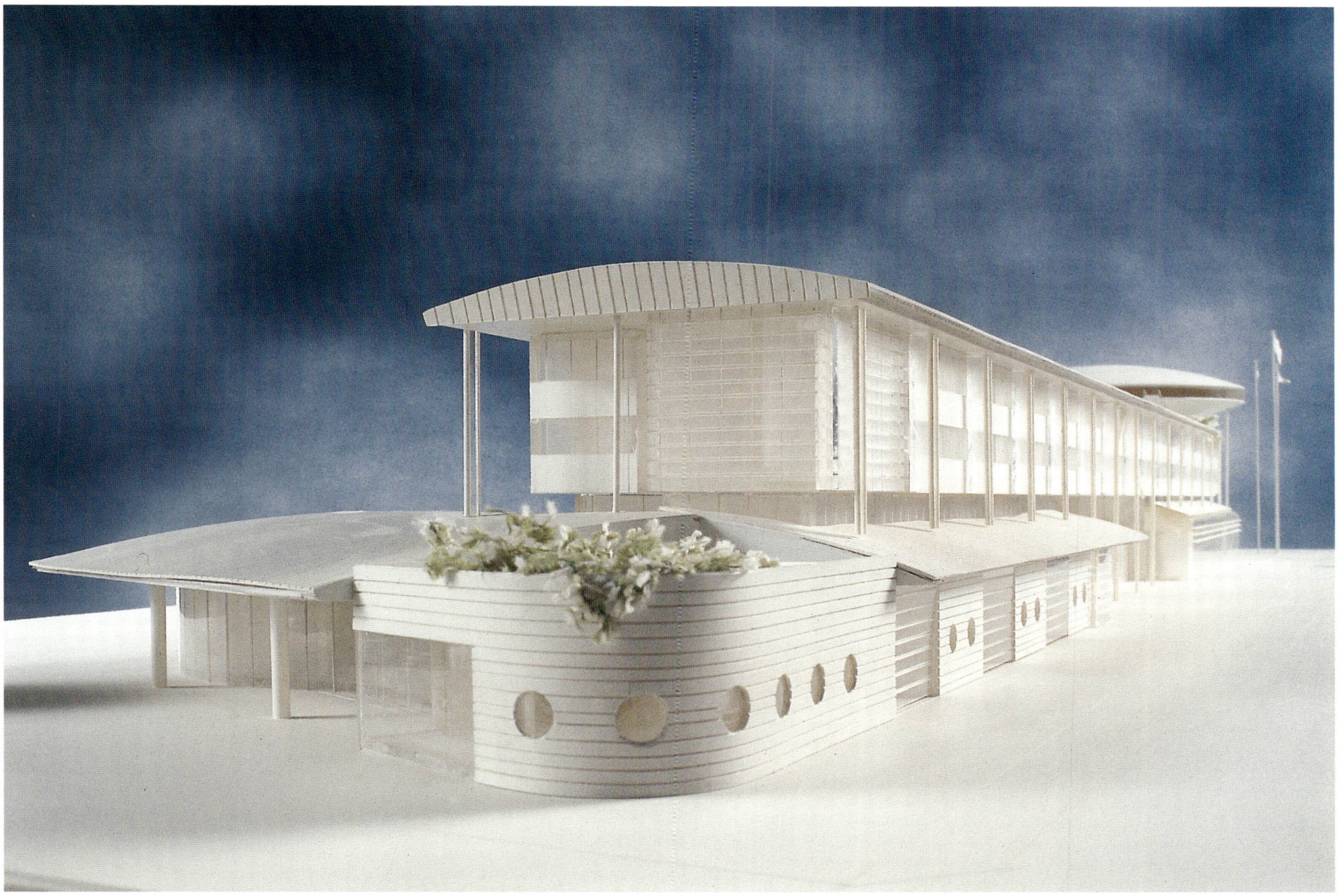

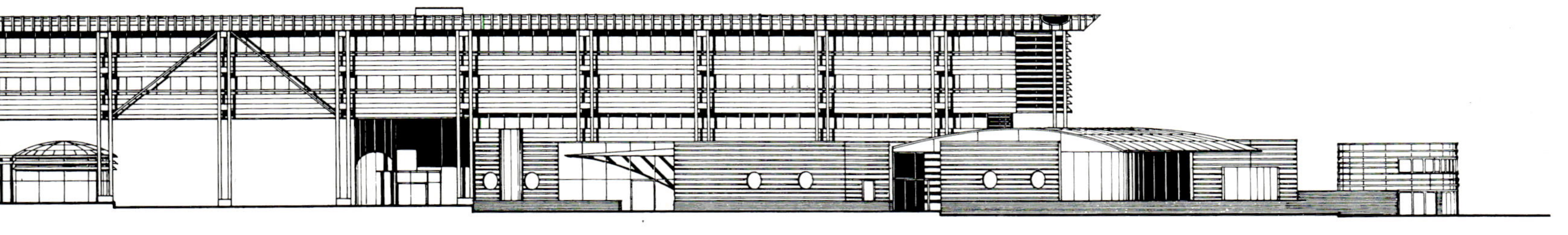

View of the model from
the south.

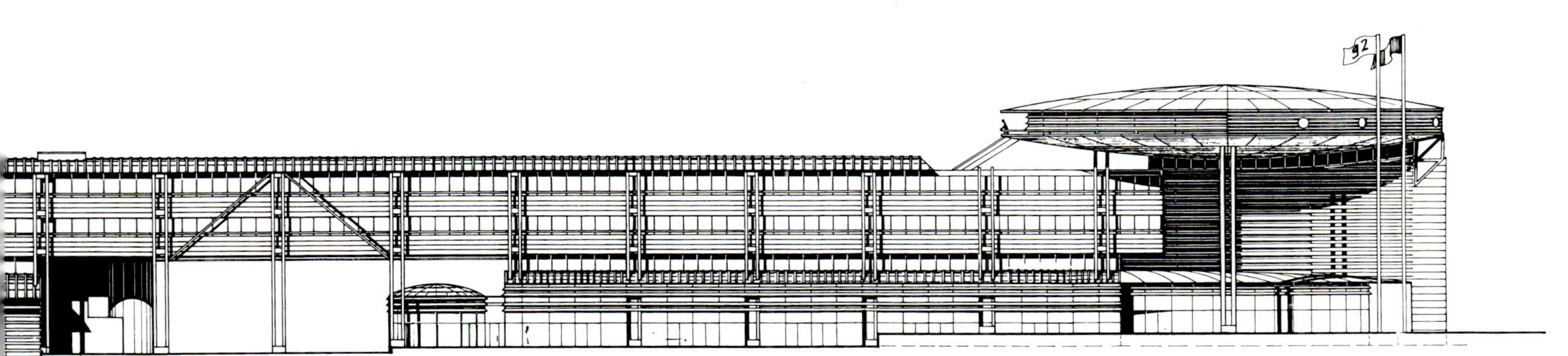

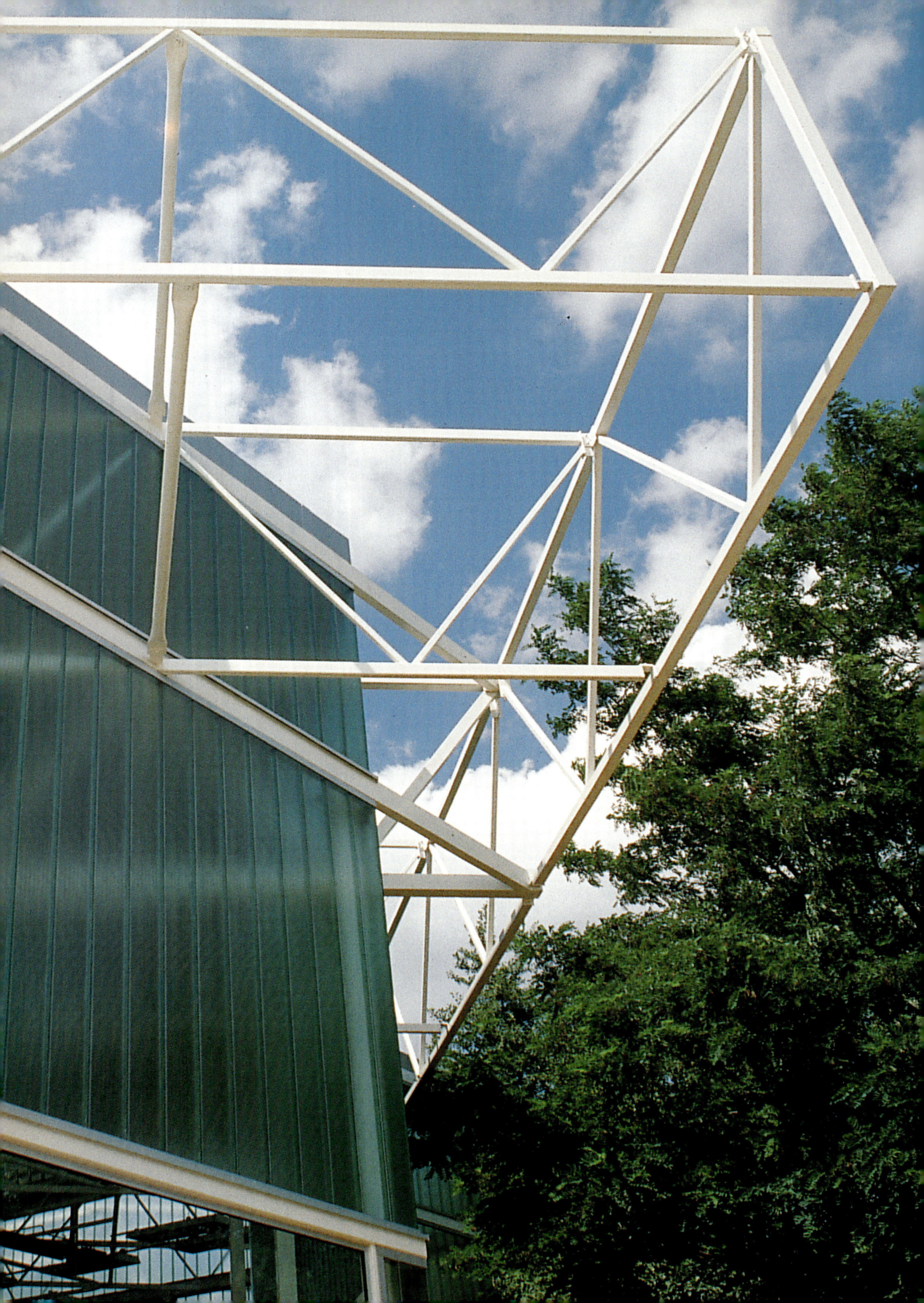

Pasteur Gymnasium
Montargis, 1992

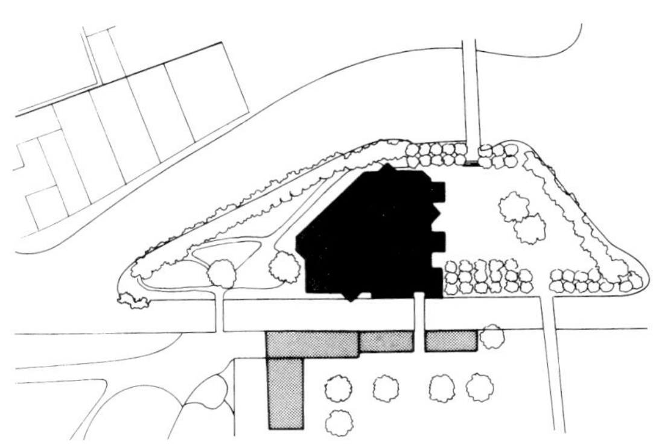

The site chosen by the town of Montargis for its new gymnasium is a superb waterfront on an island on the river Loing, near the outskirts of the town. It is in a key position near the very active gymnastics club housed in a nearby school, whose teachers also act as sports trainers.

The flaming new building suddenly emerges from the greenery in a site formerly reserved for nature. Facing south, the building actually looks onto the waterfront.

The work is discrete. It preserves the silence of the site and contributes to its mystery. It nests in the greenery, opposing tall planes of Reglit glass to the natural vegetation: the green tint of the glass against the green foliage. Only the white lines of the framework betray its presence in the landscape and define the edges of the work.

The pure and large span structure leaves the floor free of obstacles and guarantees the possibility of future remodelling. The glazing, which closes and protects the interior from the weather, does not block the view: athletics should not be cut off from nature.

In winter, radiant heaters supply warmth; in the summer, ventilation openings in the roof naturally cool the space.

It seems to breathe in the landscape. Opposing its green glass facades to the surrounding greenery, the interior perception is of transparency.

The granulated Reglit glass blurs the image but floods the space with changing light. Large bay windows made of clear glass frame the waterfront horizon.

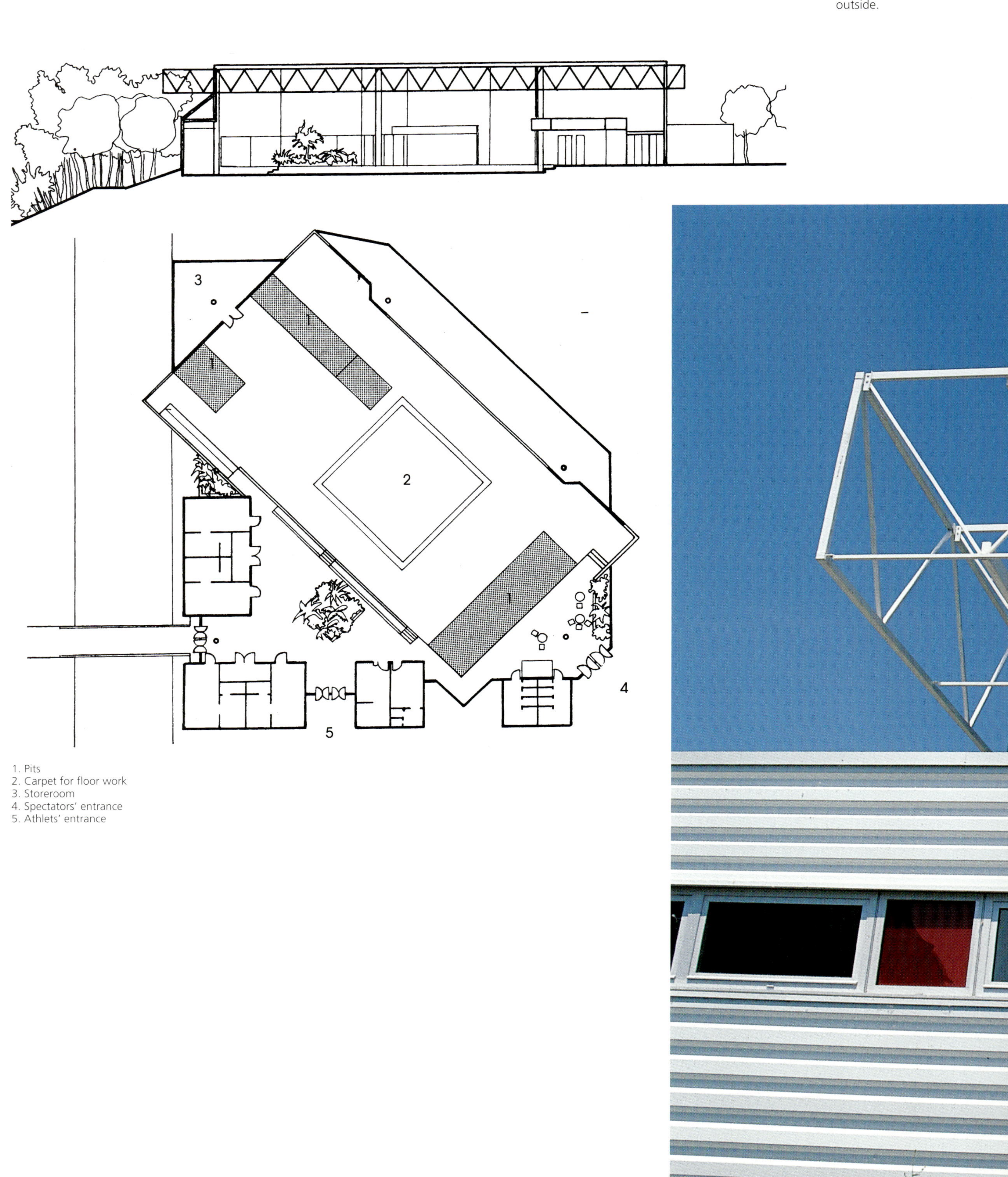

Section and plan of the gymnasium. Right and below, details of the outside facades, partly clad in metal and partly by a large glass window allowing natural light to flood in from the outside.

1. Pits
2. Carpet for floor work
3. Storeroom
4. Spectators' entrance
5. Athlets' entrance

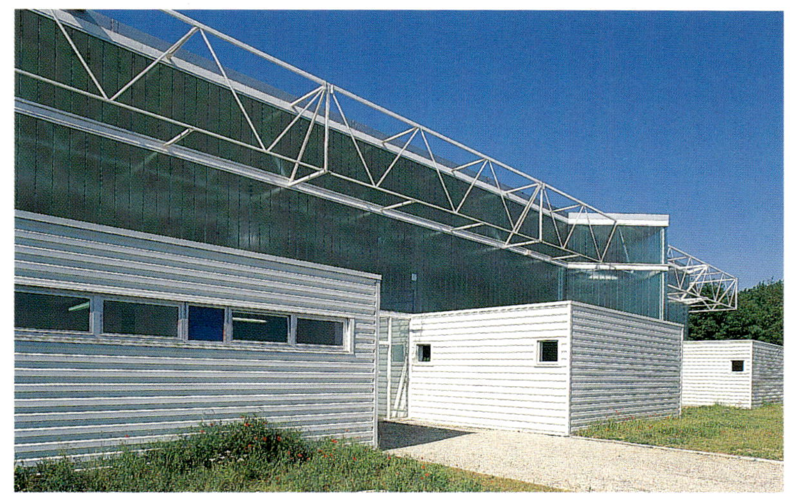
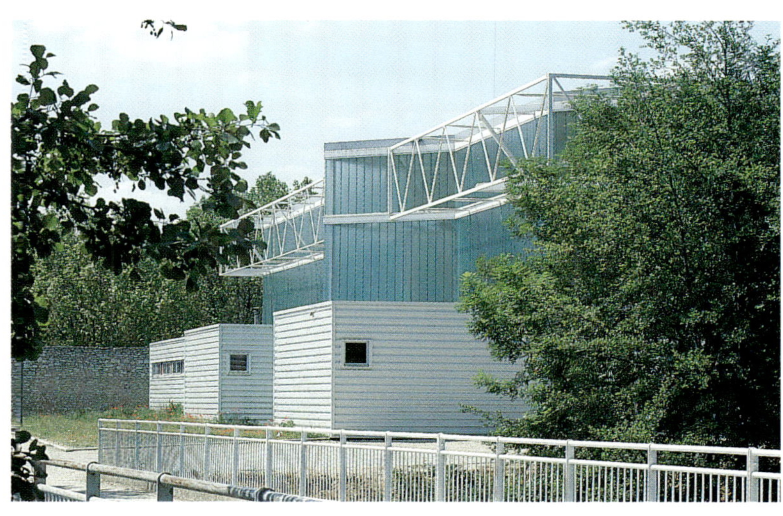

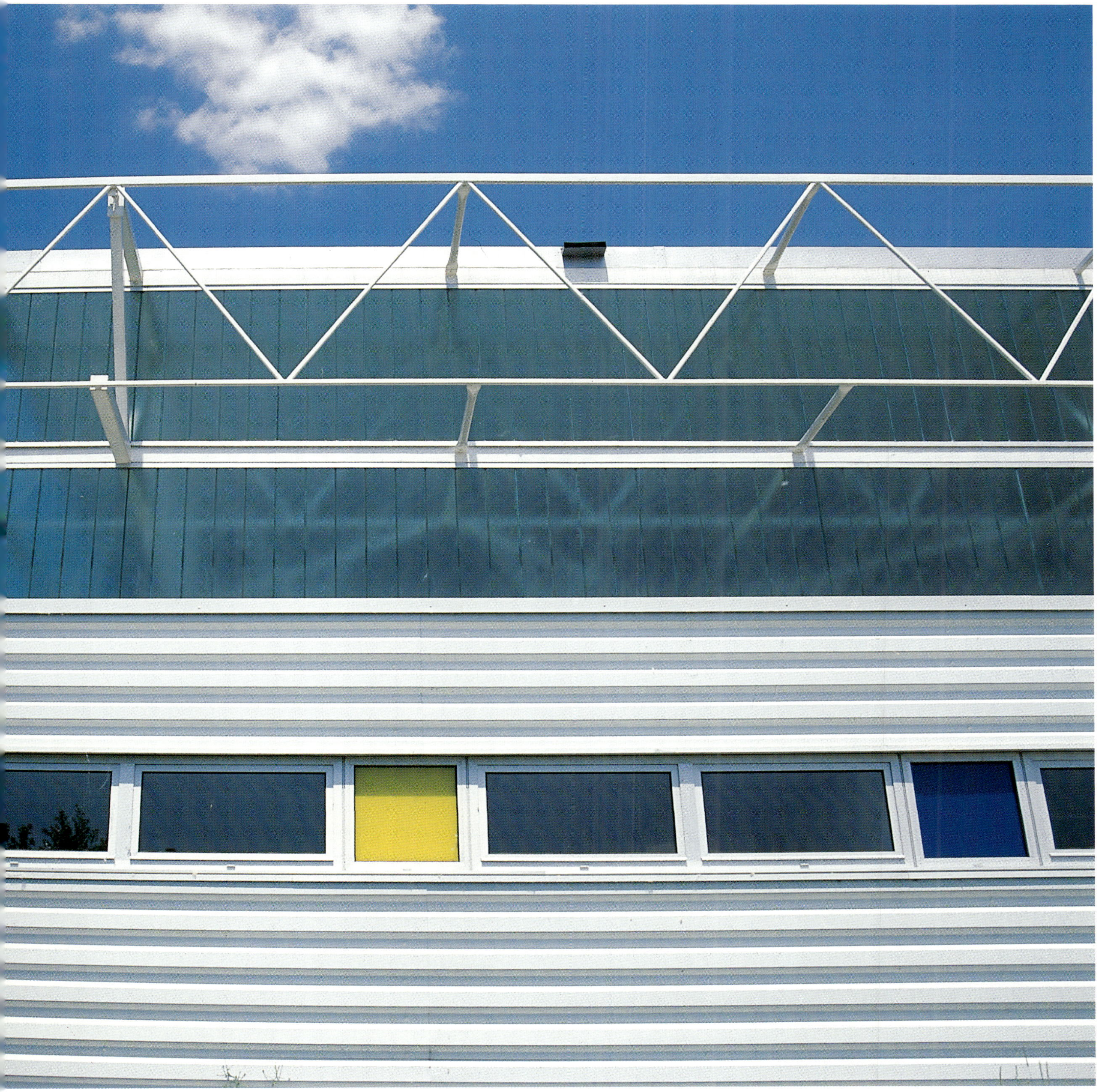

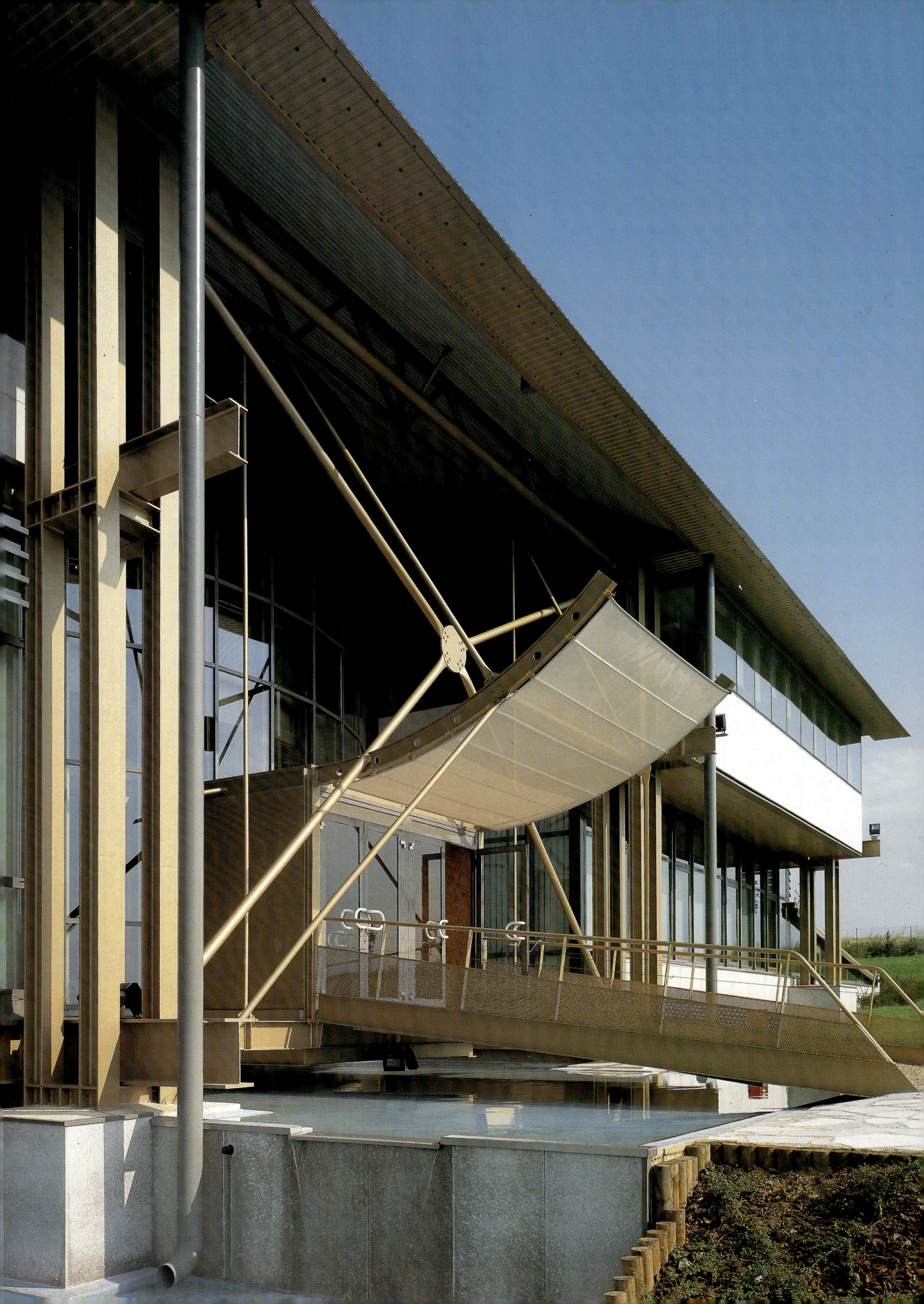

Town Hall
Gauchy, 1992

This building stands out on the cityscape due to both its position and structural architecture.

Built on top of a hill overlooking the town center, it looks like a ship's bow incorporating the main council chambers with the mayor's office placed just above, as part of a rigidly institutional-visual hierarchical ordering of space; this entire end section draws on the natural slope of the land to jut out over two sculptured columns placed along the sides of two rather unlikely little swimming pools leading through to the car parks beneath the main building (equipped with a special one-stop lift reserved for the mayor).

The local client's requirements have not detracted from the quality of this design, as exemplified by the way the structural layout transforms into the hub of the architecture without deteriorating into an exercise in style; the exposed metal fixtures serve specific functional purposes while, at the same time, weaving into a valid figurative pattern over a series of levels. There has also been an interesting choice of "light-weight" building materials (metal, mineral wool and chalk) designed to speed up the construction process and keep down the weight of the bearing structure itself.

This notably rigid structure does not require any secondary structures to anchor down the large glass thermal windows; the entire volume is extensively insulated and sheltered beneath a large classical vault-shaped roof clearly bearing Dubosc and Landowski's signature.

The decision to color the structure with a golden bronze coating turned out to be extremely effective, adding (together with the fancy interior cabinets) a touch of Baroque-type nobility and craftsmanship to the overall design.

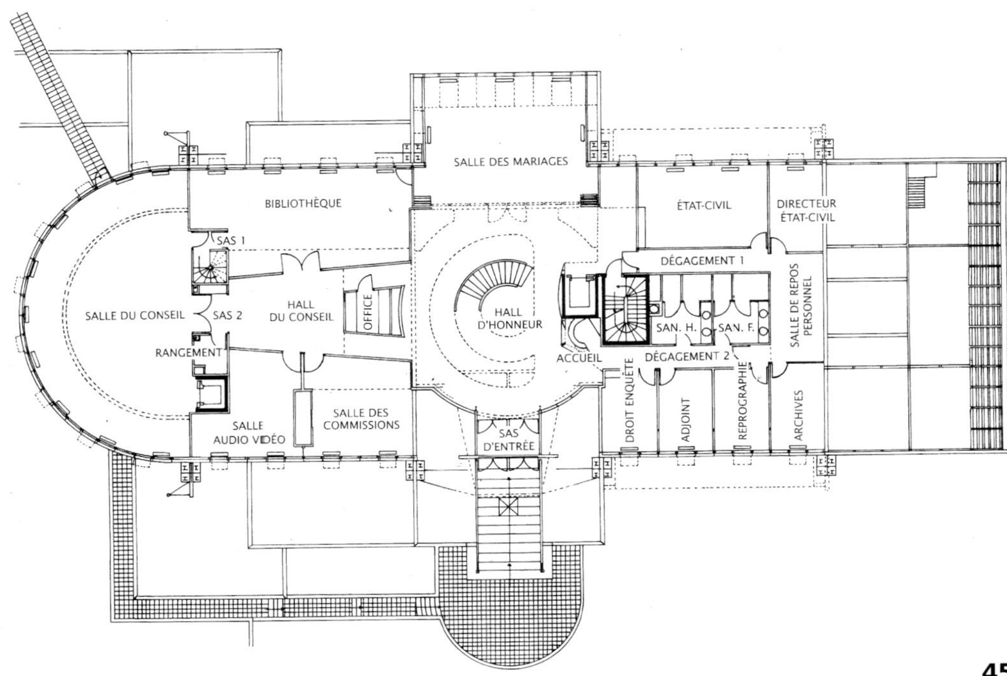

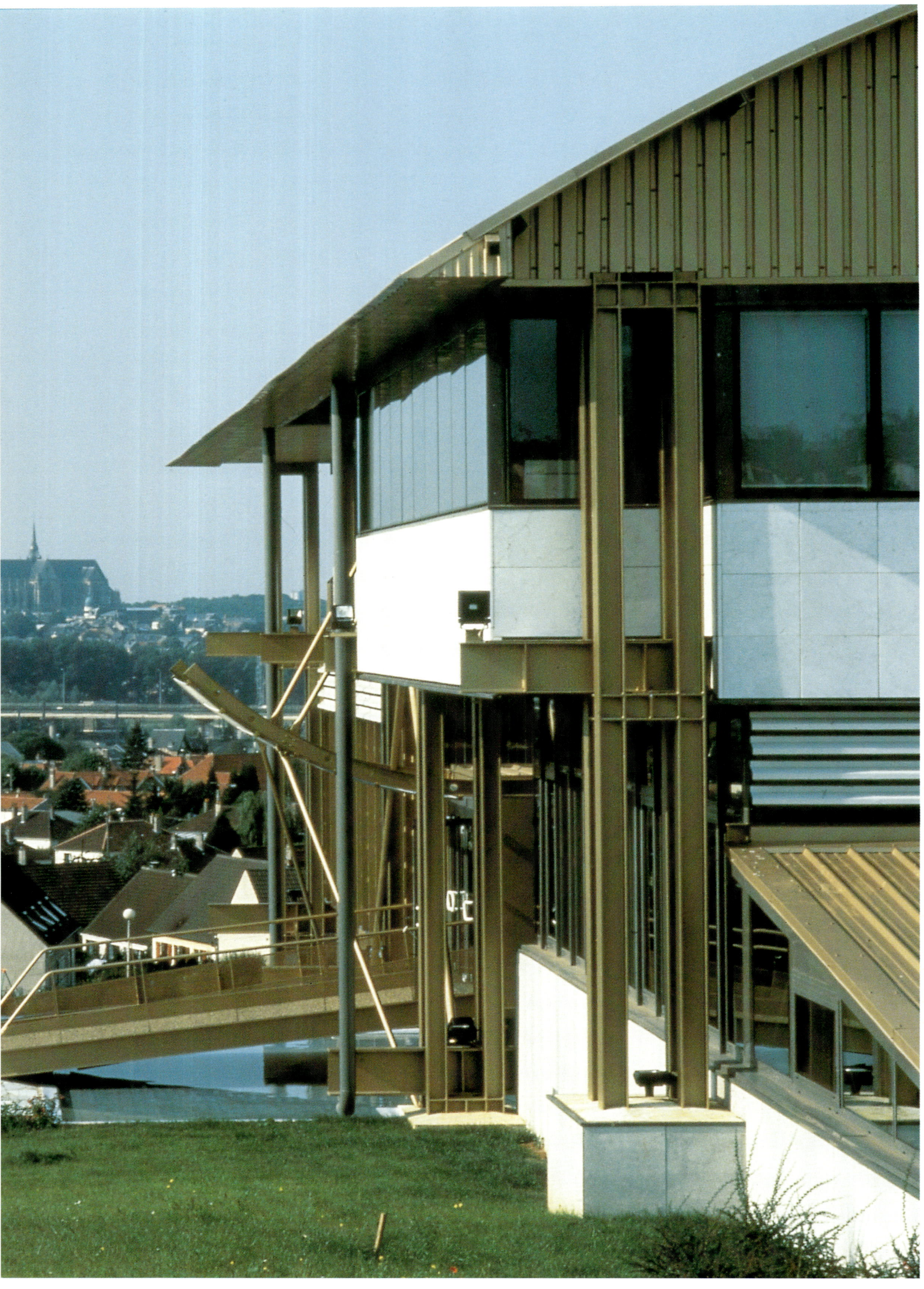

Below, longitudinal
section and general
view. Opposite, side
view of entrance facade
with the urban context
of the town hall.

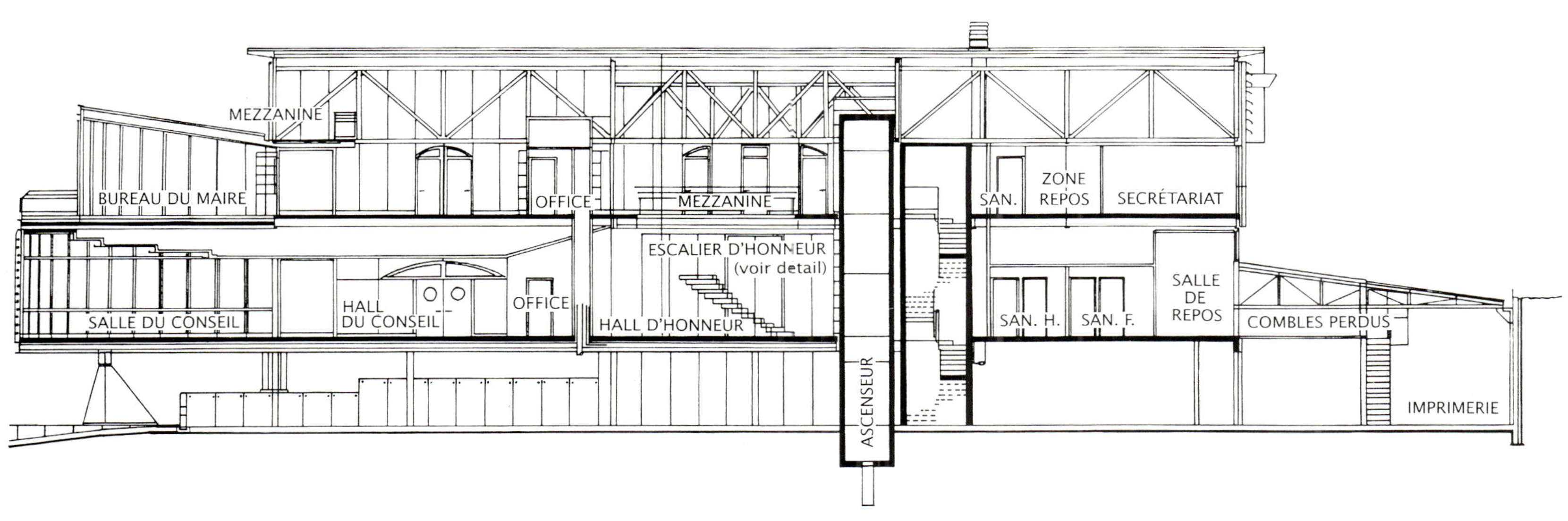
MEZZANINE
BUREAU DU MAIRE
OFFICE
MEZZANINE
ZONE REPOS
SAN.
SECRÉTARIAT
ESCALIER D'HONNEUR
(voir detail)
SALLE DU CONSEIL
HALL DU CONSEIL
OFFICE
HALL D'HONNEUR
ASCENSEUR
SAN. H.
SAN. F.
SALLE DE REPOS
COMBLES PERDUS
IMPRIMERIE

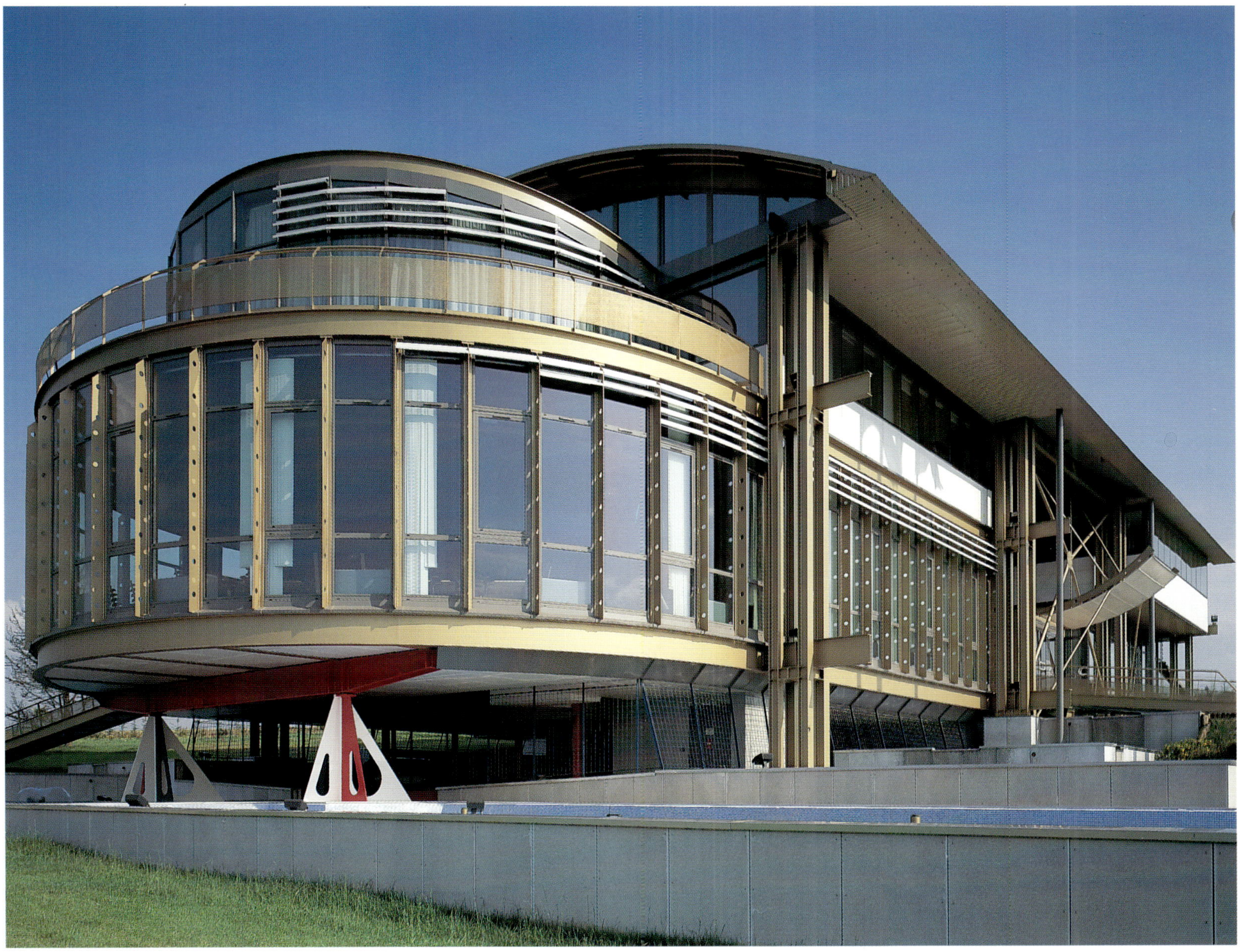

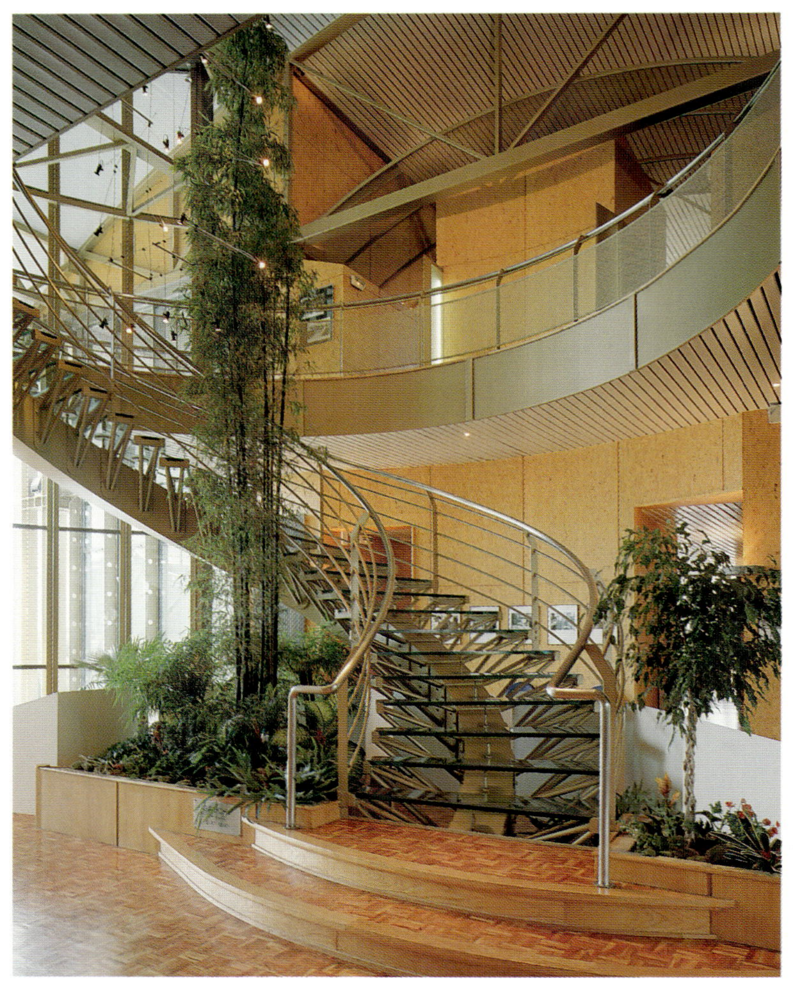
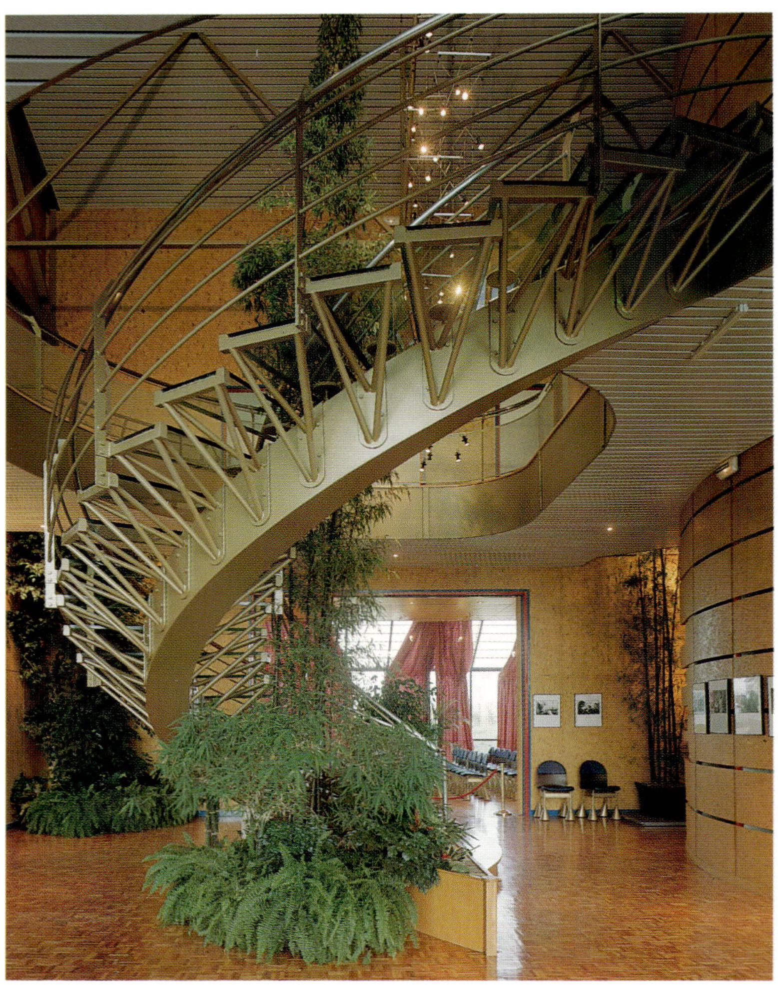
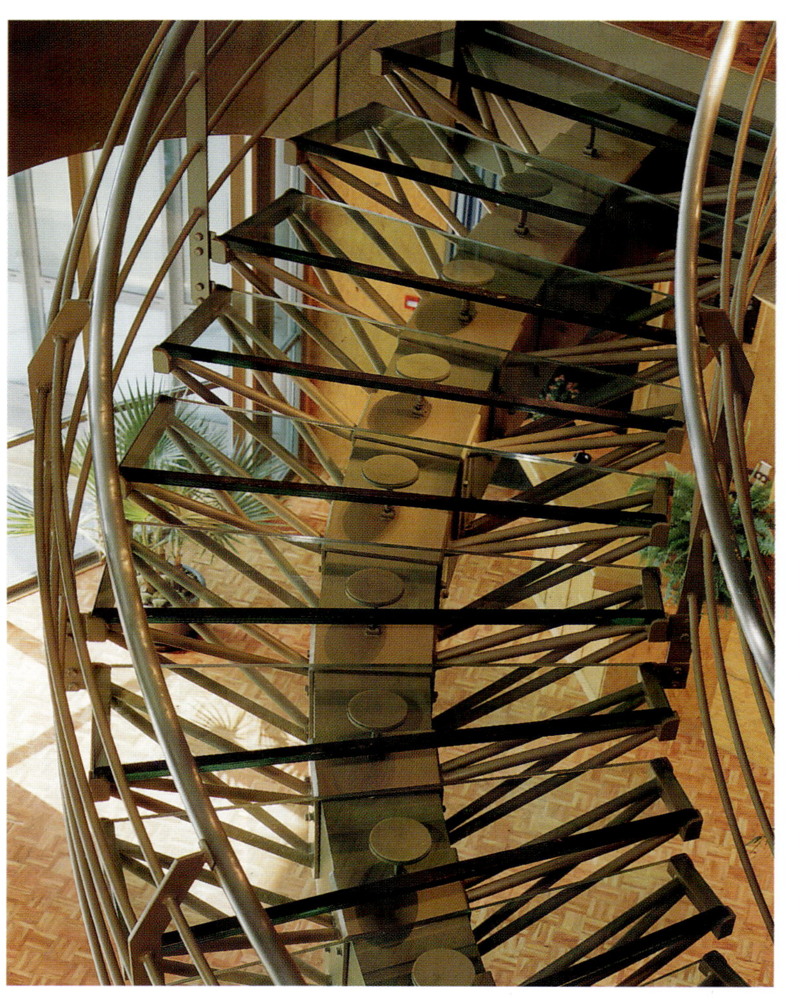
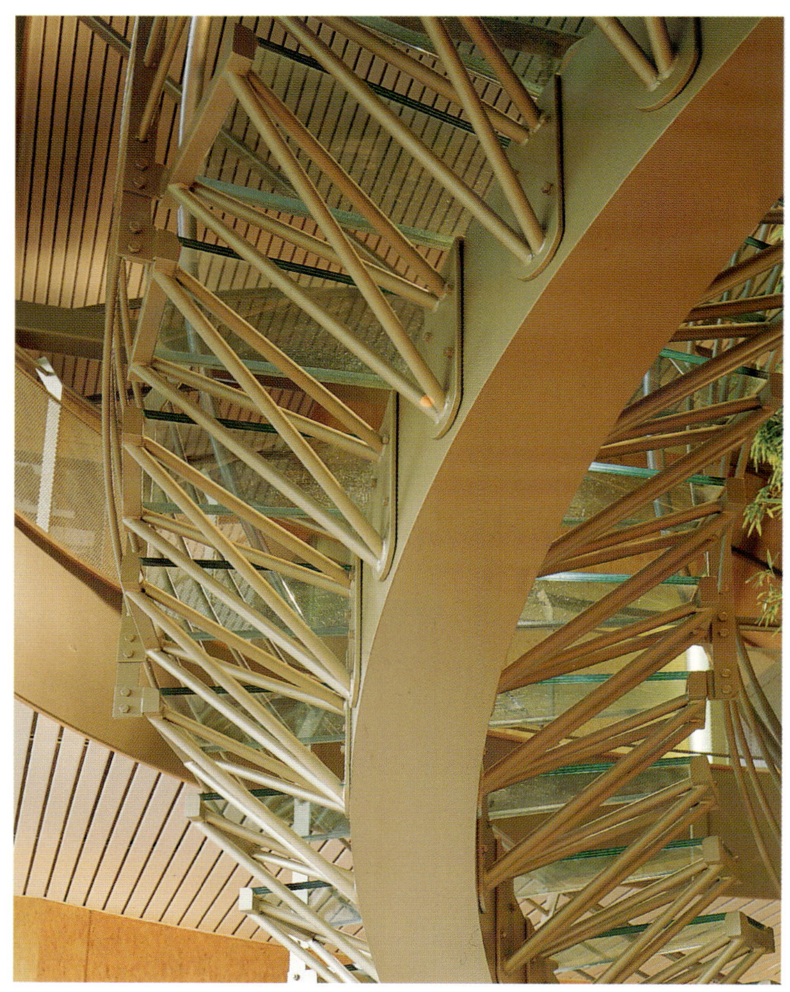

Below, the mayor's
office. Opposite page,
the grand staircase
running from the
entrance hall to the first
floor, where the offices
of the mayor and
the general secretariat
are situated.

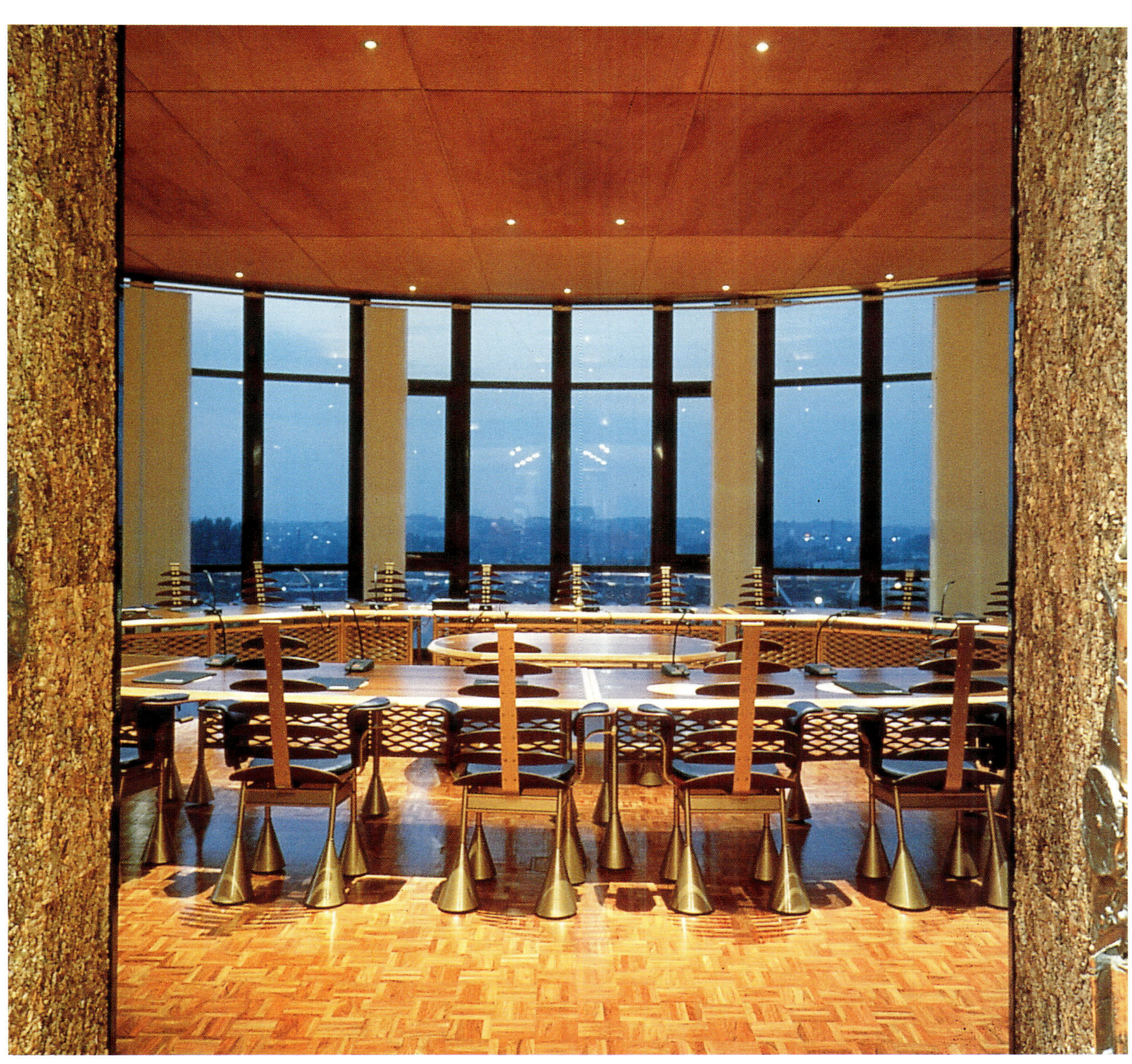

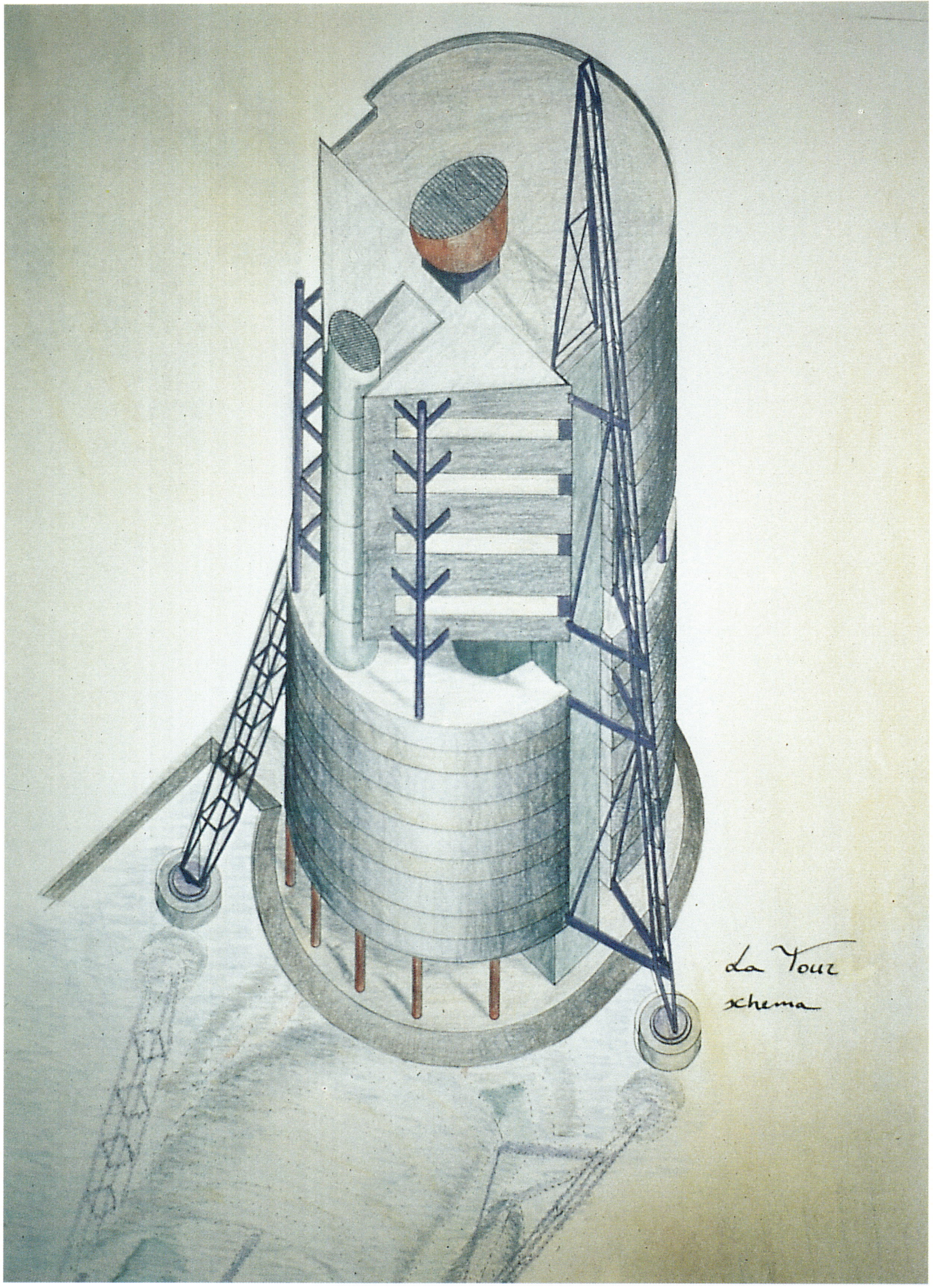

La Tour
schema

D'Auguesseau Housing Complex
Clermont Ferrand, 1992

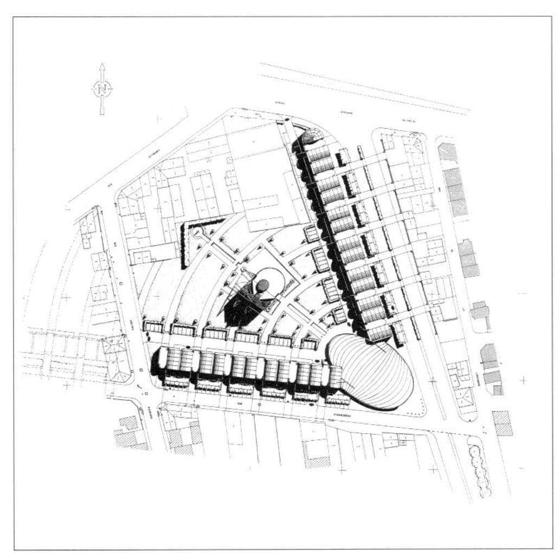

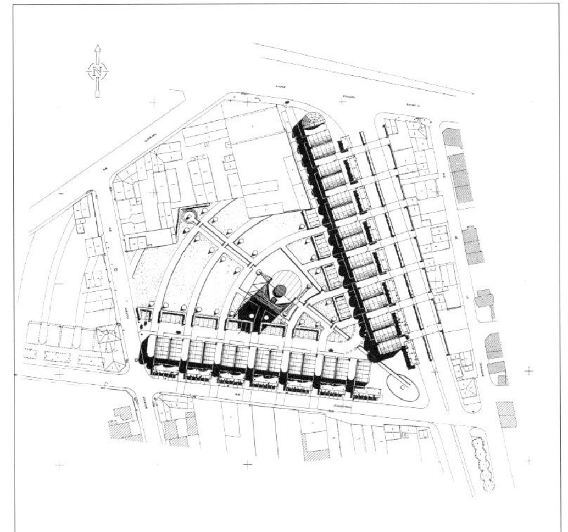

This project is designed to ground an urban development scheme in a classical architectural composition drawing on the latest building technology.

Interaction with the urban fabric takes advantage of a "4-way system" to create an urban-type sequence without interferring with the carefully controlled atmosphere of this small neighborhood.

The same classically inspired geometrical forms exercise their organising force on the landscape, road layout and buildings, in order to keep the visual situation under strict control.

Architecturally speaking, it is the facade that dicatates the overall design, as with most projects designed by Dubosc and Landowski. Great care has also been taken over the surfaces of the facades, exploiting the appearance of the materials used and their contribution in terms of thermo-acoustic efficiency, ease of construction assembly, and ageing properties. The interiors mirror a dynamically innovative concept of space.

Here again in this project, these two French architects have used the potential symbolic force of forms to send out an ideological message: the tower, firmly entrenching a design hinging around a pool of water, projects up into the sky to express a feeling of confidence in the future. It also constitutes a powerful landmark and, at the same time, is ideally reflected in the bell towers in the old town center,

built, as it is, out of the same deep black Volvic stone.

These two designers are convinced that the delicate problems associated with living in the new suburbs should not be treated superficially or reduced to mere socio-economic conflicts. They could draw great benefit from a modern rendering of the positive aspects of humanism applied to the construction of architecture; the project is, in fact, designed to prove this very point.

Drawing showing
the internal partition
of space.

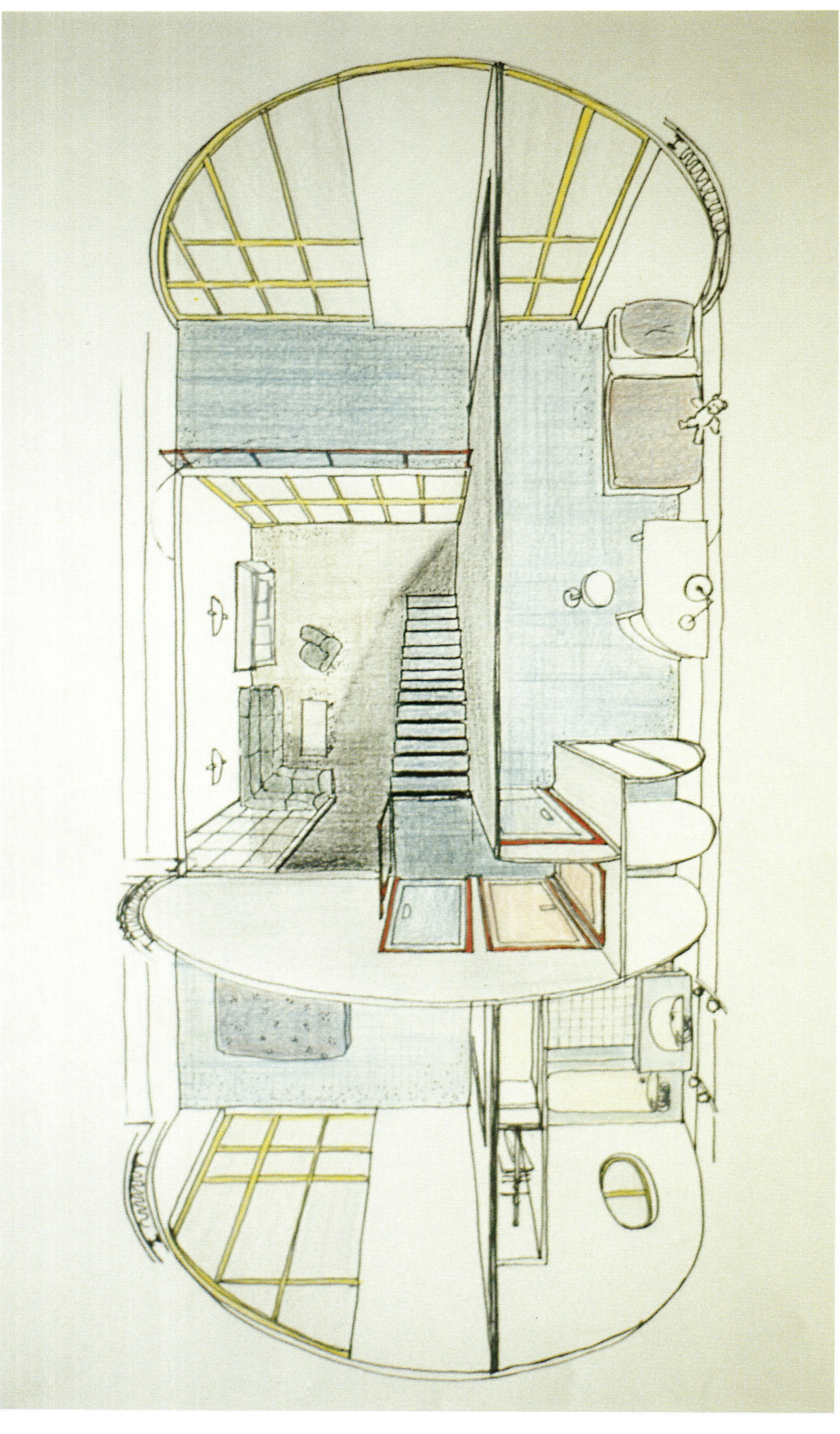

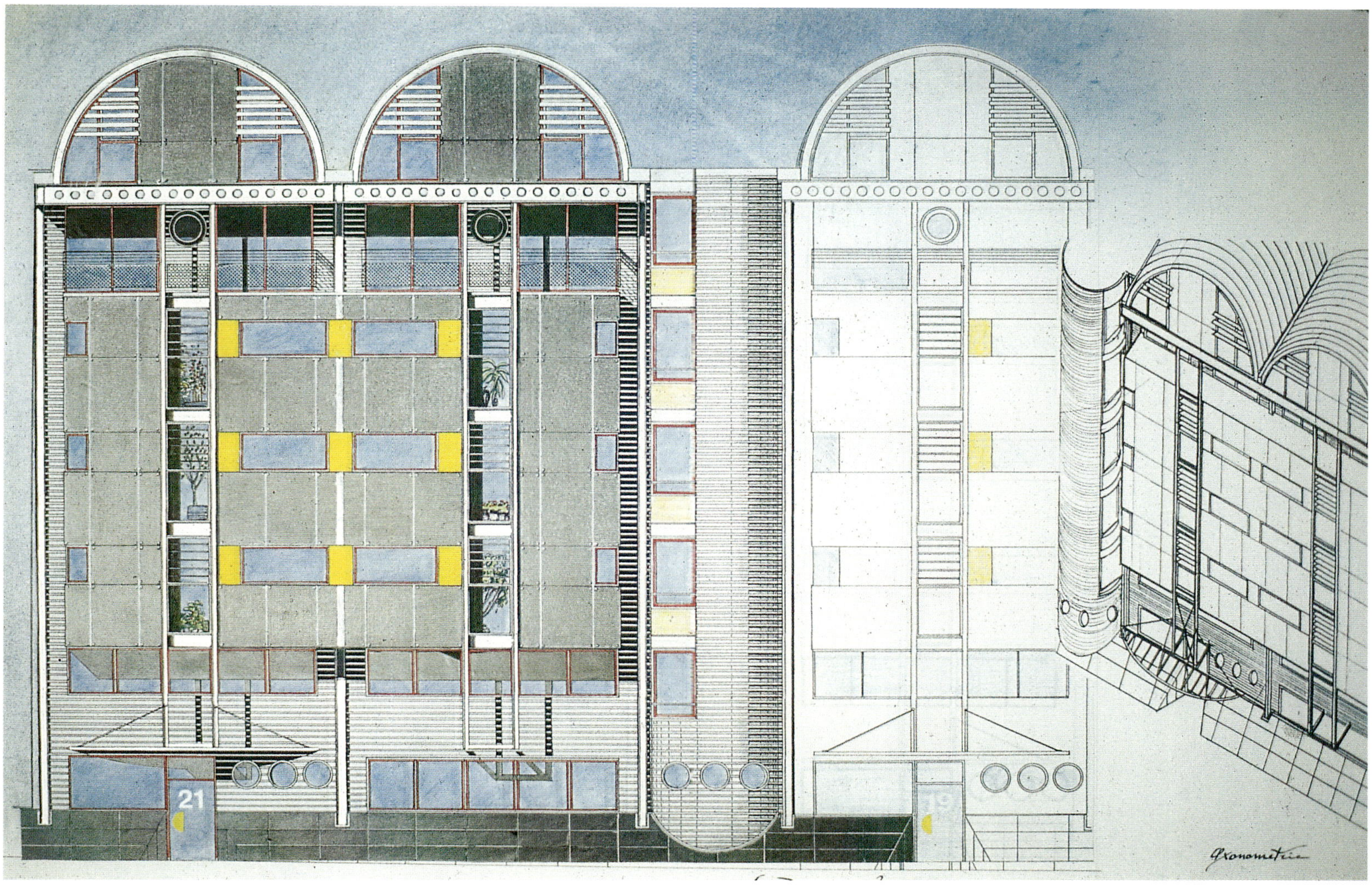

Elevation, section and perspective view of the front of the housing complex and, below, main elevation.

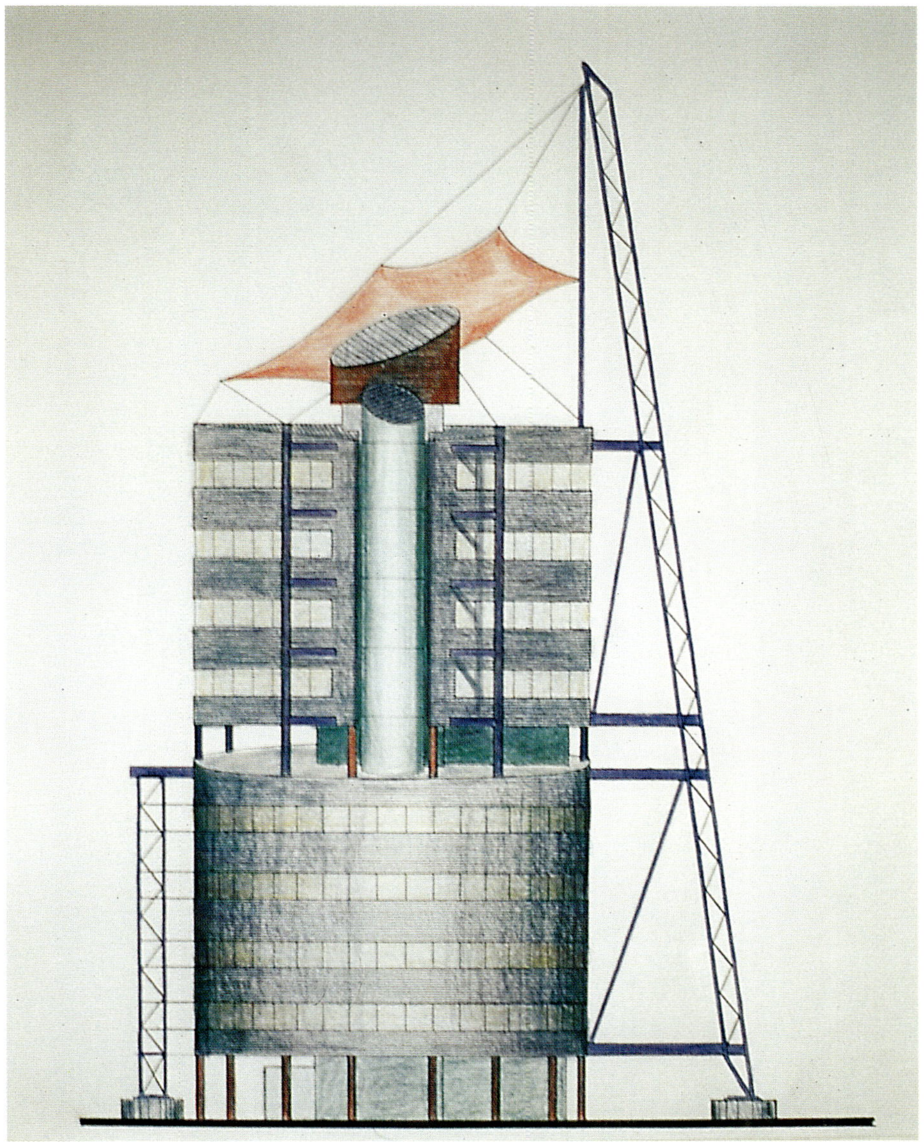

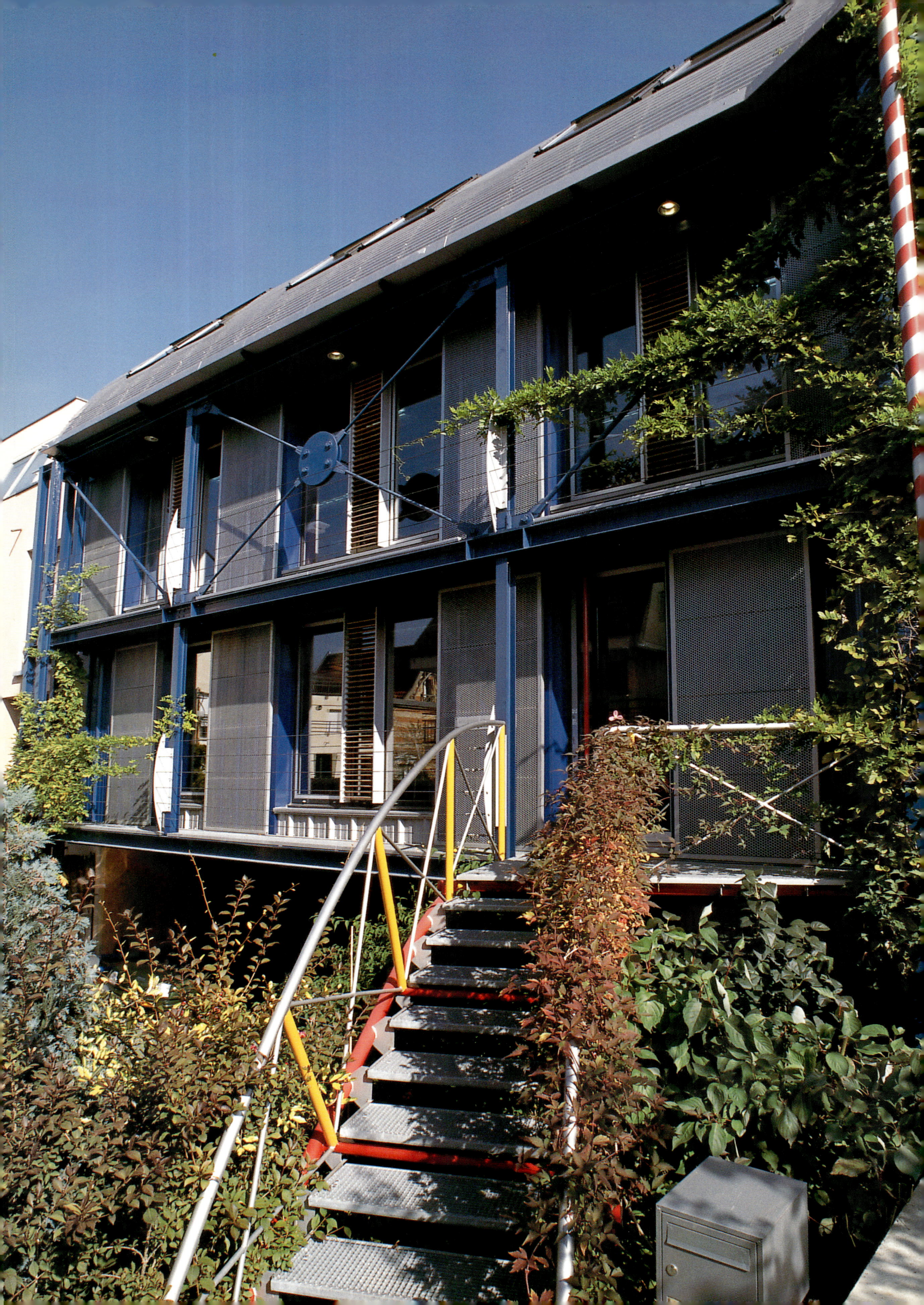

Architecture Atelier
Issy les Moulineaux, 1993

This building, constructed on a 570 square meter lot, is designed on the basis of a simple post and beam structure, yet, despite the simplicity of the construction technique, the building surfaces are highly stimulating on a perceptual level.

The entrance overcomes a certain difference in height in the surrounding terrain through a sloping bridge design of great metaphorical force leading into the entrance area.

The layout of interior space is aimed at creating a series of different internal viewpoints and, at the same time, to foster interaction between work teams, without making the space seem noisy or dispersive; the floor design draws on the staggering of two half sections separated by a central space planted with greenery.

The roof over the top floor is constructed out of a huge barrel vault, a characteristic feature of much of Dubosc and Landowski's architecture, fitted with three pairs of skylights on each side.

Two projecting wings at the rear of the building create a wide balcony and interrupt the flatness of the facade design.

The use of a metal structure simplified the construction work on a site where access was very difficult. The structure also allows the possible re-adaptation of the building to house, eventually, different types of activities.

The facades are composite and lightweight. They are made of plasterboard and wooden panels. The outer skin is composed of ribbed steel cladding pre-lacquered with PVDF in shining blue, with a transparent grid of perforated aluminium sheeting superimposed to create the impression of a bridal veil. Sliding shutters made of the same material and brise soleil add a sense of depth and softness to the facades, as well as insuring quality thermal comfort.

The combination of perforated sheets and colored cladding gives remarkable lightness to the construction.

This concept machine allows intimacy as well as dialogue: architectural design in this studio is both an individual and a team process.

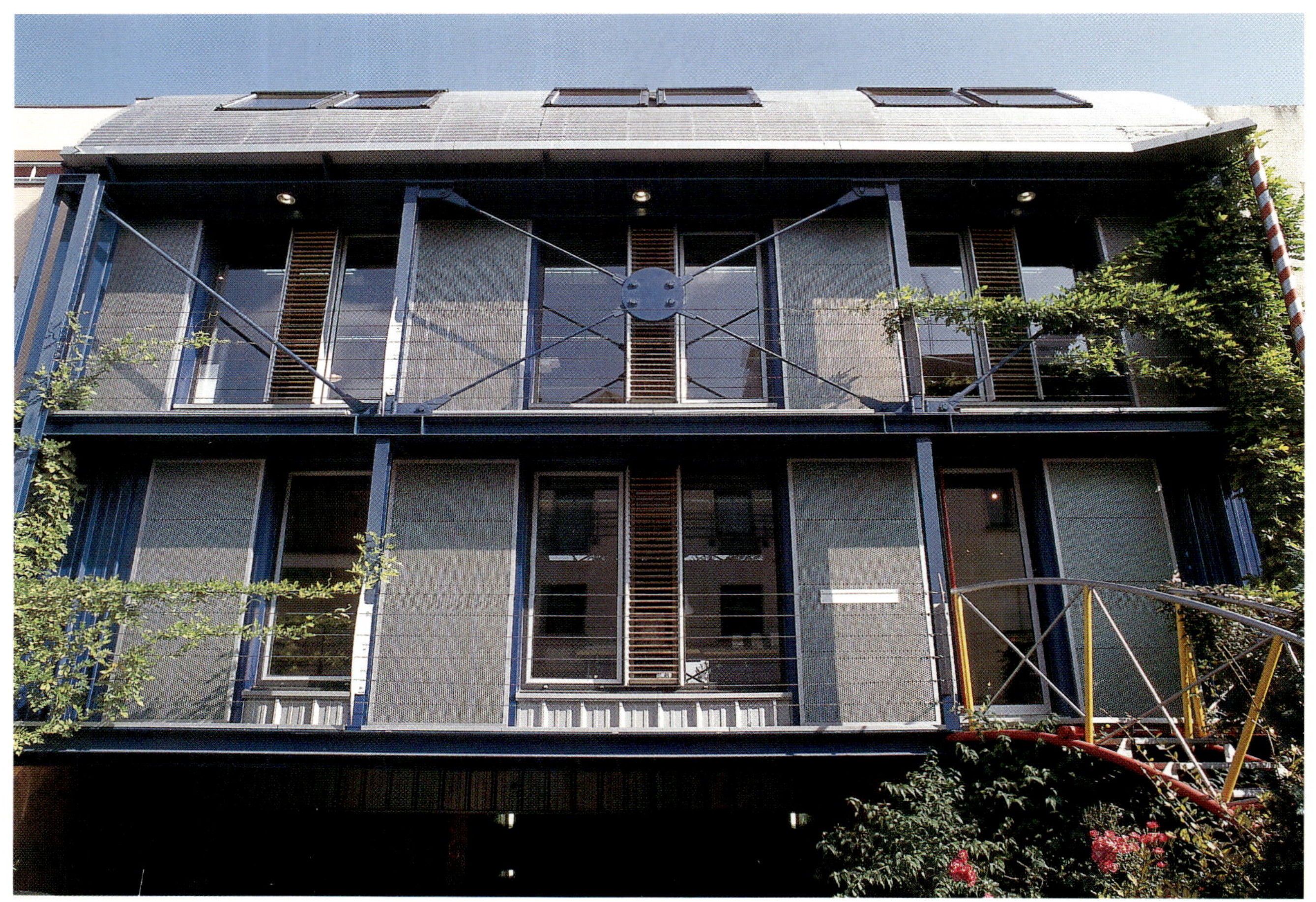

Above, general view of the building housing Dubosc & Landowski's studio. Right, axonometric cut-away, plan and cross section. Opposite, detail of the rear facade with its two distinctive round overhanging structures housing the meeting rooms.

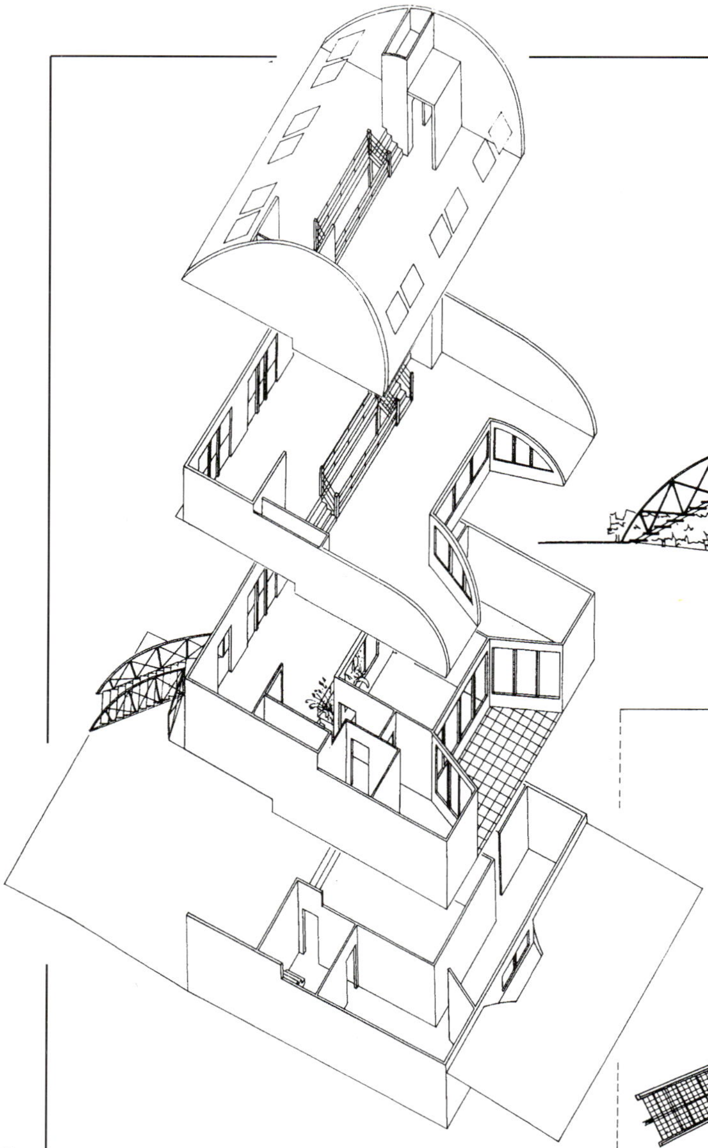

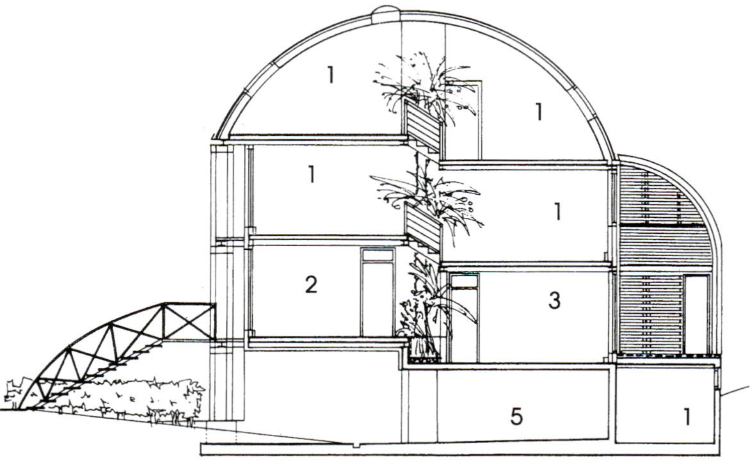

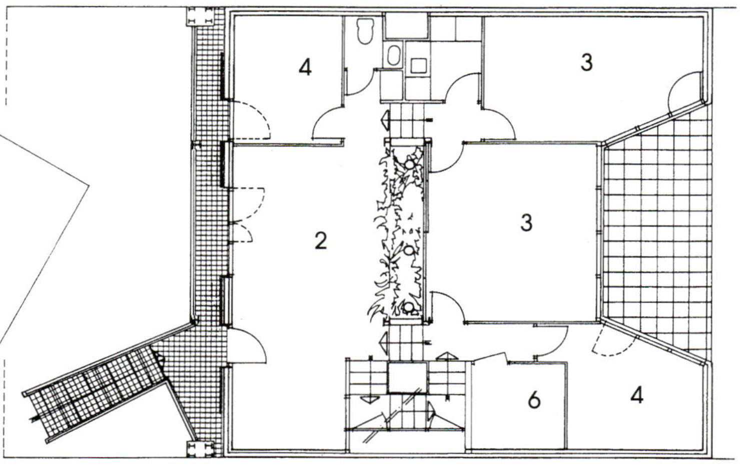

1. Studio
2. Reception
3. Meeting room
4. Offices
5. Garage
6. Archives

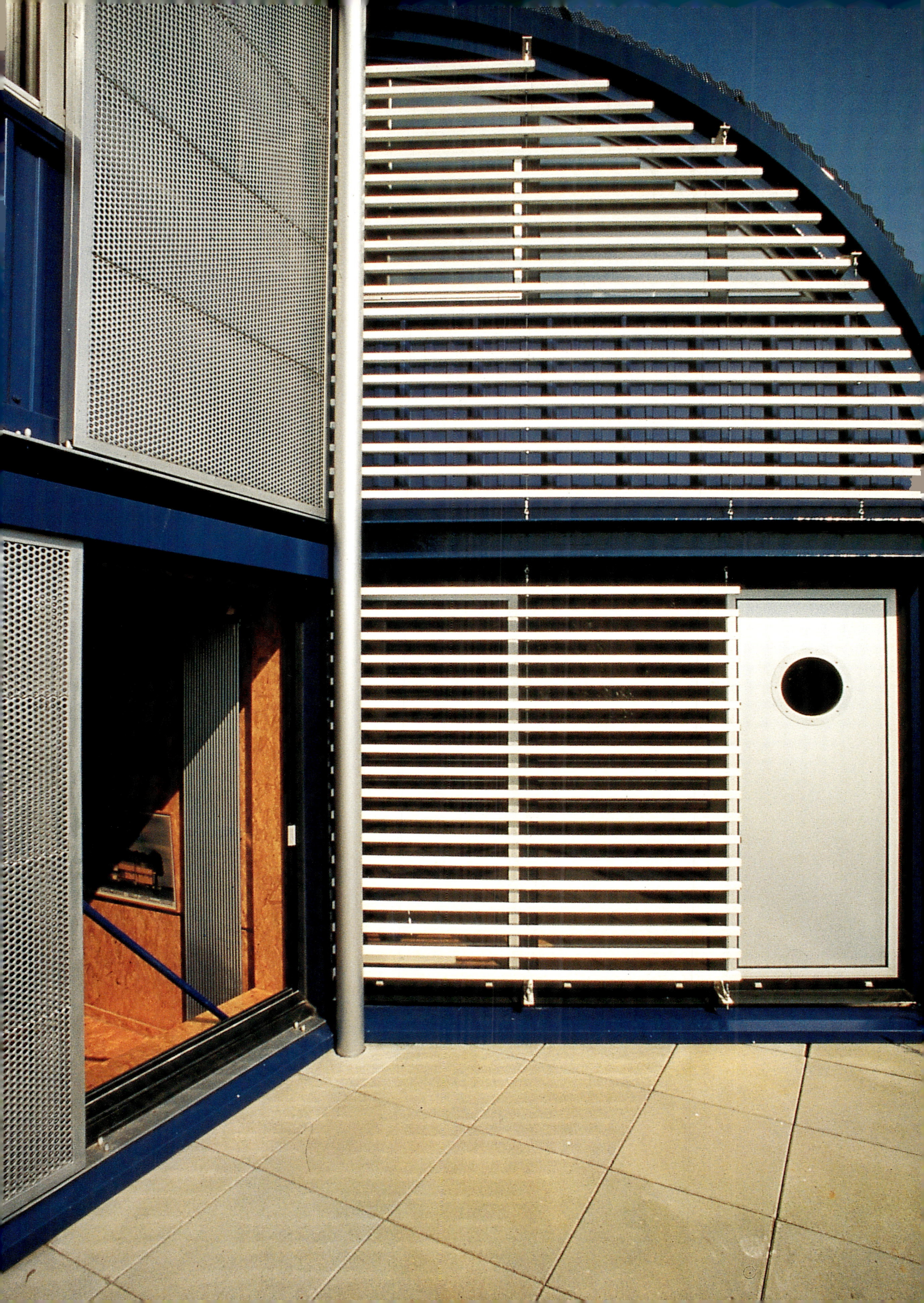

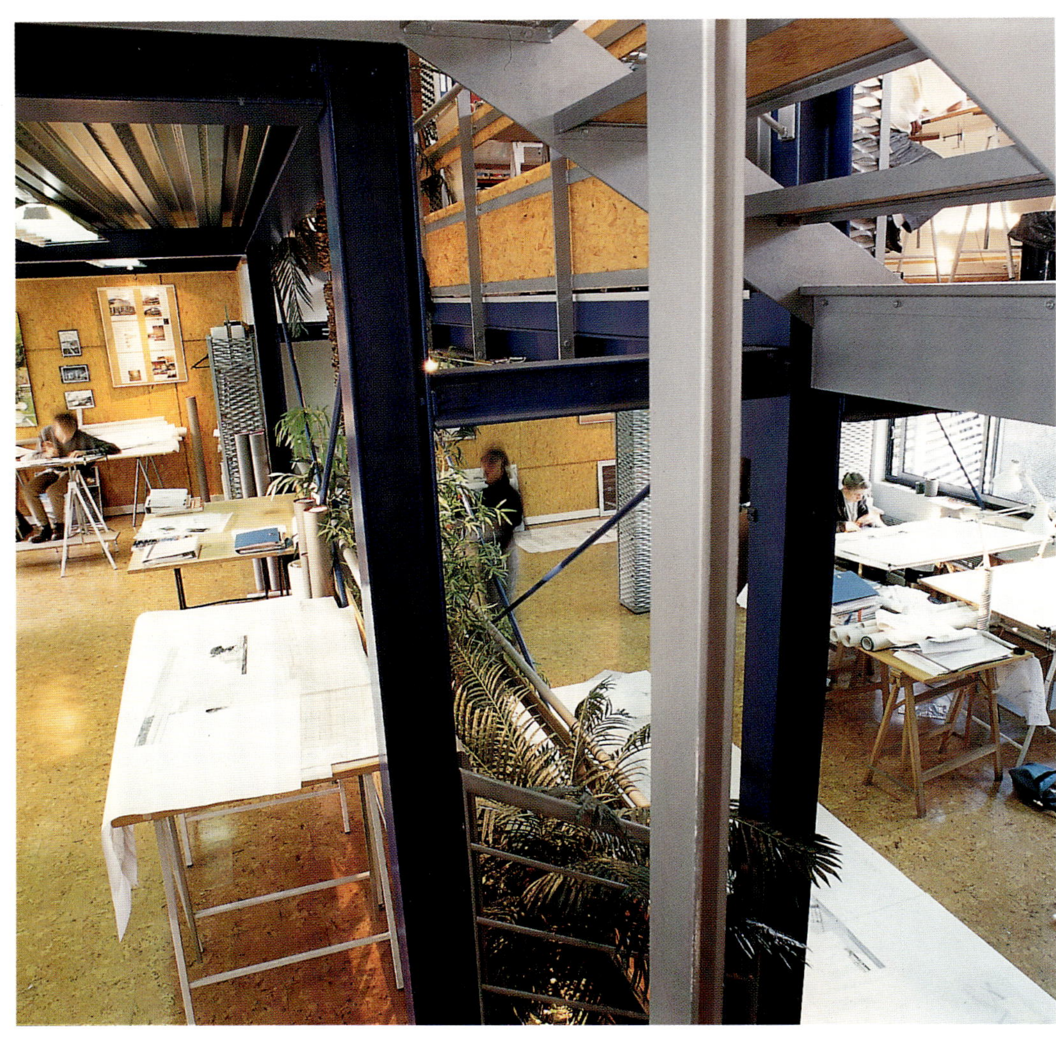

The inside of the studio,
whose interior layout
is designed to create
a series of different
viewpoints and
encourage team work.

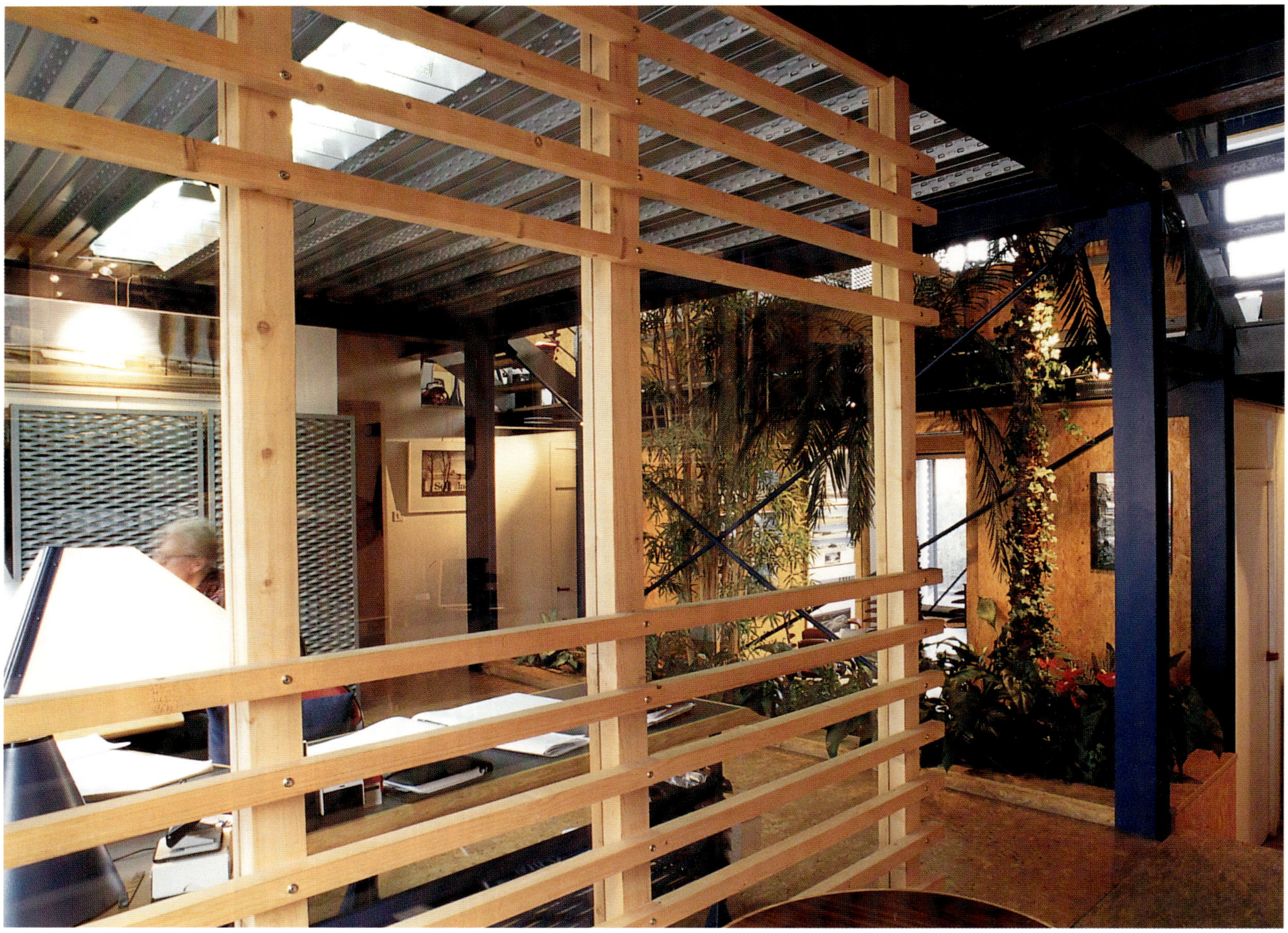

Right, the meeting
room and, below,
one of the offices.

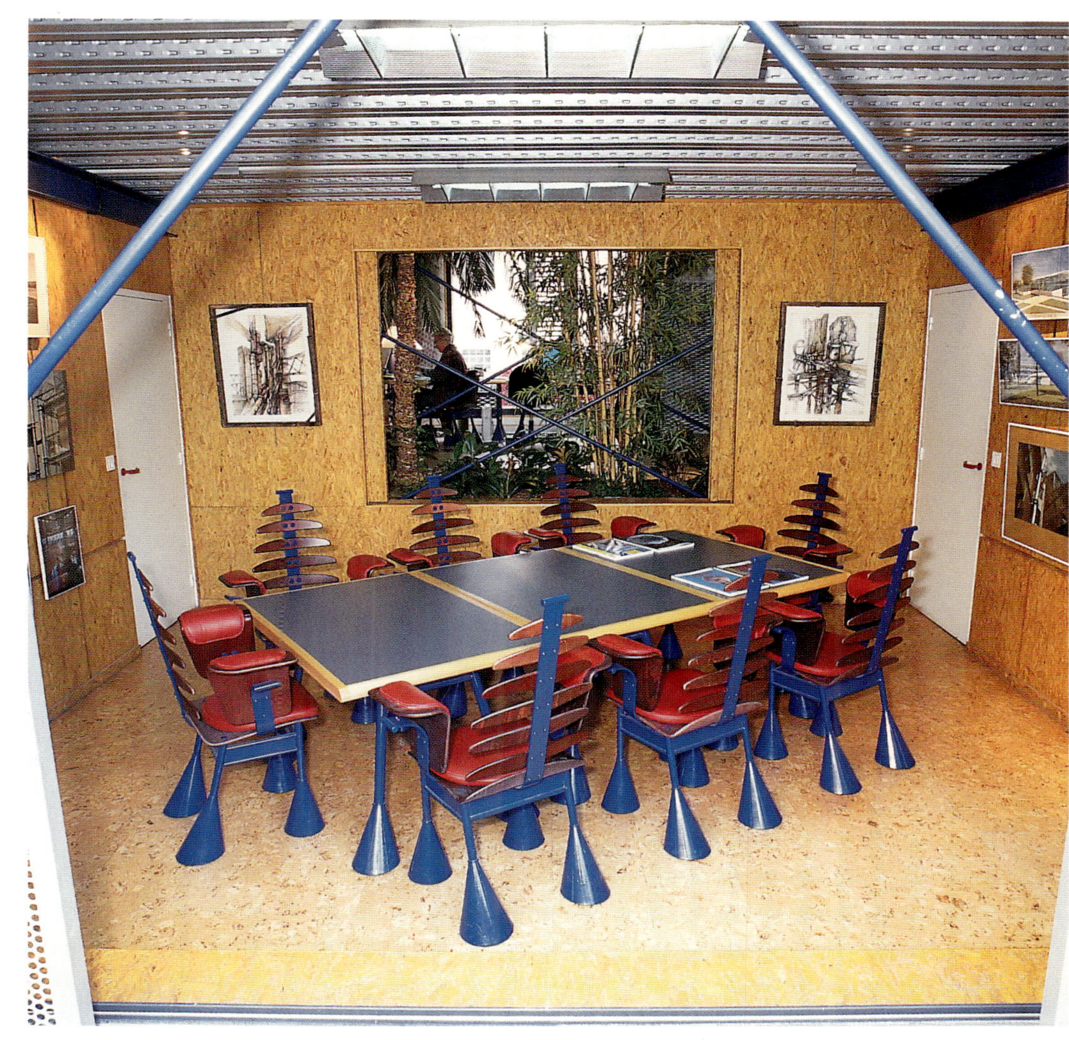

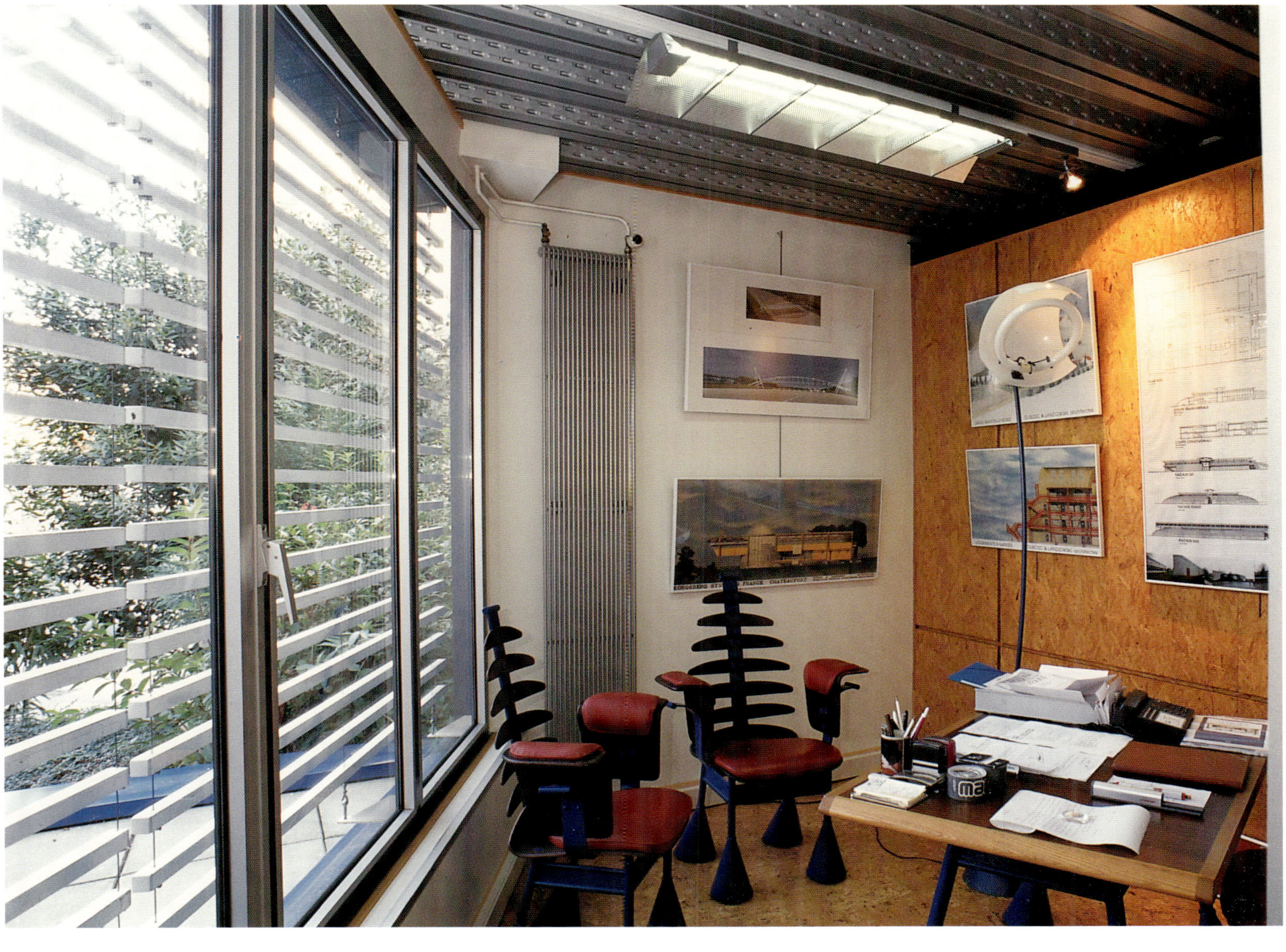

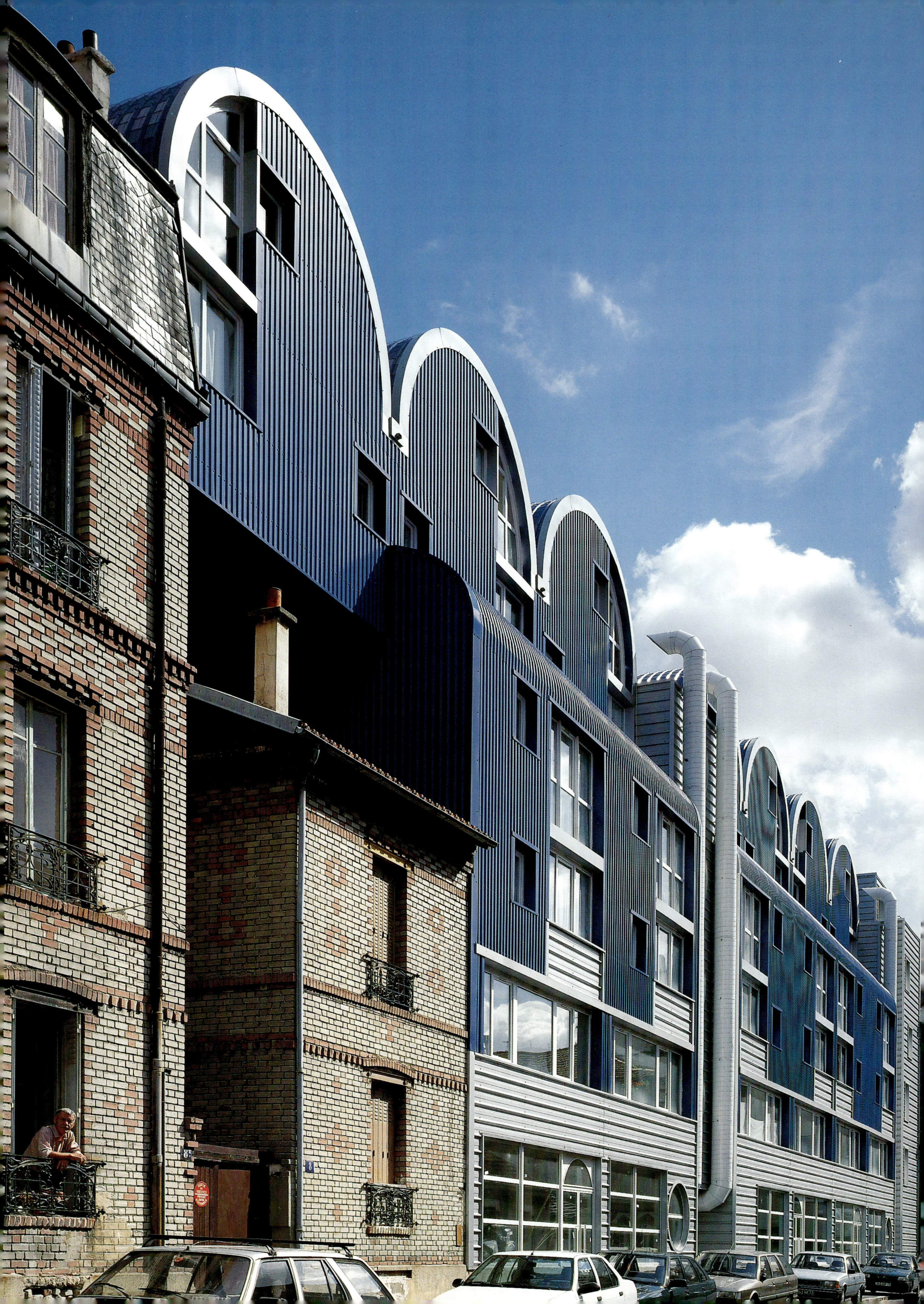

Amitié Housing Complex
Montreuil, 1993

Here thirty-six apartments, five studios and five commercial spaces integrate a dense, heterogeneous urban fabric of often dilapidated housing, shops, and small studios, in an area in the process of being rehabilitated. The building imposes itself as a sign of renovation.

In order to preserve the remarkable structure of the city, the building presents a homogenous front, an alignment which relates strongly to the proliferate urban fabric. It respects the composition of the neighborhood through a structured combination of housing, studios and other activities. The building opens onto the Friends Garden through the hallways and studios on the ground floor. A regular pattern of vaults marked by two entrances emphasises the monumental scale of a building which is nonetheless designed on housing layout grid (approximately 6 meter span).

This building is constructed out of superimposed "houses", all the apartments are duplex so that hallways were only required on one of the two levels. The steel post and beam construction system frees the housing space between structural points designed over freely partitioned height levels.

The interior space is free to evolve in time. Each occupant may redefine his/her needs and the function of each room.

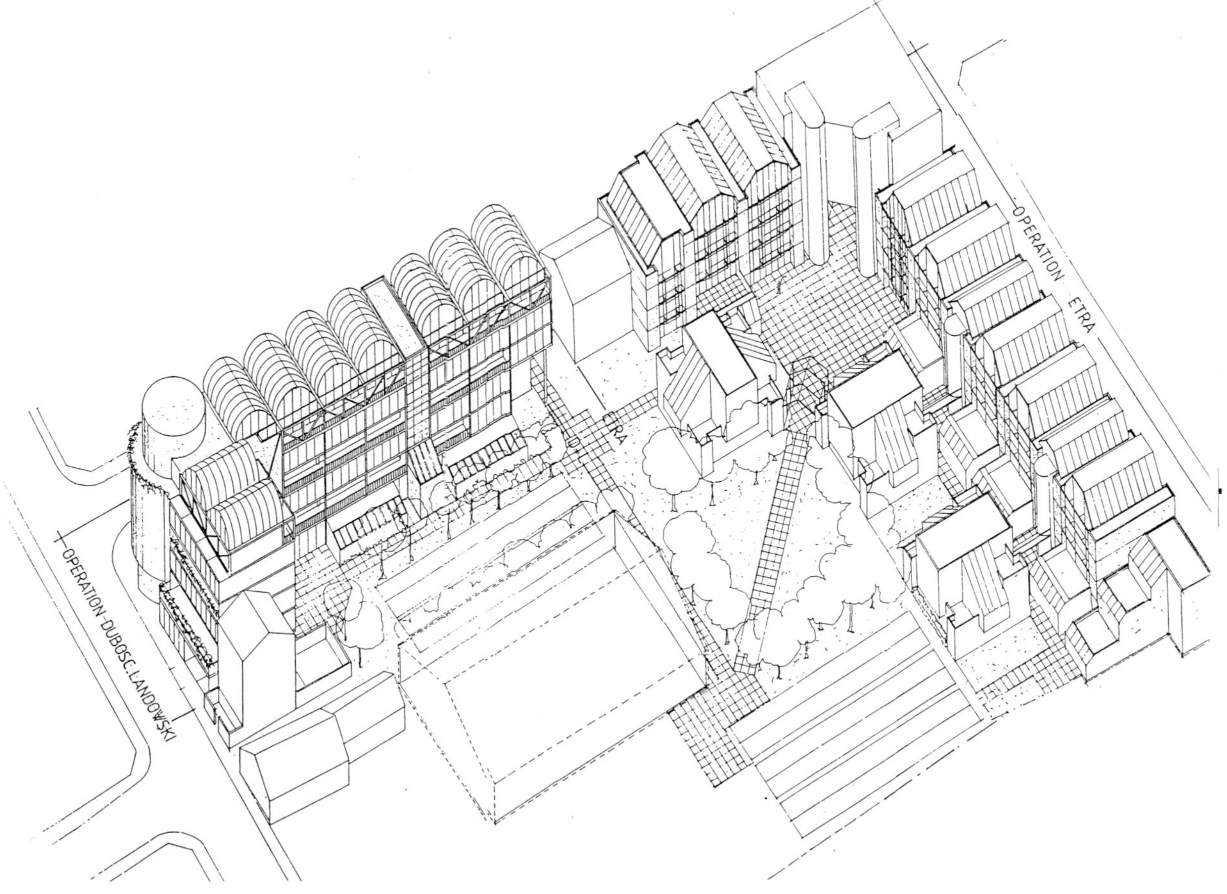

General view of the
complex, which
contains 36 flats,
5 studios and 5 shops.
The building is a new
landmark on the
cityscape. Right, detail
of one of the two main
entrances.

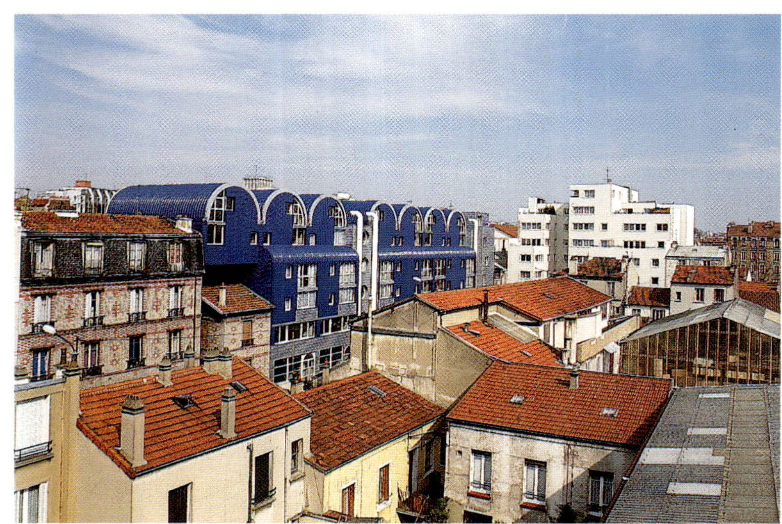

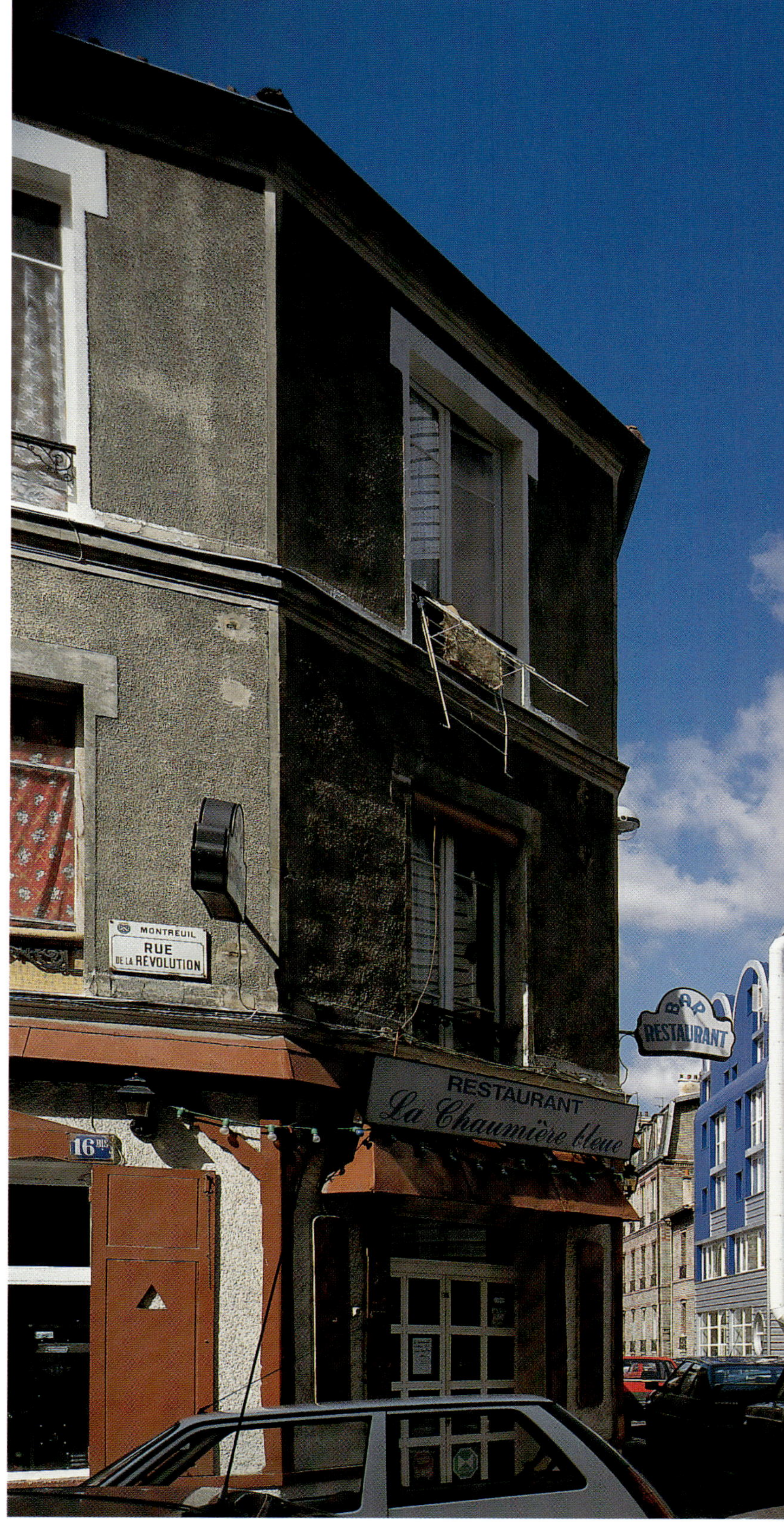

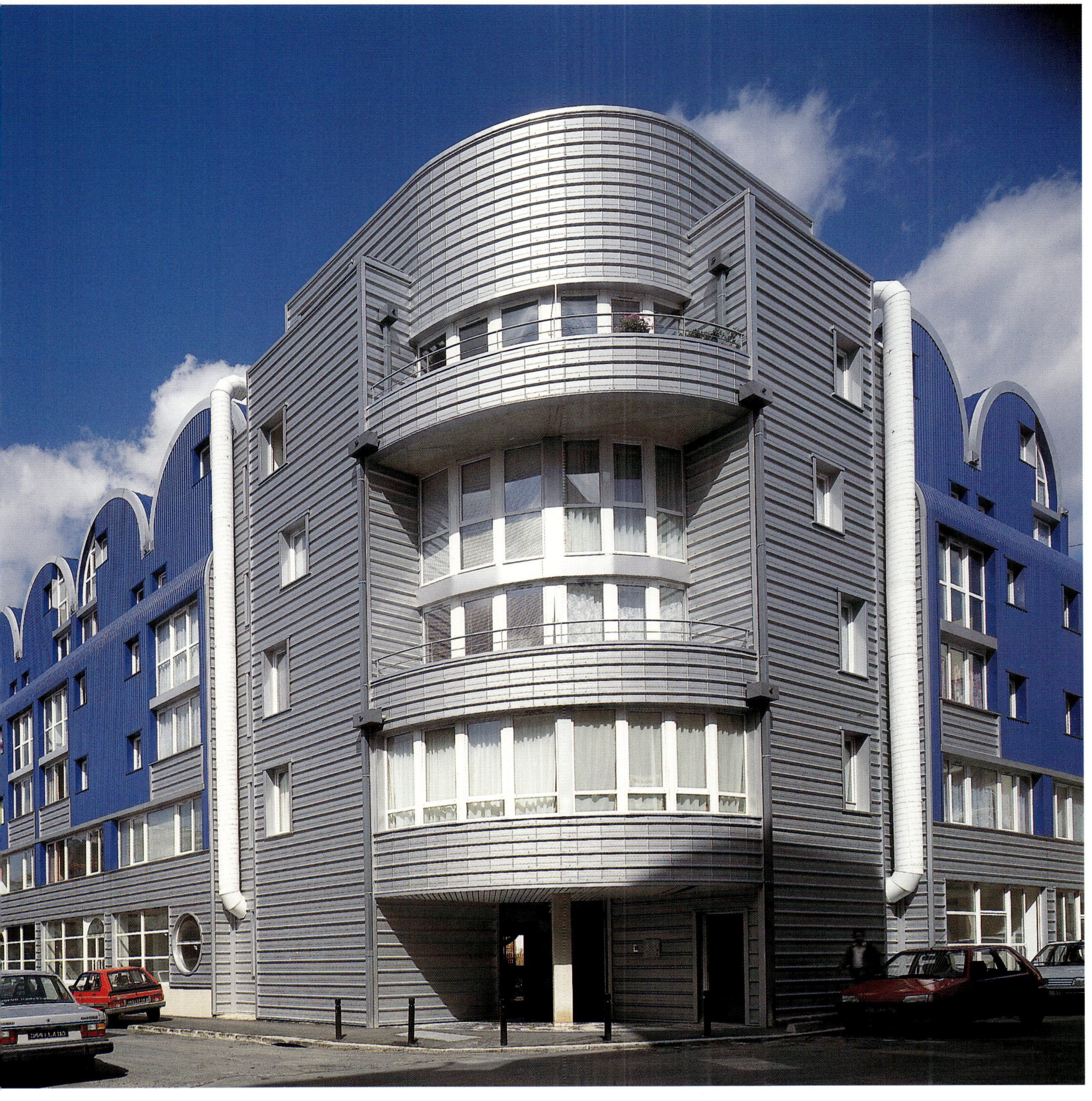

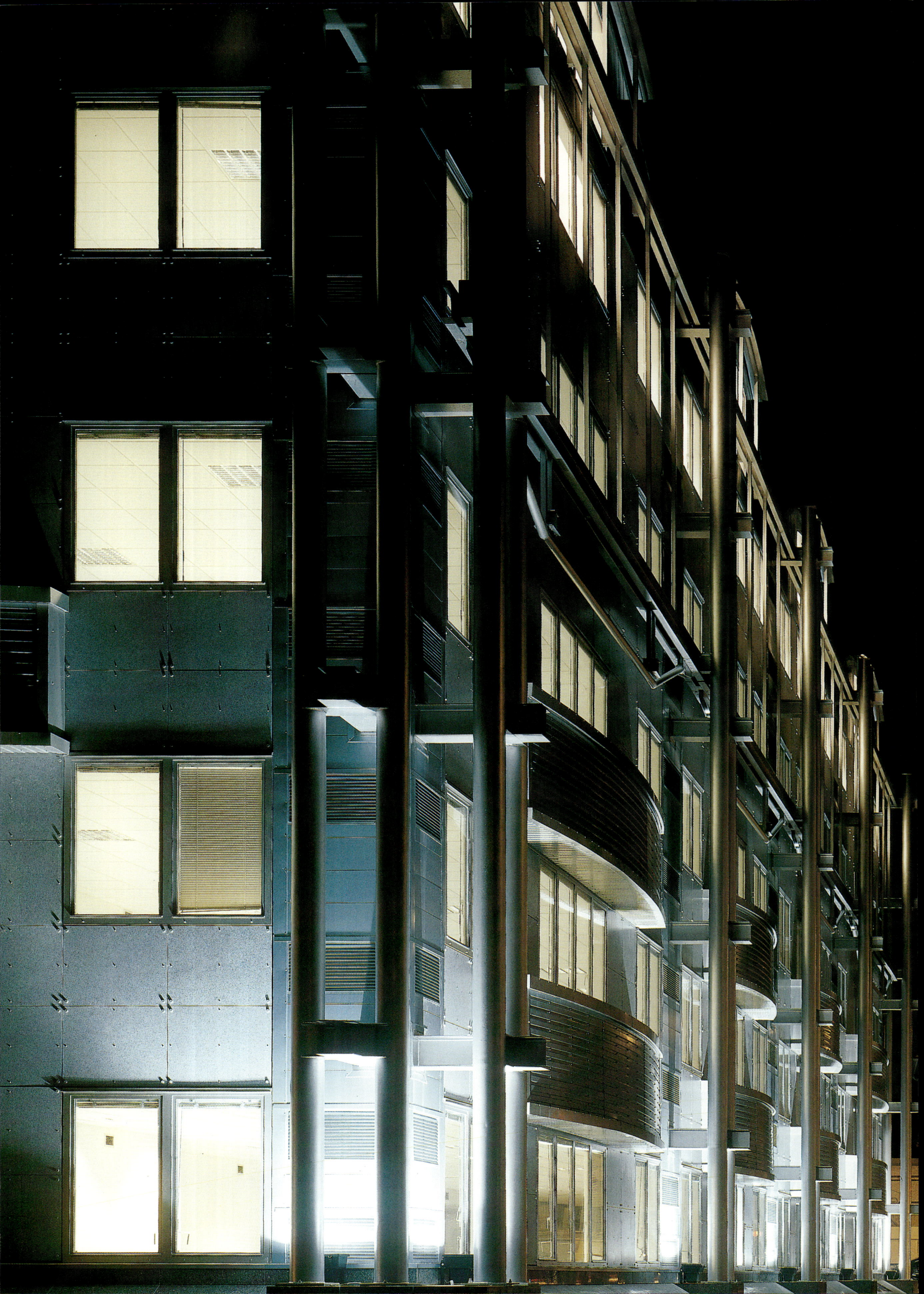

West Side Complex
Suresnes, 1994

Runner up in the International Hylar Award, (Ausimont, U.S.A.) 1994
Winner of the Gypse d'Or Prize, Paris, 1996
Runner up for the Plus Bel Ouvrage de Charpente Metallique (Best Work in Metal Structure), Paris, 1995

Two insurance companies, UAP/AGF, united under the name SCI Richelieu, owned this commercial-office space on a one hectare lot in Suresnes. The previous building, constructed out of a metal structure, was almost completely destroyed by a fire. Considering reconstruction, the client called on Dubosc and Landowski for their experience in the domain of metal structured construction systems.

However, due to projects for widening a road bordering the lot and to various recommendations issued by the town planning offices, it was soon decided to rebuild the entire lot, while redefining the functional program. This was reoriented to include thirty-two housing units, a large public retail space, various activity spaces, offices, underground parking, and a public garden.

To favour mixed use as well as possible developments in the future, the client wanted the building to have a transformable structure.

This meant using a post and beam constructive system with dry composite partitioning; a concrete stern and slab construction would have hindered any chance of future modification.

The client planned to reconstruct the building using contemporary technology designed to enhance its image.

The facades are designed on a narrow grid (0.90 meters) to provide the greatest flexibility for partitioning and to allow for abundant light. The glazing is insulated and clear. The upper floors are covered by a vaulted roof space. The building has a sophisticated internal circulation system, the vertical connections are numerous. It is equipped with a monitoring system to control energy consumption, entry, and circulation.

The building is bordered by three streets with discontinuous front elevations made of heterogeneous materials.

Faced with this lack of coherence, the architects chose to create a powerful, orderly building to counterbalance the disorder of the neighborhood. The vertical metal structure of the building, made of a double pipe pillar, is visible from the outside. It has a 12 meter deep span, identical to the width of the roads bordering the project.

The filled and glazed panels of the facade are designed on a vertically dominant scheme.

The shell is actually behind the structure; this gap animates the elevations through the interplay of shadow and superimposition of the structure upon the face. The lower part of the building is made of polished granulated concrete forming a socle for holding the tubular columns.

The color of the materials, which varies from smooth or speckled grey (glossy or matt) to pale blue, tone down the impact of the contemporary character of the building.

Drawing showing
the new complex in
its urban context.
Right, the main facade
featuring a grid filled
with clear glass
insulating panels that
let in natural light and
help regulate the air
inside, and detail of the
framework of beams
and uprights designed
to allow maximum
flexibility for future
extensions.

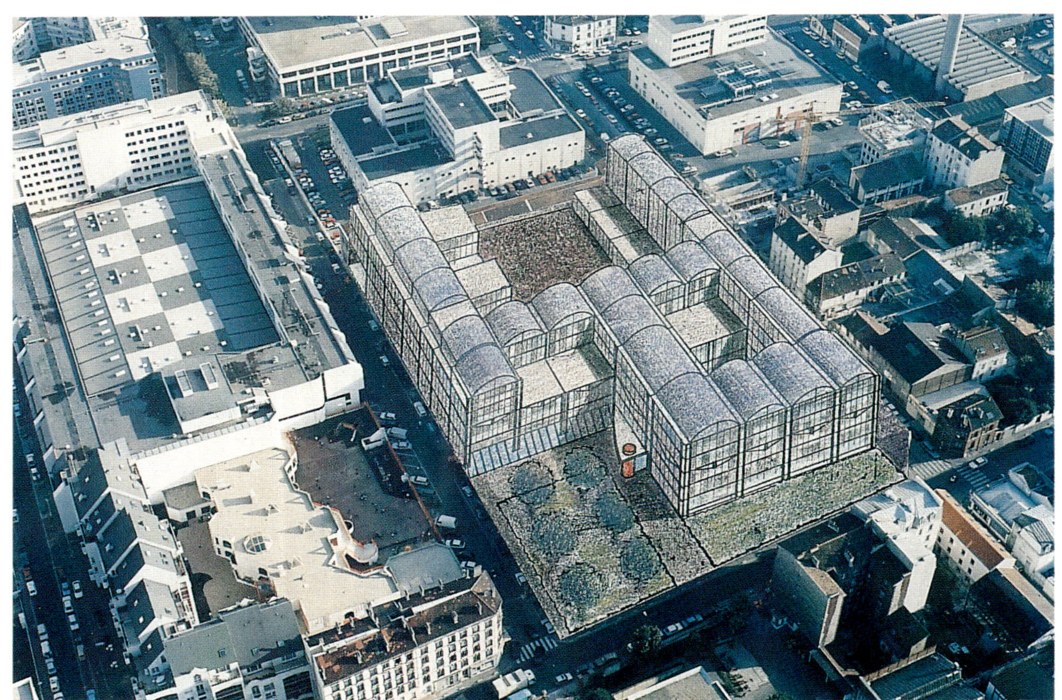

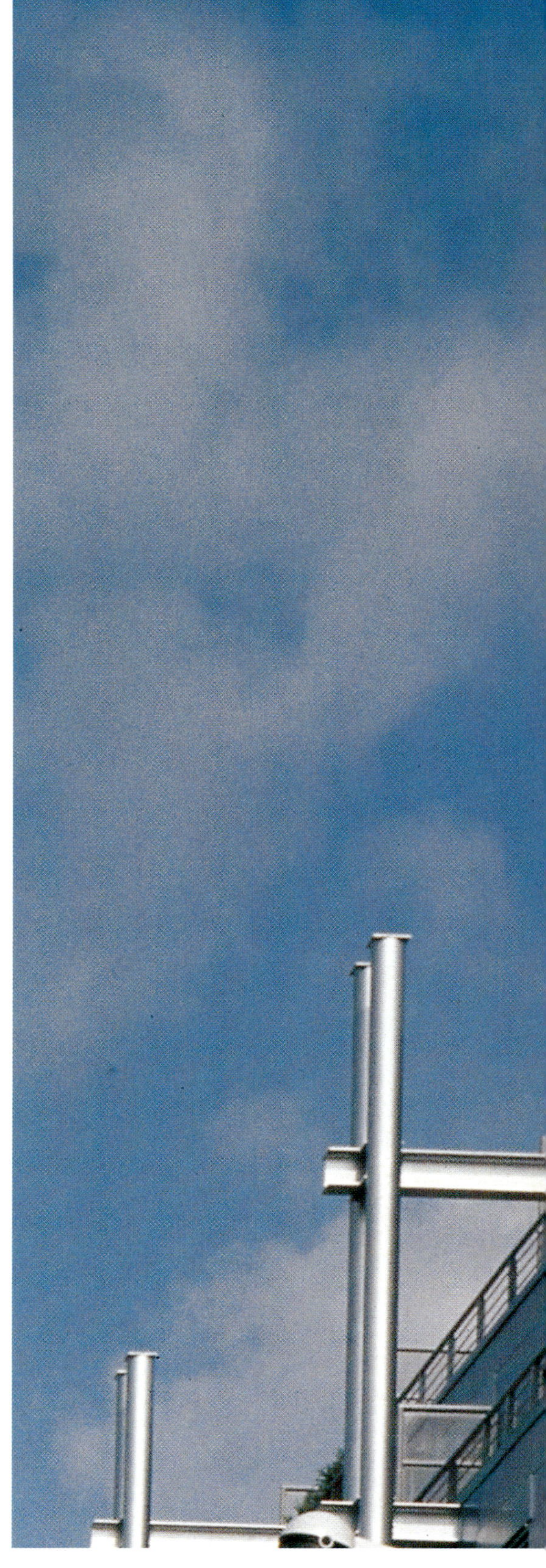

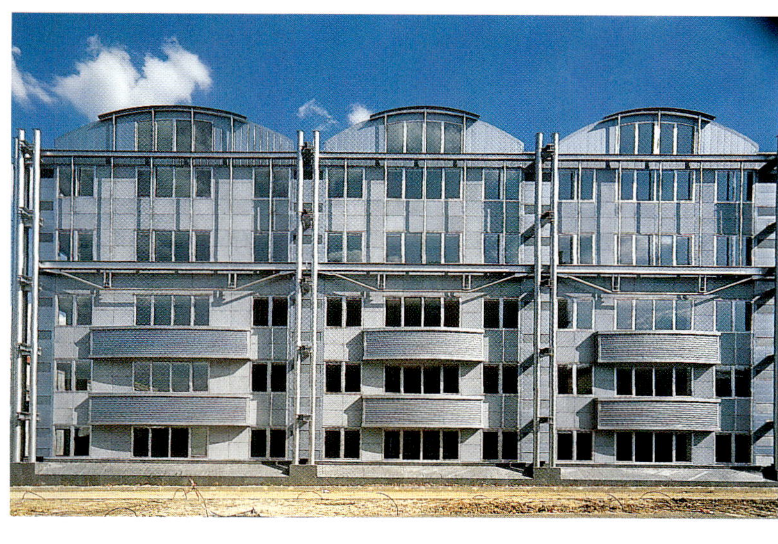

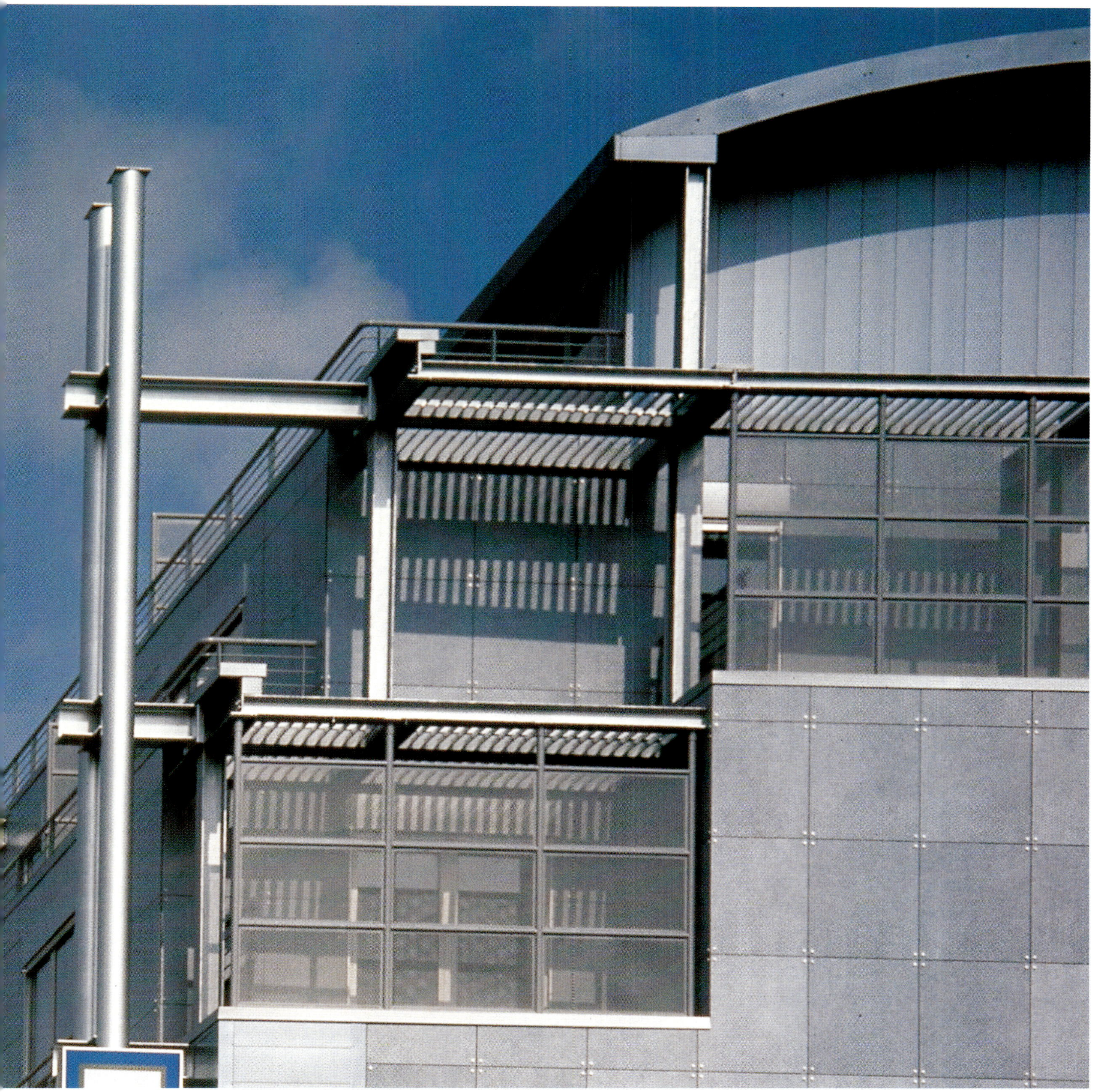

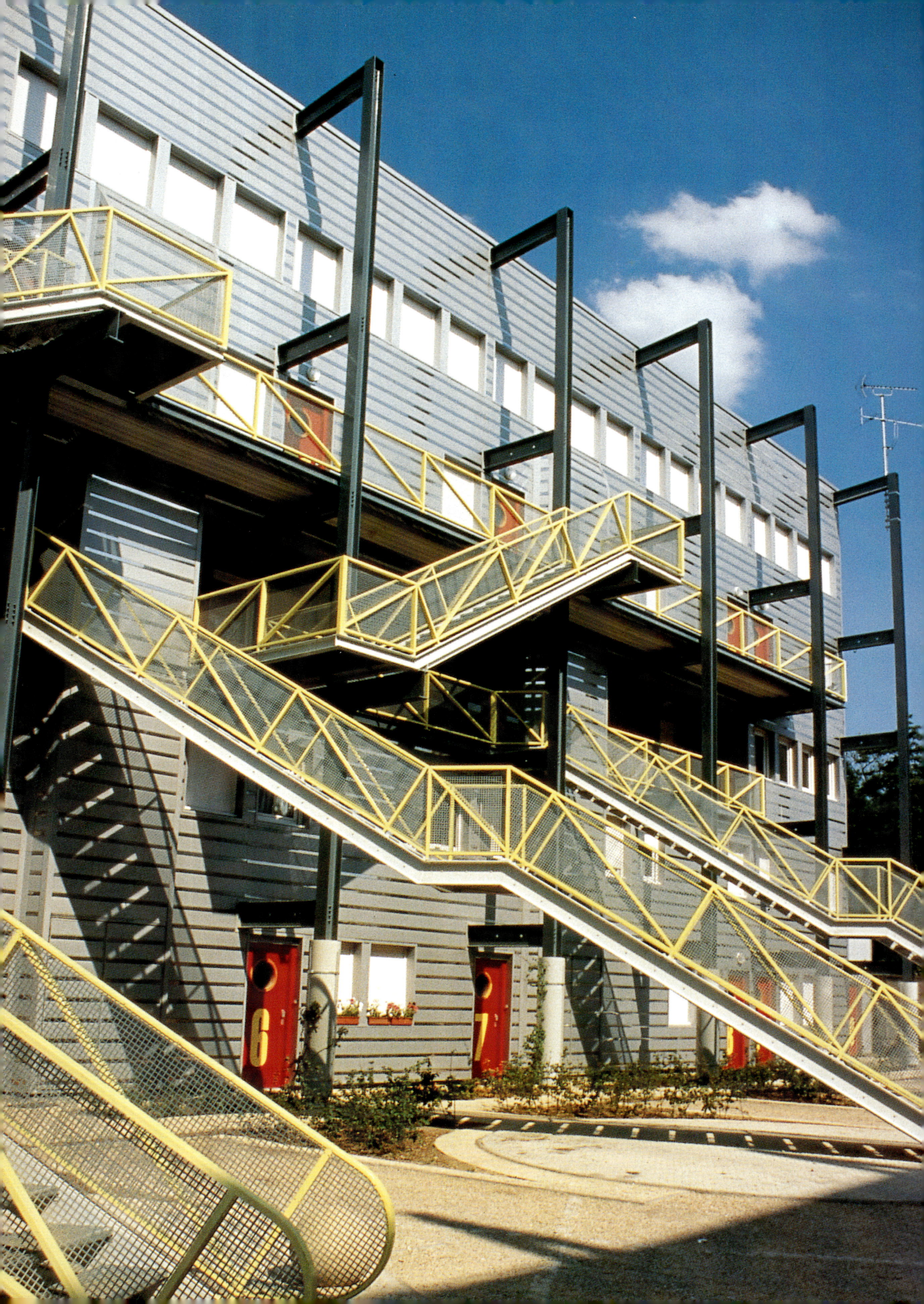

La Vénérie Housing Complex
Montargis-Le-Franc, 1994

The housing operation, La Vénérie, in the city of Montargis in the Loiret Region marks an important stage in the research of the Dubosc and Landowski architecture studio. For ten years the studio experimented first on metal works, then on the structure casing sequence, and subsequently with this project on "Dry Interactive Composite Systems".

The materials used weigh up to six times less than their traditional counterparts and special attention has been focused on horizontal structures and the possibility of re-using and disposing of these materials. For this "Assessment Building" a proposal was devised to be presented to the Ministry of Equipment and Housing Construction Planning for a research grant.

A grant was given for an acoustics study, the public authorities being very interested in improving the standards of housing acoustics. La Vénérie was to serve as a rest site for different acoustical results, particularly horizontal transmission through the floor from one apartment to the next. The idea was also to make a cost evaluation of supplementary acoustical comfort standards in comparison with those corresponding to the strictest current regulations; tests were carried out in two morphologically identical buildings with two different acoustical standards.

It would be interesting to know if they have different rent rates to.

The first view of the buildings is astonishing. They look more like some kind of technical "body" than buildings. There is no traditional culture of living at all, no compromise in form, matter, or color. Whether or not this meets the demands of people looking for a home is a difficult question, which has to do with the role and the right of architecture to change people's habits. Between the initial shock of a new culture and then the surprise at finding such unaccustomed finishing quality, the viewer is usually perplexed: is this acceptable, wonderful or intolerable?

The architects wanted inhabitants to converse from one gangway to the next and meet on the open stairways. The facades on the central space are rhythmically marked by fine polished stainless steel joints, which reflect the lightness and darkness of their surroundings, and larger mat aluminium bands.

The other elevations are cased in shallow profile pre-lacquered aluminium which moulds the curves and counter curves of the main structure.

The organisation of the apartments is simple. The large three or four bedroom units are in duplex on the ground and first floors, with independent entrances and small private gardens. Smaller, one-bedroom units are situated on the second floor. And, crowning the buildings, there is another series of duplex two-bedroom units occupying the rounded roof space.

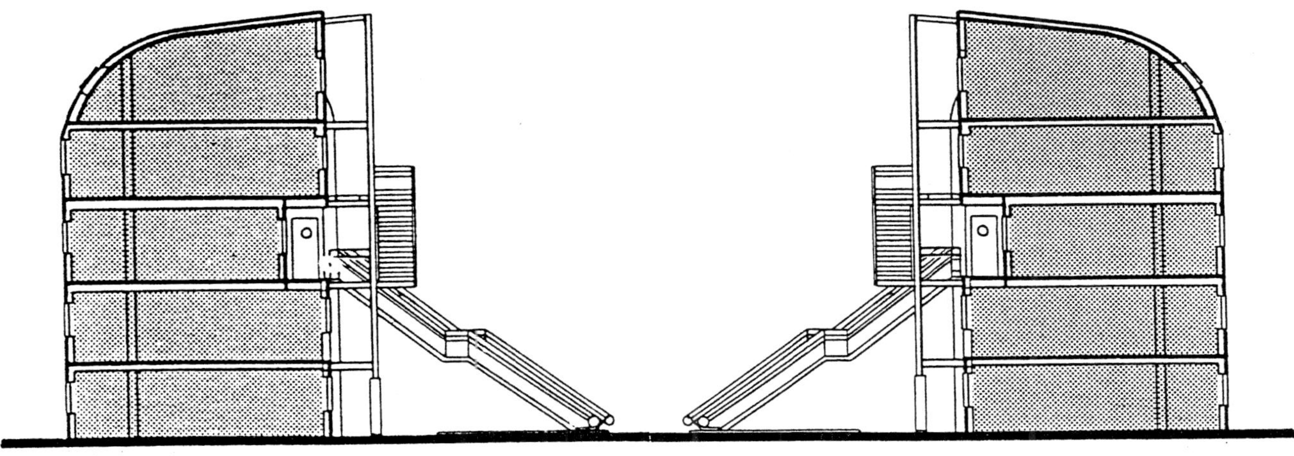

Below, the two facing
blocks which form the
housing complex. Right,
the interior facade of
one of the two building
blocks marked
by a screen of metal
partitions making
the building look like
a high-tech machine.

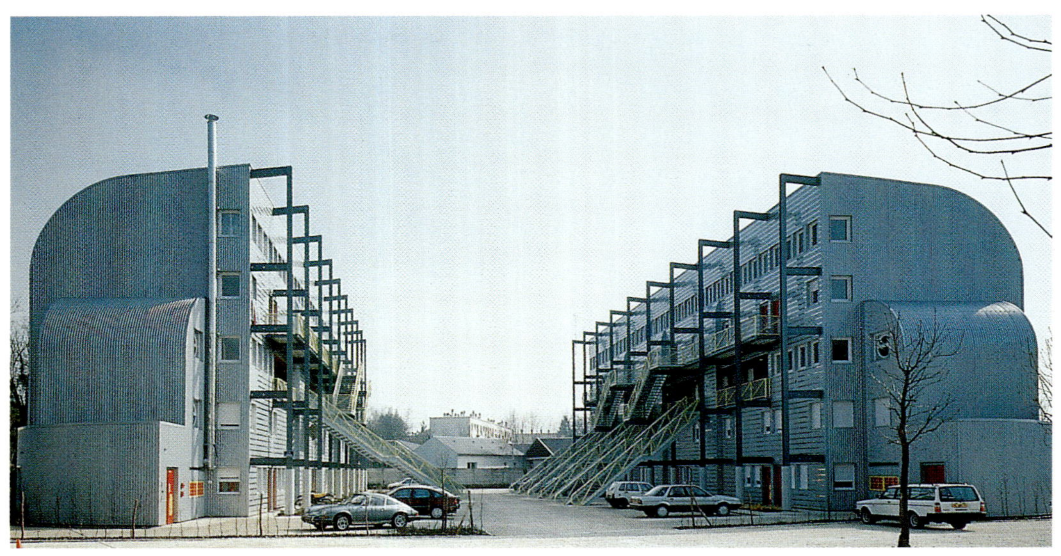

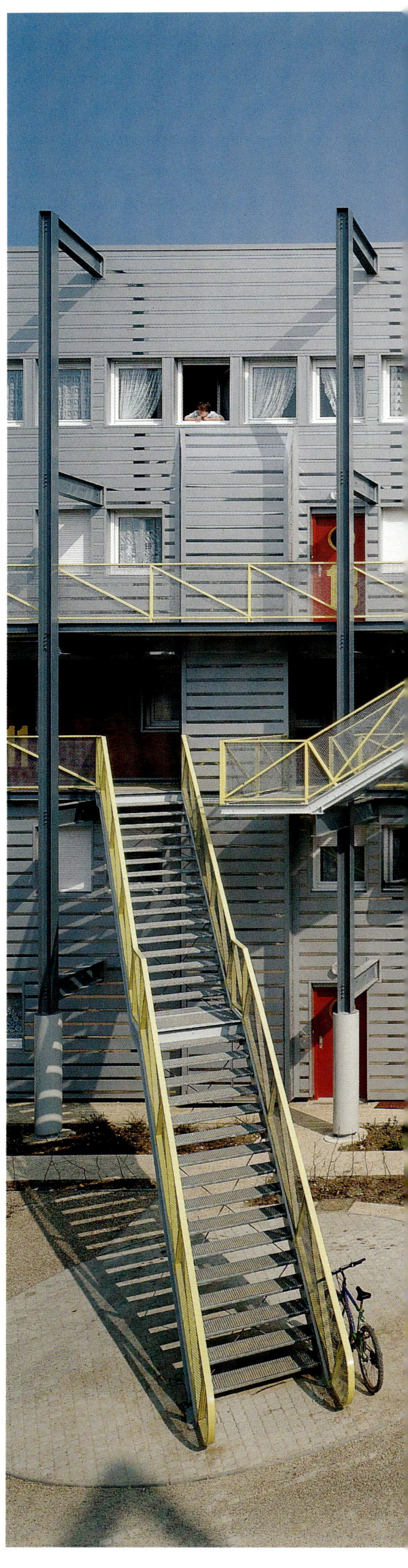

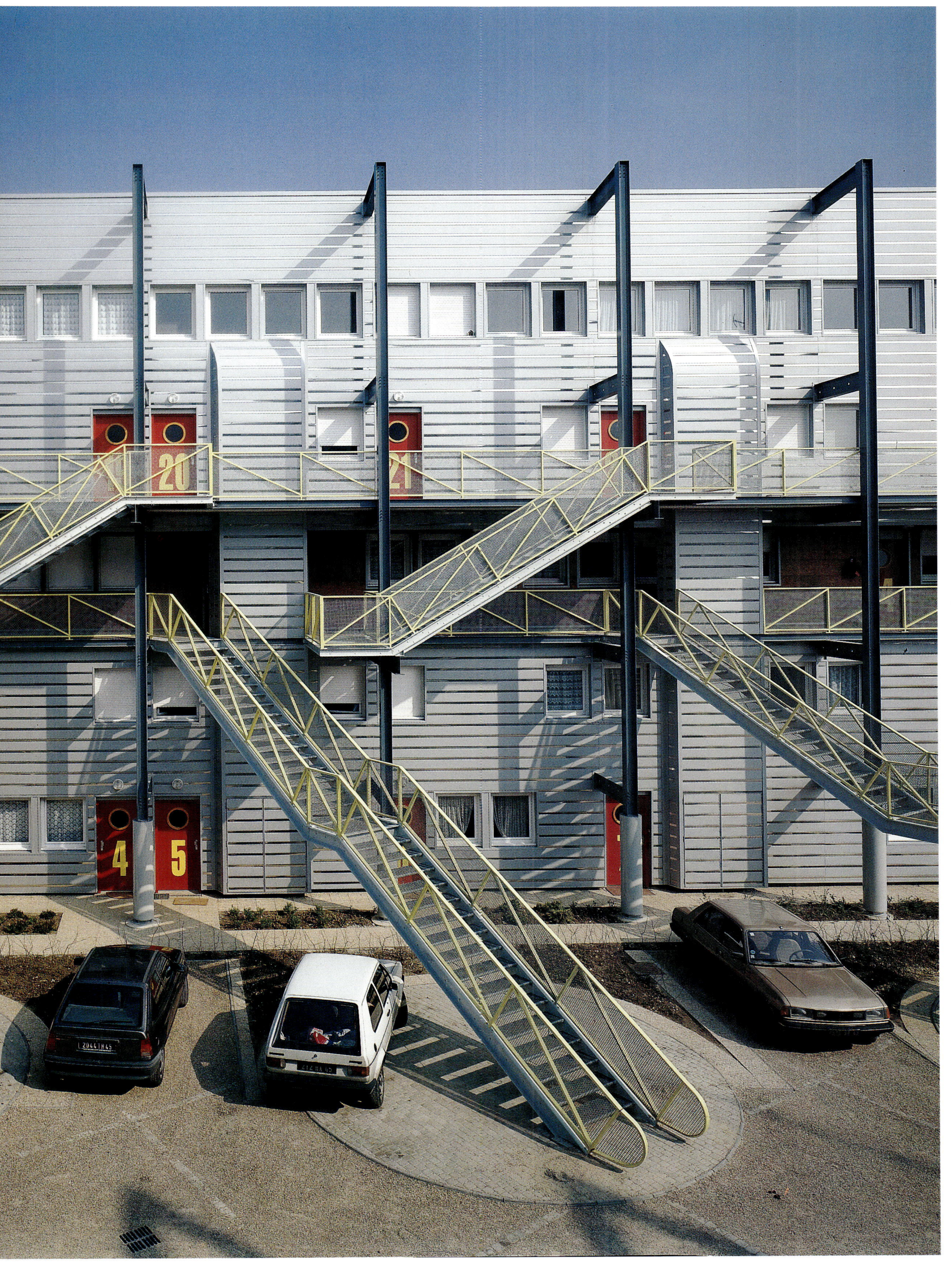

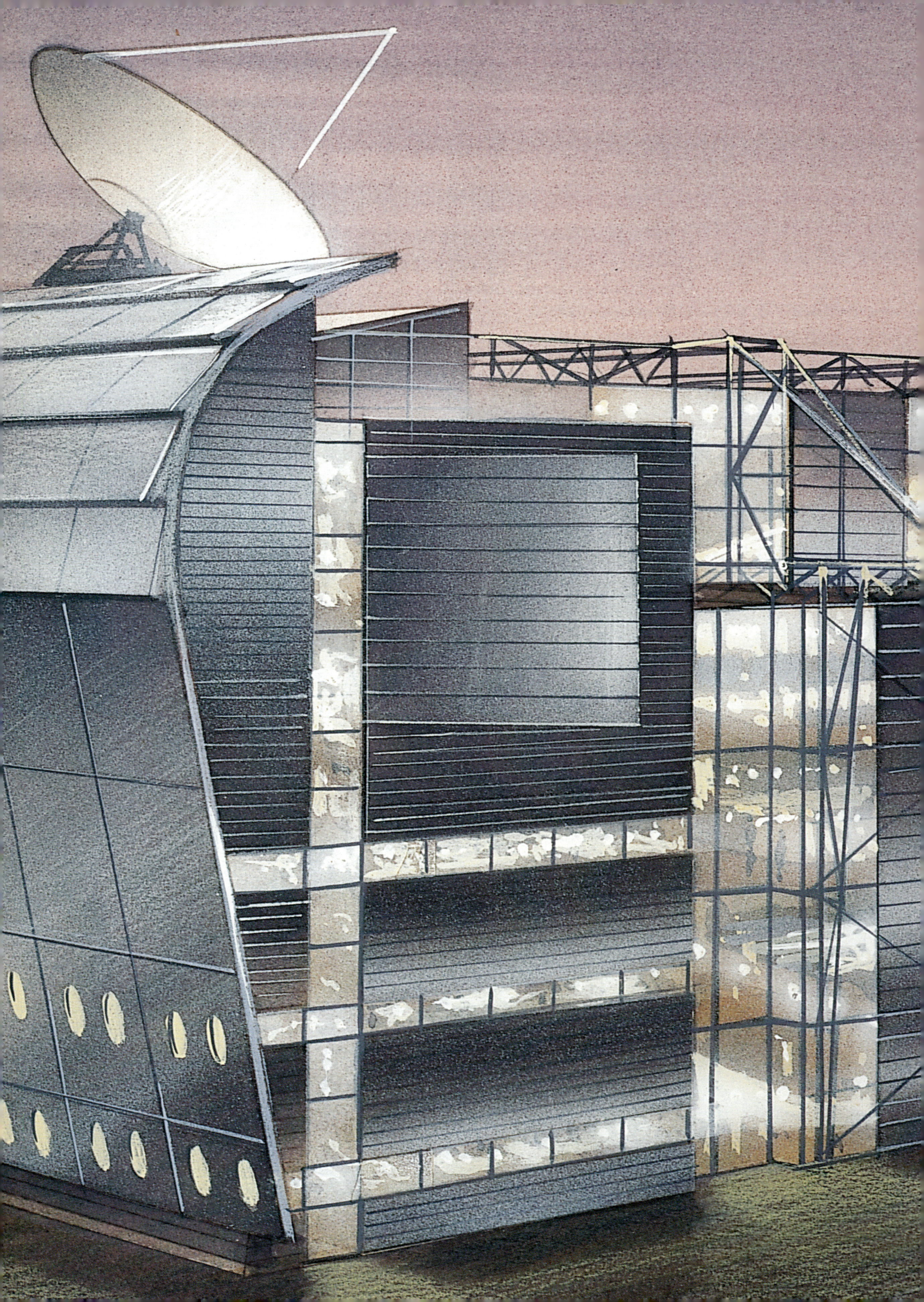

Space Museum
Les Mureaux, 1994

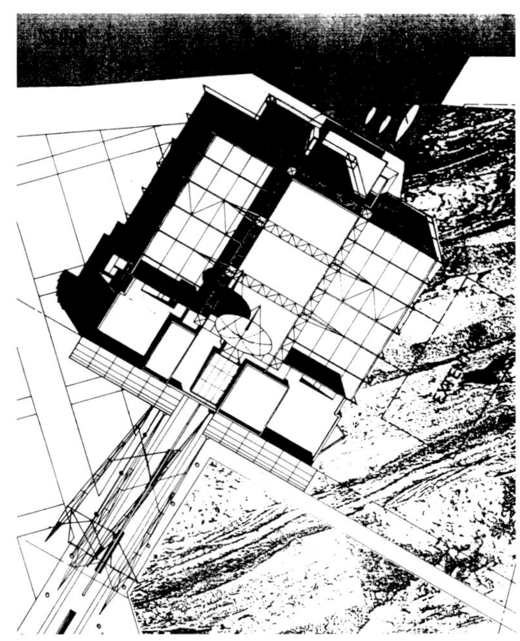

This museum, known as the "Space Port", is designed to host major events in the aerospace industry, not just missiles, satellites and rockets, but also conferences, research and teaching programs.

The building was planned to be built on the edge of the River Seine; the waterfront site would enhance and reflect the building. A large open space was deliberately left around the building to create an unusual landscape. This "lunar" landscaping would accentuate the isolation of the building and underline its essential feature as a space port.

The site can be reached via land or river boat. A sort of landing strip leads through to the building entrance.

The building needed to be compact. Large, tall volumes are necessary to display missiles and satellites "in the air" in a spectacular way.

The building is devised to be "useful" or, in other words, entirely devoted to its function: presenting the items displayed inside and therefore neutral and modest so as not to interfere with the viewing of the exhibits. However, due to the high-tech image that the architects aimed to achieve, there may well be some rivalry between the architecture and the technological elements inside. The idea was to create screens from which to hang missiles, satellites etc. These elements would define, both inside and outside, the architecture of the Space Port.

The steel structure, constructed out of reticular poles with four main sections on a square base, supports platforms, facades, and roofing, of course. It is also designed to support the elements on display. From the inside its presence is very discrete and undistracting.

Natural light is brought in to the building from three sides and it is possible to open the roof using sliding panels. It is an interactive building. The tall interior structure may be partitioned vertically as well as horizontally. The platforms may be hung at different levels.

The design of the structure and platforms allows flexibility and adaptation to museological or programmatic additions.

The transparency of the service grid (stairs, glass elevators) affords a global view of the functions of the building. Its transparency displays the interactivity of the building, each element is exposed to every other.

Plan and renderings
of the Space Museum
designed to host events
related to the world of
satellites and research.
The building is designed
out of a light-weight
metal structures and
wide glass sections to
give it a more futuristic
appearance.

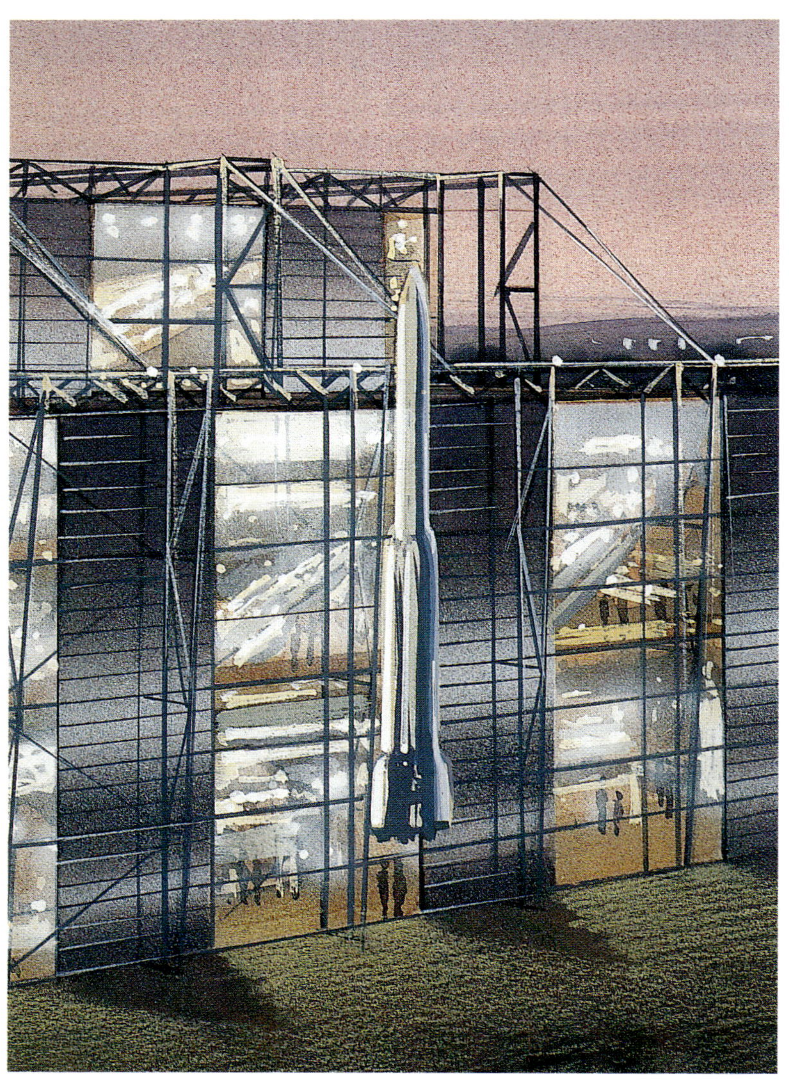

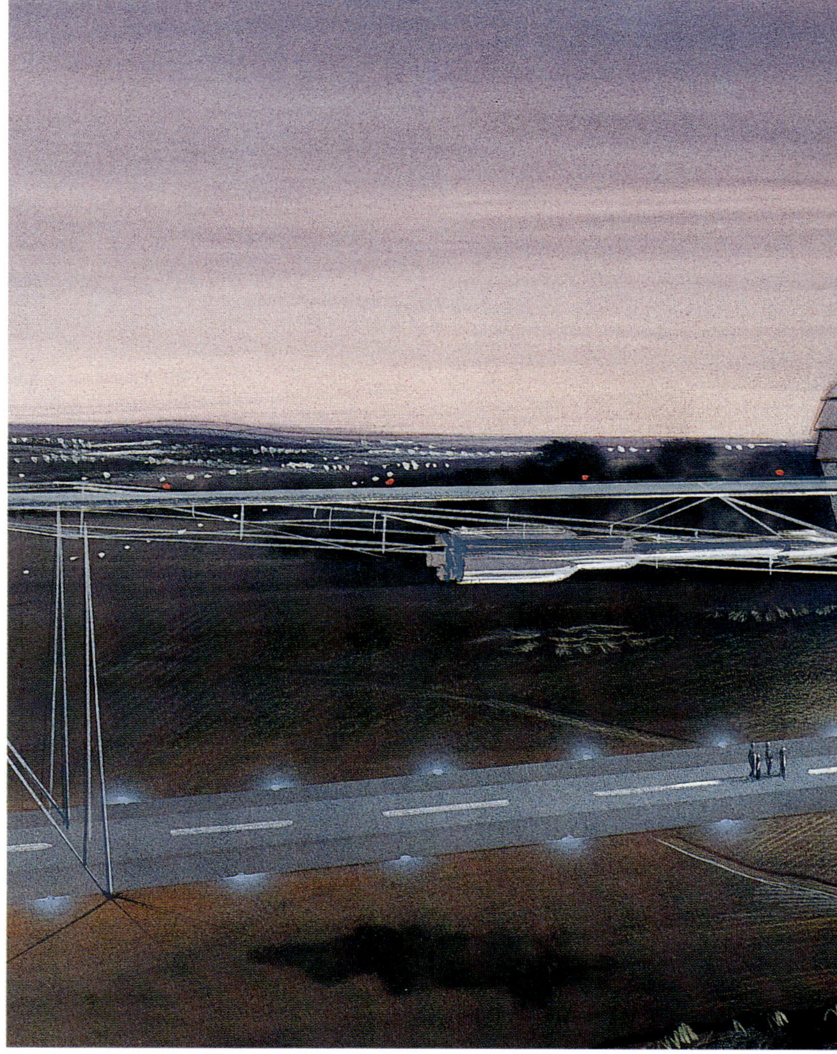

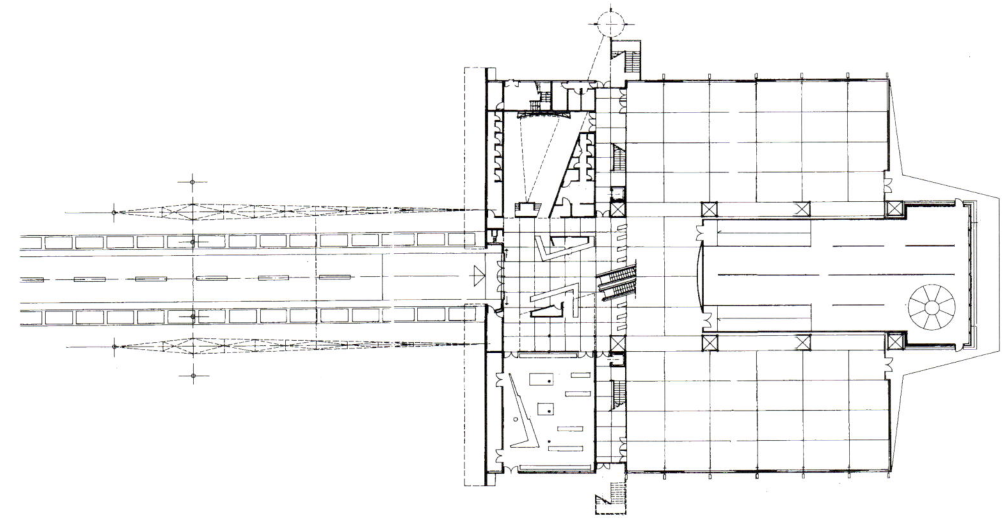

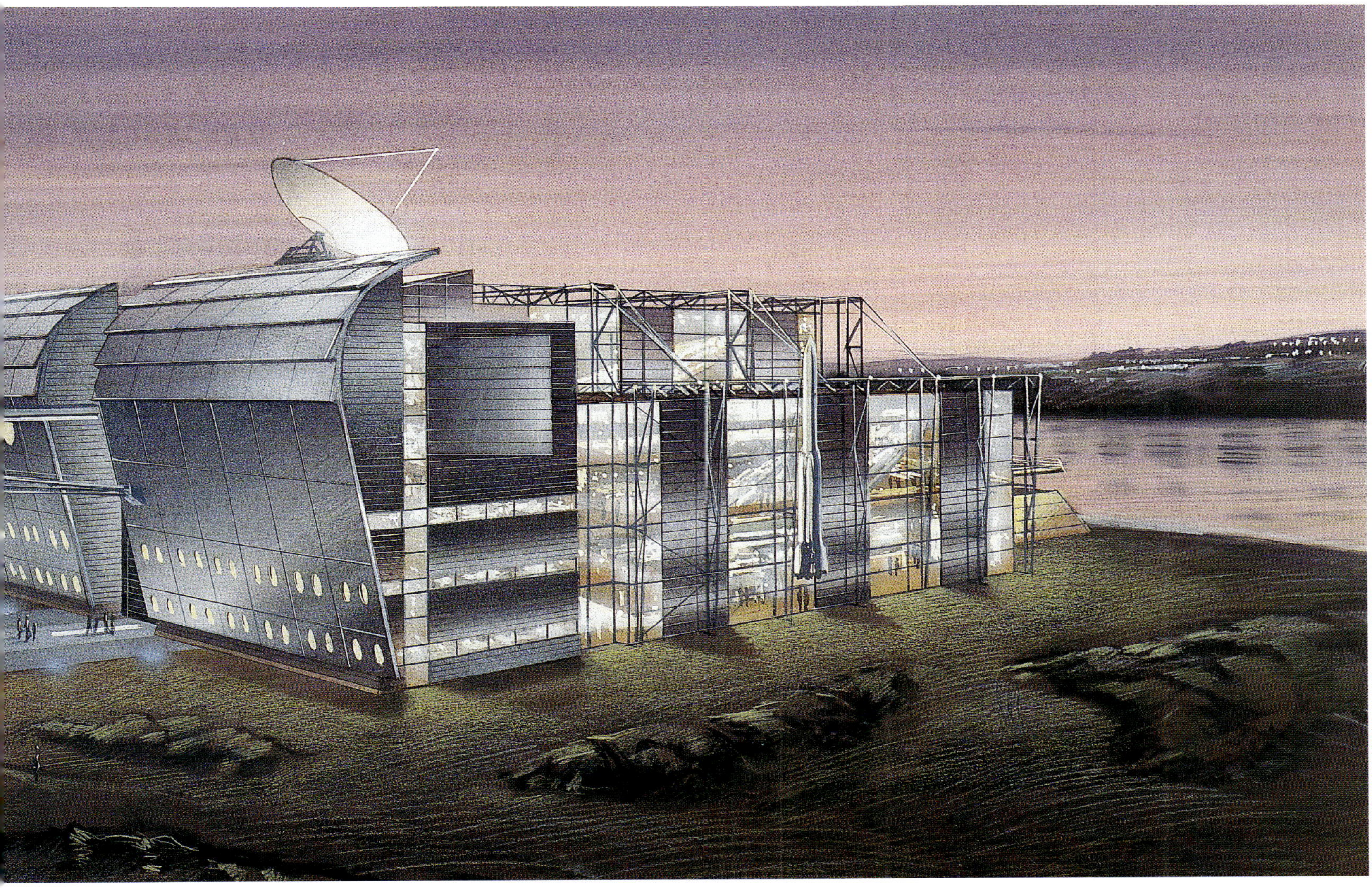

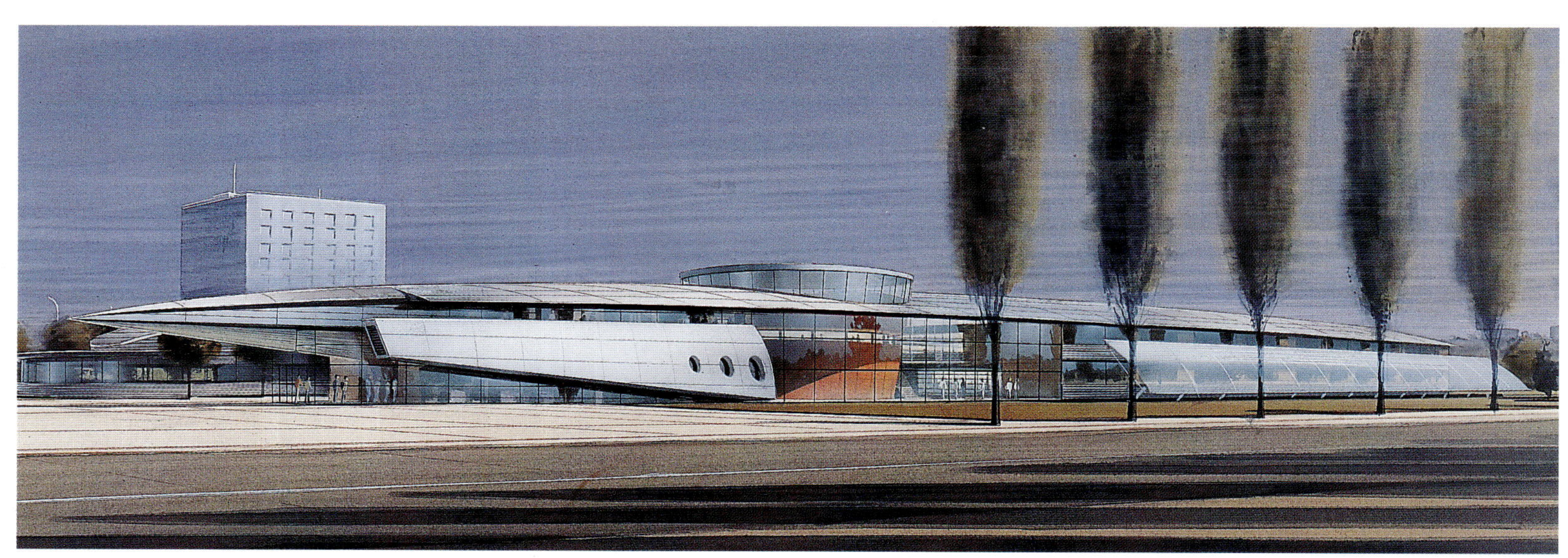

Gérard Philippe Elementary School
Aulnay-sous-Bois, 1994

The site of the project is unstructured: it consists of an accumulation of volumetric objects, houses and buildings, as well as a poorly constructed road system.

The avenue is bordered by a row of poplars, lending force and structure to the general confusion. This affirmative architecture geared to the avenue's powerful image will add strength structure to the neighborhood, simultaneously acting as a landmark and bestowing identity.

It is important for public schools, considering the important role they play in the society of today, to be easily identifiable in the urban environment.

The cultural diversity of the students excludes the idea of devising architectural forms deriving from any common sense of historical roots. What these children have in common has nothing to do with the past of the place where they live, but only their future.

The architects worked on this idea to create an avant-garde building, a building for tomorrow, a building that will be a common symbol for all.

It developed into a sort of space vessel, with a very spectacular prow pointing towards the crossroads, powerfully manifesting its presence.

The building's distinctive appearance is also playful; perhaps facilitating how the students perceive it.

Three buildings occupy the site: the school itself, a restaurant facility, and a school building.

The school is separated from its cafeteria, so students can leave the school building and relax in a different environment.

The classrooms are distinctive, they are "protected' by a "fore-class", an exterior garden. The gardens are bounded by a convex closure in perforated aluminium, a semi-transparent veil.

These elements accentuate the sense of calm in the classrooms, protect them from the noise out in the streets, and help concentration. At the other end of the building, the gardens may be used as classrooms in good weather.

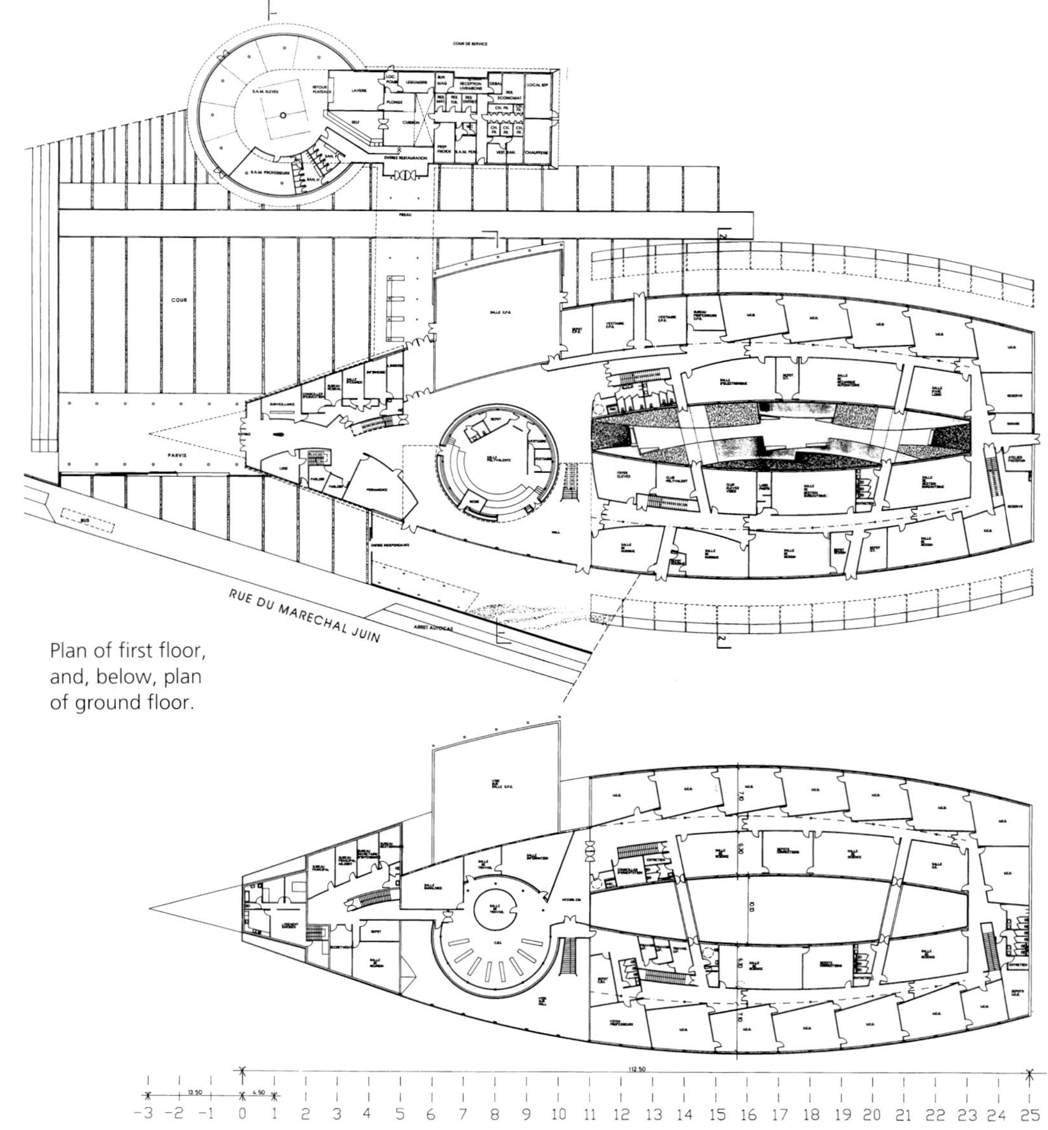

Plan of first floor, and, below, plan of ground floor.

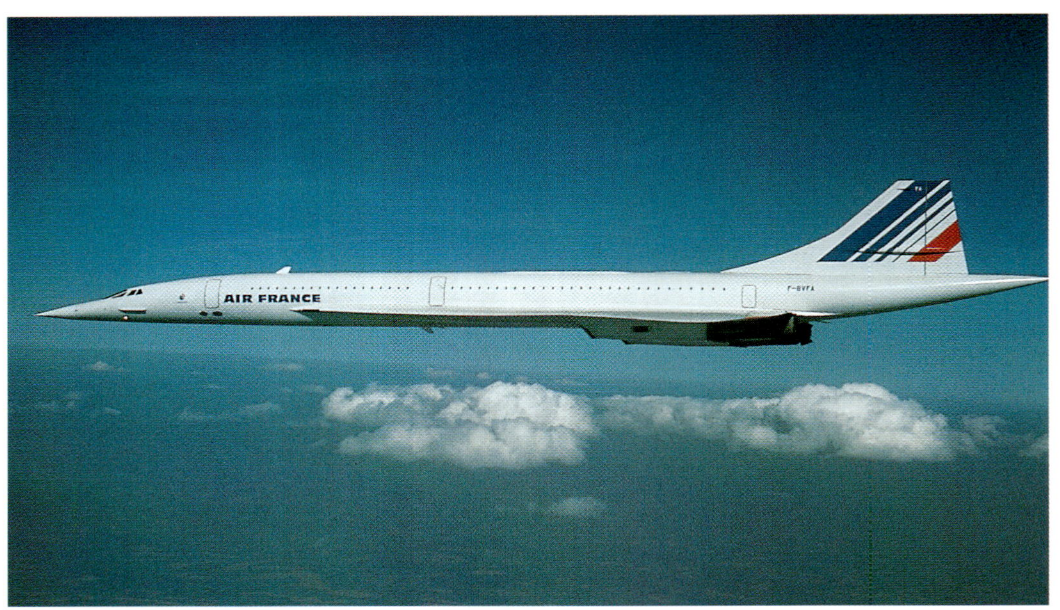
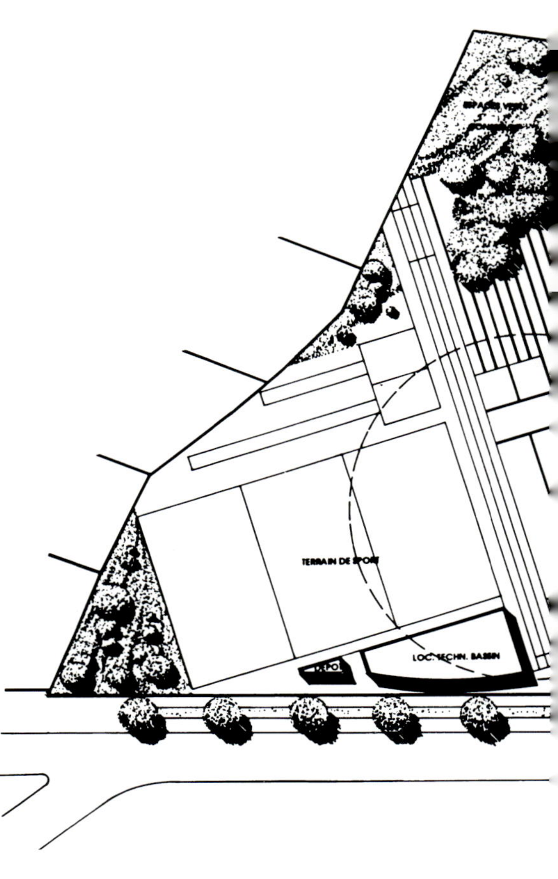

Above, the Concord aircraft, whose fluid form inspired this project. Below, rendering of the futuristic school building designed for Aulnay-sous-Bois.

Right, site plan of the complex.

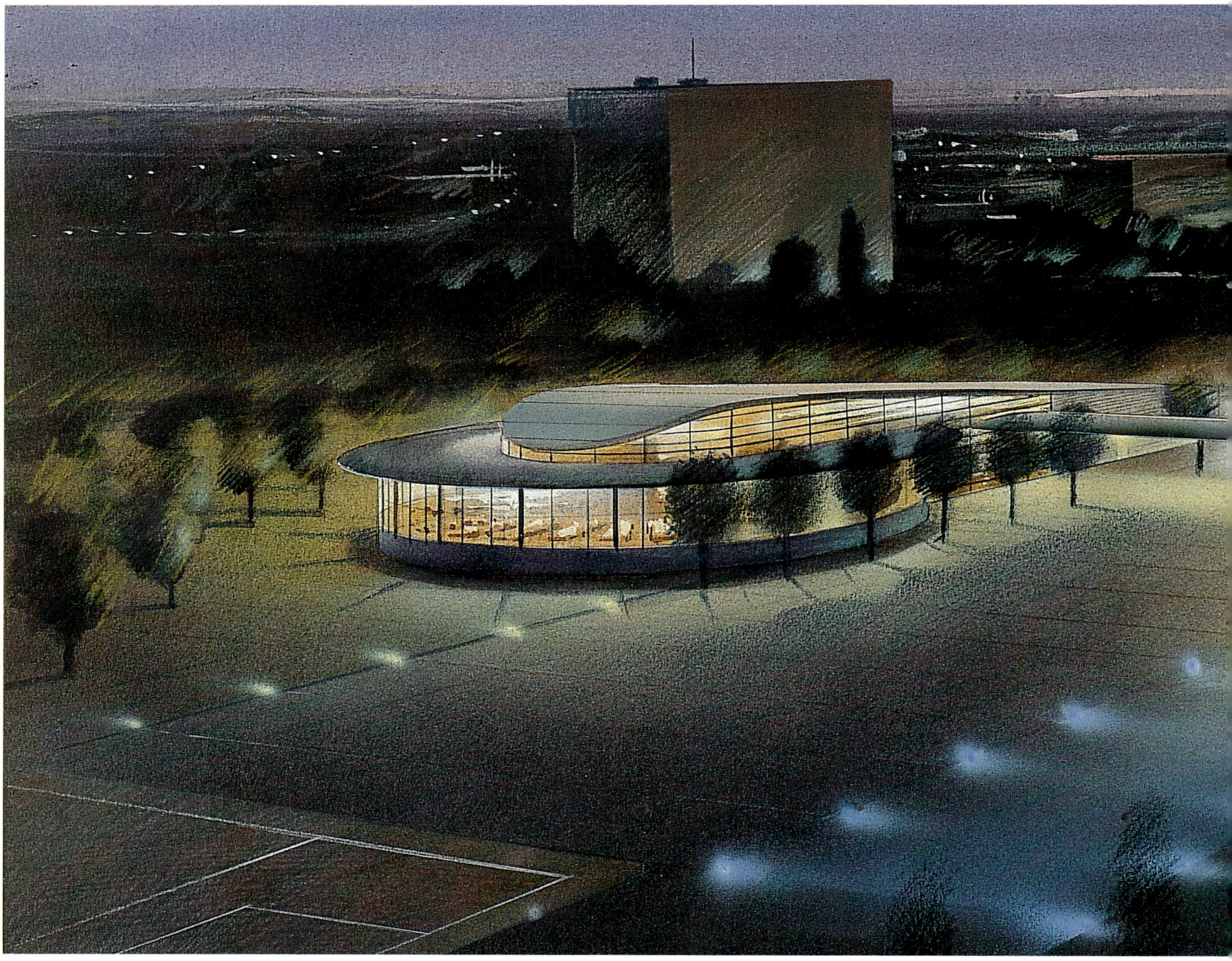

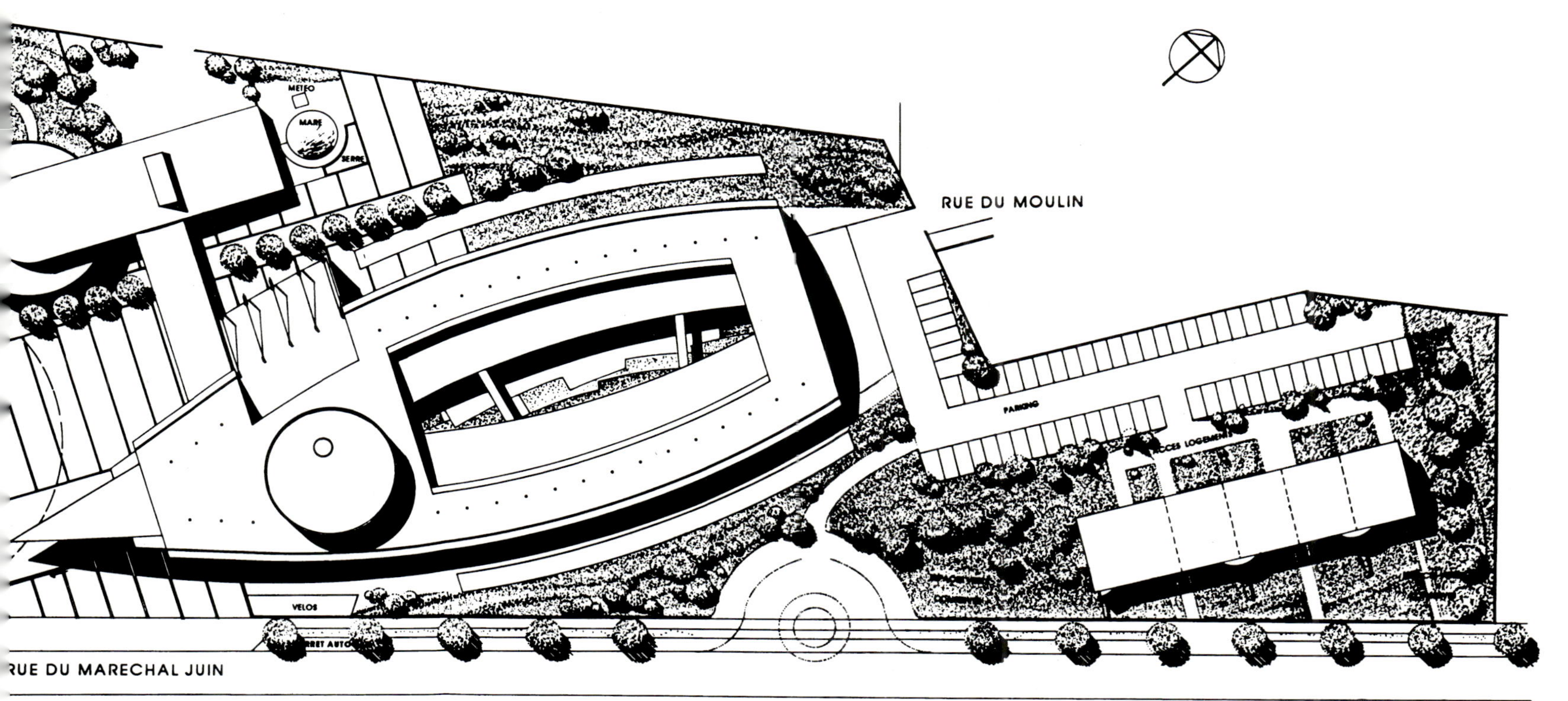

METRO
MARE
RUE DU MOULIN
PARKING
VELOS
RUE DU MARECHAL JUIN

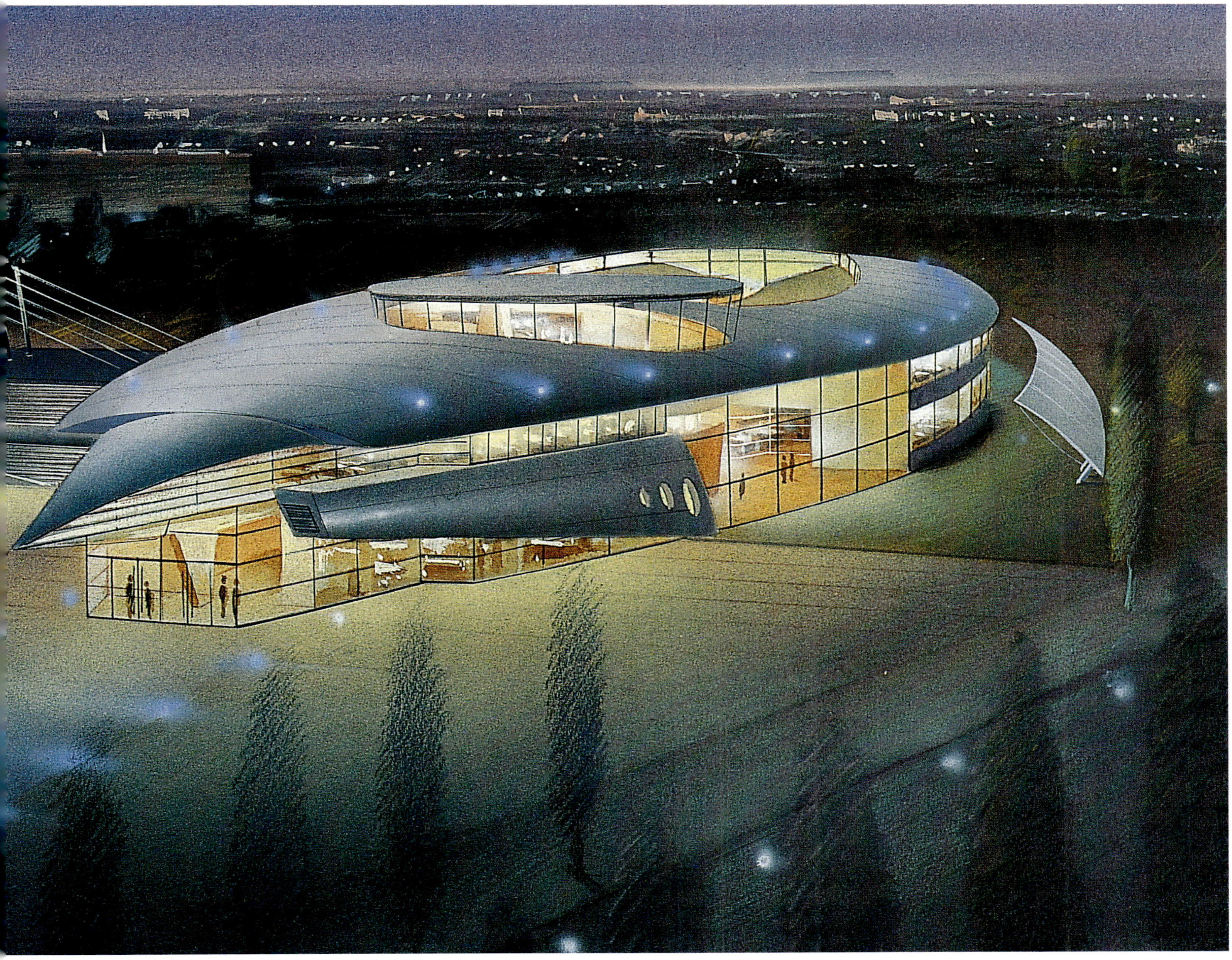

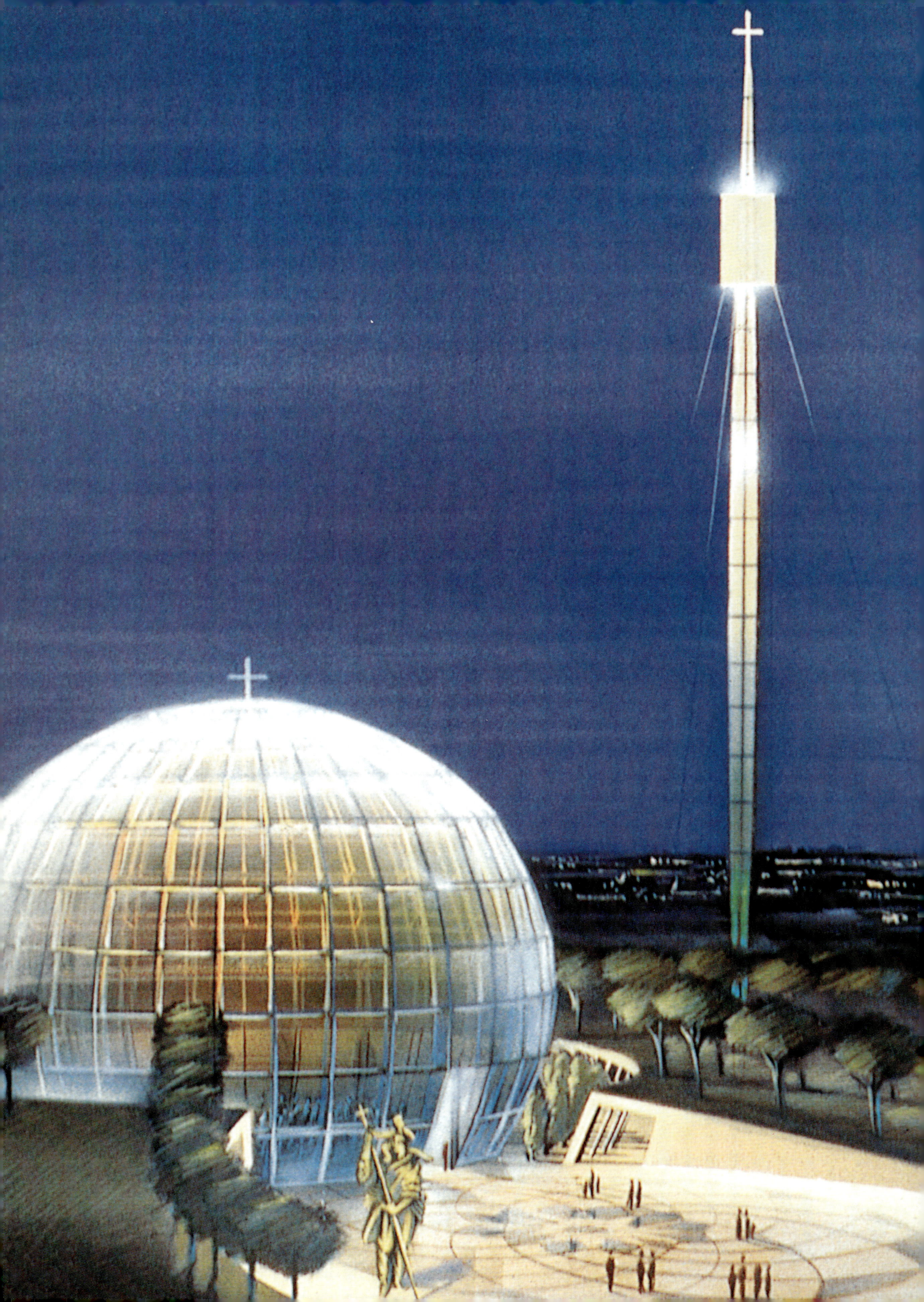

Proposal for a Church
Rome, 1994

The church sits on the axis of the perspective formed by two imposing housing blocks. It is an active part of the neighborhood layout, a sort of landmark. The church and other two buildings envelop the congregation area in front of the church. As in the past, the churchyard is right in the heart of the neighborhood.

The church itself forms a near perfect sphere, a natural evolution of the dome: the sphere is the current symbol of the earth, just as the dome was in the past. The church is situated in a crater whose outer slopes are planted with vegetation and it seems to rise straight up from the ground as if the world were being born. The churchyard's ground pattern evokes the Campidoglio. The church itself is bordered by a modern cloister surrounded by a peristyle leading to the annex rooms and chapel situated under the embankment of the crater. Its design symbolises both the earth and a metaphysical mediator.

The shell of the building is made of stainglass through which we can see the light of the sky in all its variations from storms and sunrises. The messages it sends out is of the universal return: we go to church to commune with the entire cosmos and God is present now and forever.

The layers of steel frame the sphere with a space of 1.20 meters between the stained glass. The color effects change as you walk thorugh the church as they overlap and superimpose. The glass is duller in the bottom section to safeguard the privacy of prayer, gradually growing brighter and brighter as it rises up to the tabernacle. The contrast with daylight is magnified by a double layer of colored glass.

The gap between the glass adjusts the church temperature (powerful, silent ventilation or excess heat, and also allows the inner panes to be cleaned.

The inner layer is made of toughened glass, while the outside layer in the bottom section is protected by a perforated aluminium grill to safeguard against break-ins and vandalism.

The absence of interior bearings allows a clear view through to the choir. The church floor contrasts with the splendour of the churchyard, since it is a simple concrete slab with radiating joints originating at the tabernacle.

A *campanile* carries the bells on high. It is actually made of steel and glass and, just like the church, it may be lit up from inside so that it can be seen from a distance.

Both are made of lacquered stainless steel. The project is designed to create contemporaary architecture for the present day: to inject high technology into a message for our age.

1. Entrance
2. Main hall
3. Conference hall
4. Associations' rooms
5. School rooms
6. Sacristy
7. Offices
8. Chapel

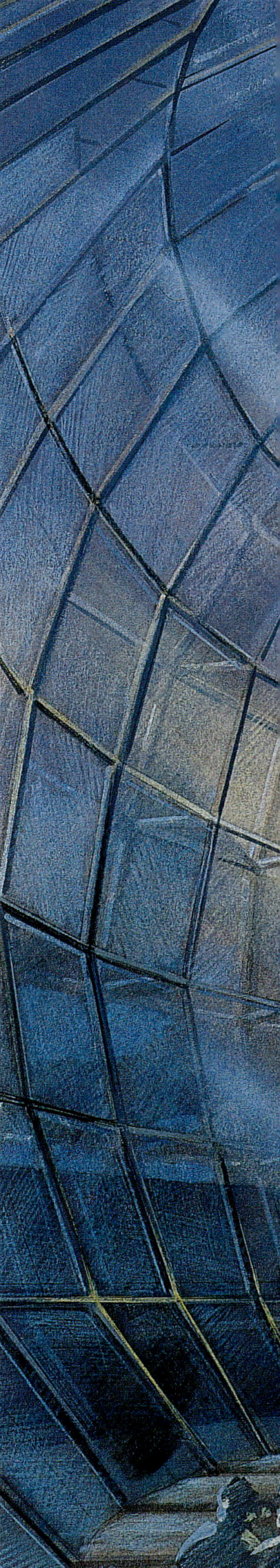

Left, ground floor plan.
Below, internal view of
the main congregational
hall.

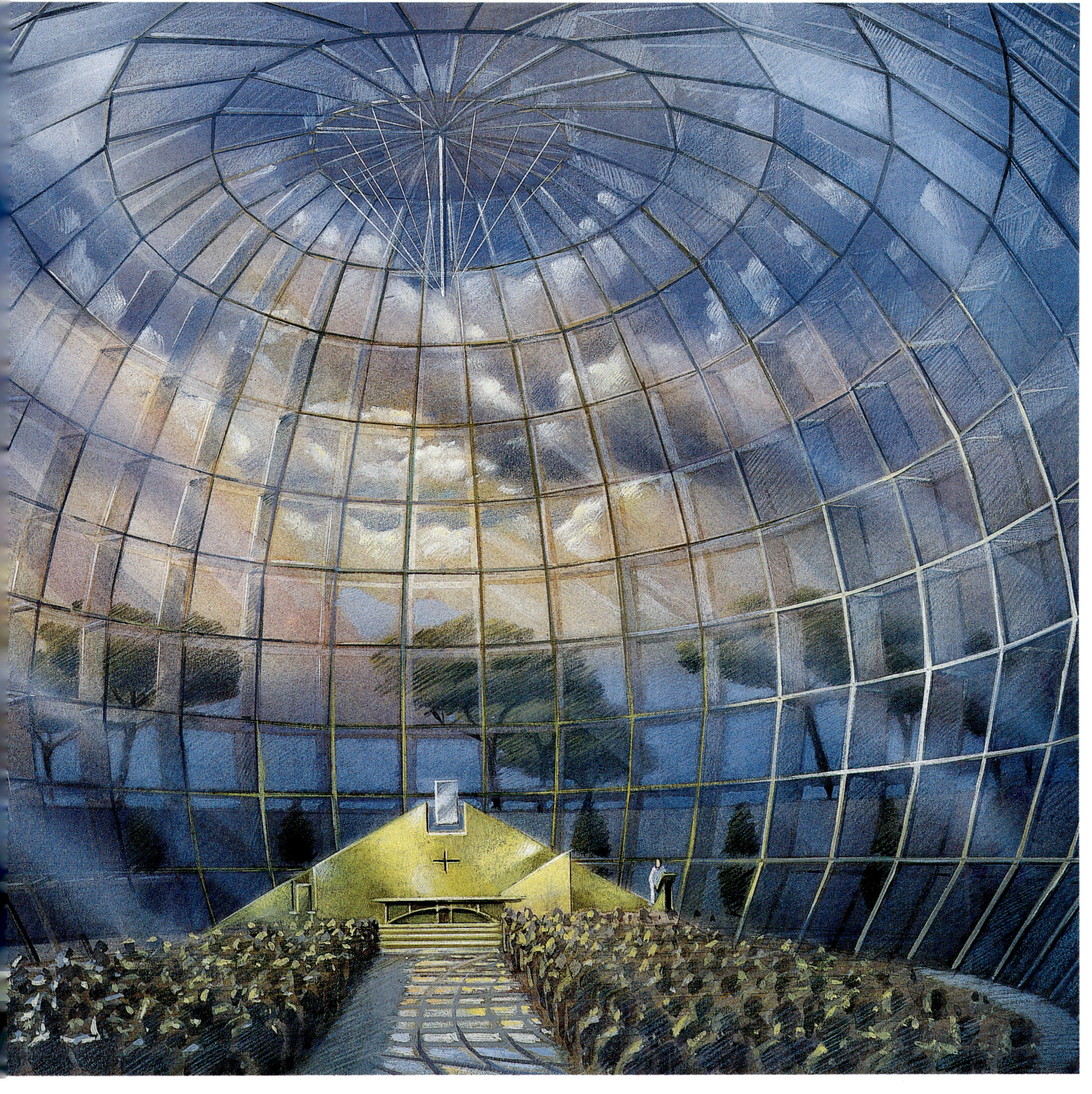

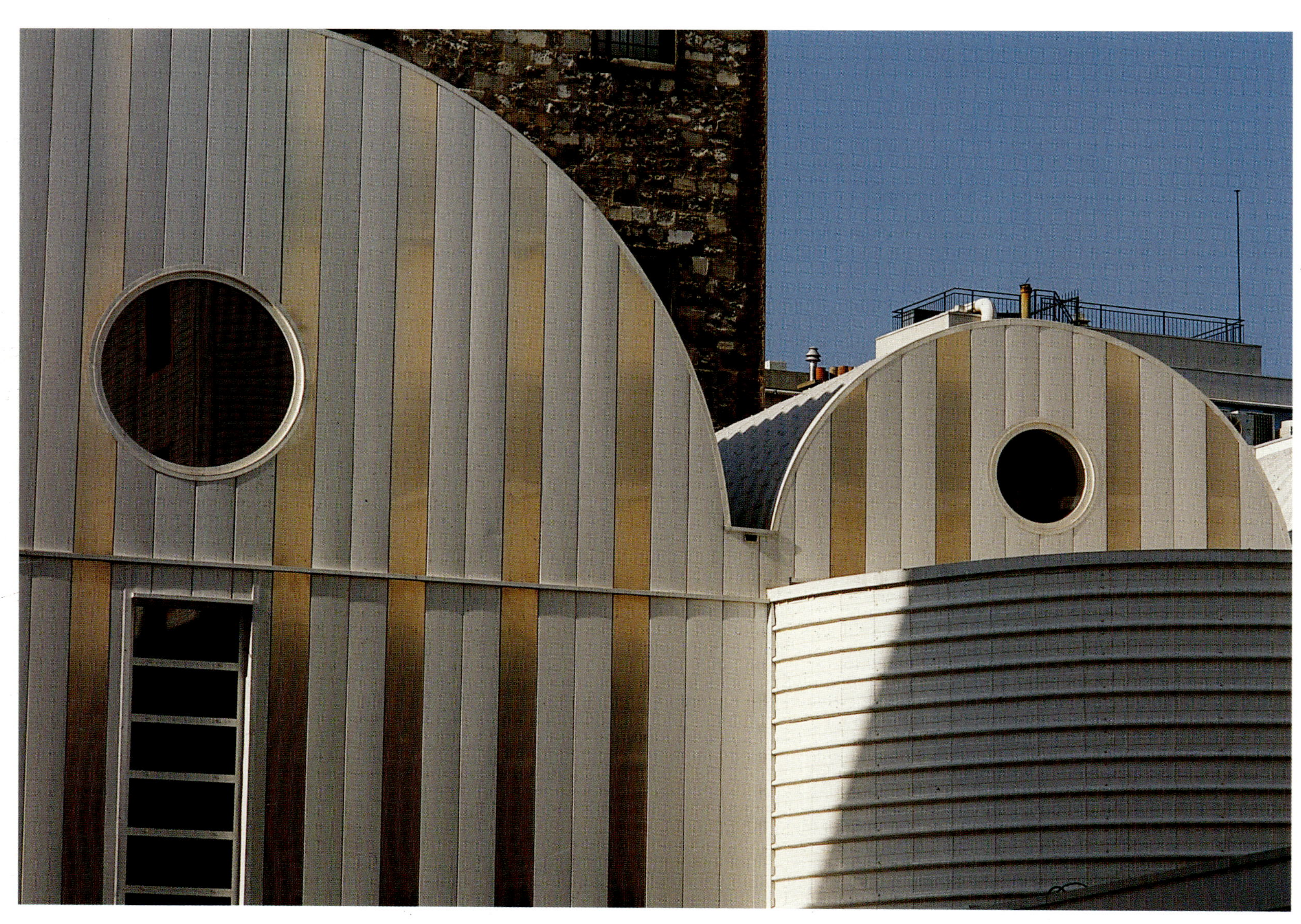

Synagogue
Paris, 1994

Built on a very complex parcel, practically inaccessible to construction veihicles, in a historic neighborhood of Paris, the synagogue houses a large prayer room with a mezzanine, as well as a school with class and meeting rooms in a space in the basement.

The construction system uses large steel arches that support a vault clad in prefabricated plasterboard. The mezzanine is suspended. The effect of this large volume in its very small ground space is very effective.

The simple, sweeping curved forms of the outside surfaces draw on the patterns described by the ribbing of the materials and alternating clear and opaque finishing.

The inside and outside interact through large circles of light projected through the glass windows with vertical uprights and a rectangular grid. The interior lighting is entirely indirect and designed to exalt the roof vault through its reflecting white surfaces.

The architecture is very contemporary and directly evokes the cultural roots of Judaism. Both the site location and the simplicity and effectiveness of the synagogue's interior and exterior space, that concede nothing to decoration and opulence, are ideally suited to the characteristic features of Jewish liturgical space. Rather than focusing on the stylistic features and symbolic force of this space, the design is geared to the uniqueness of a synagogue standing in such a strange, "hostile" context.

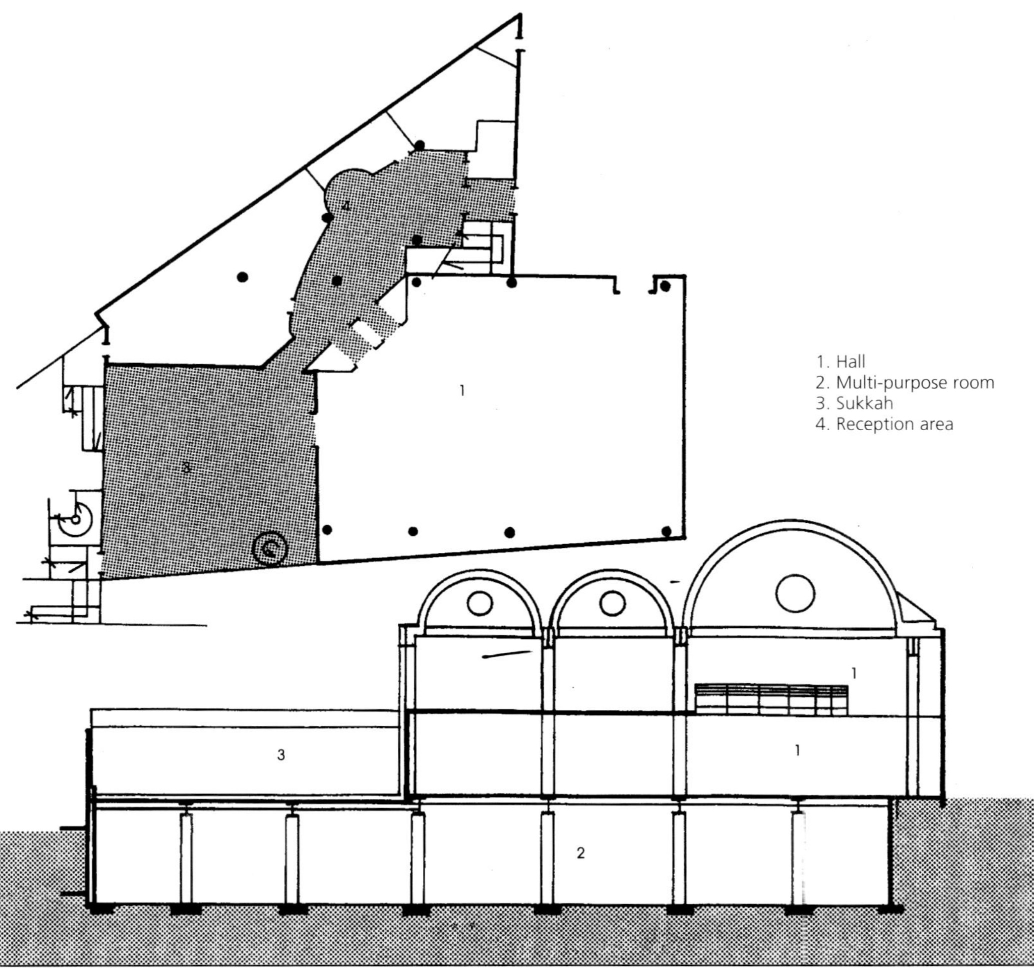

The Synagogue, which
is constructed out of
a system of steel arches
supporting the vaults
clad with prefabricated
plasterboard panels.

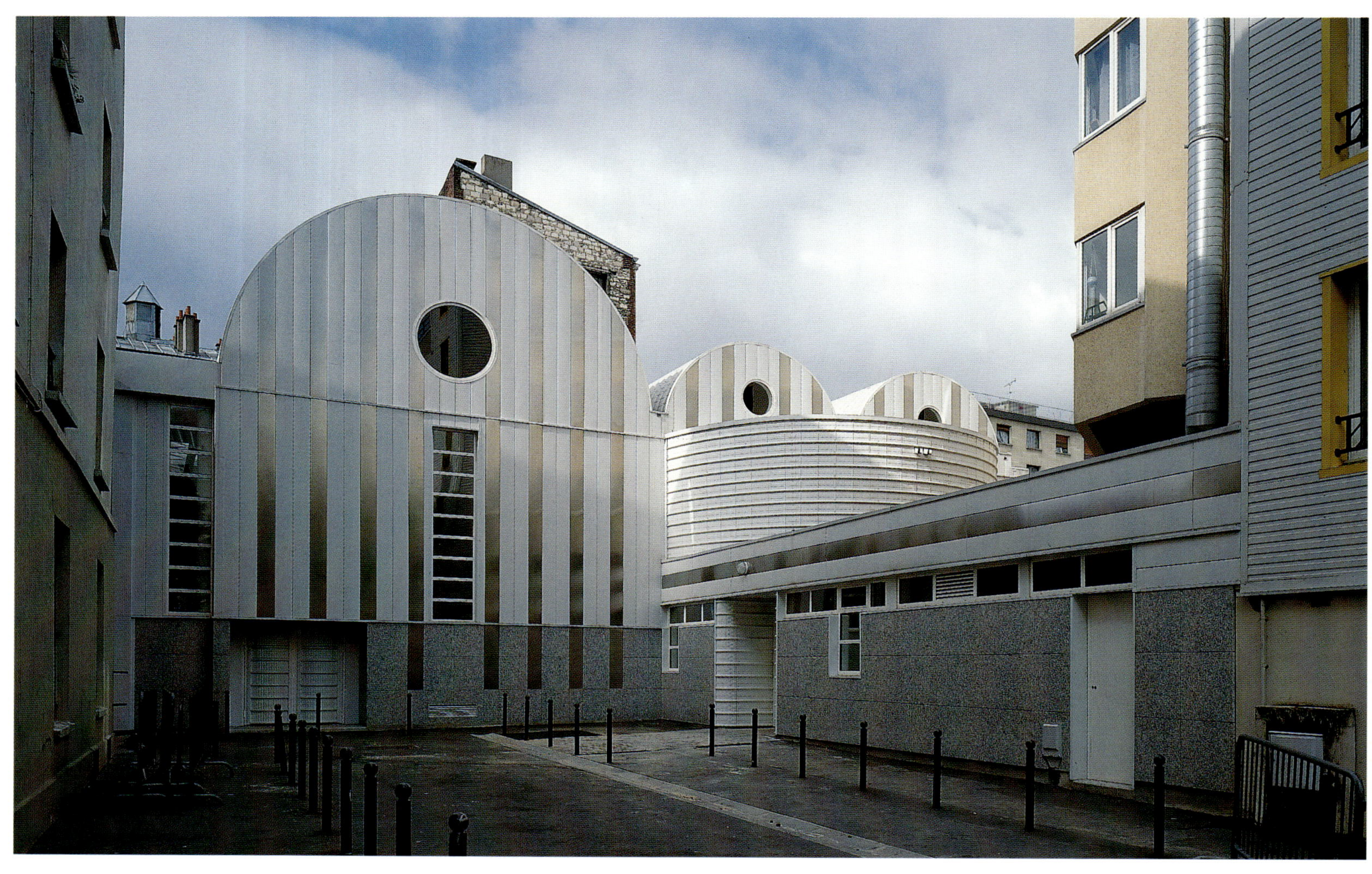

Details of the interior
showing the suspended
structure at mezzanine
level. The interior
lighting is all indirect
and designed to
highlight the roof vault.

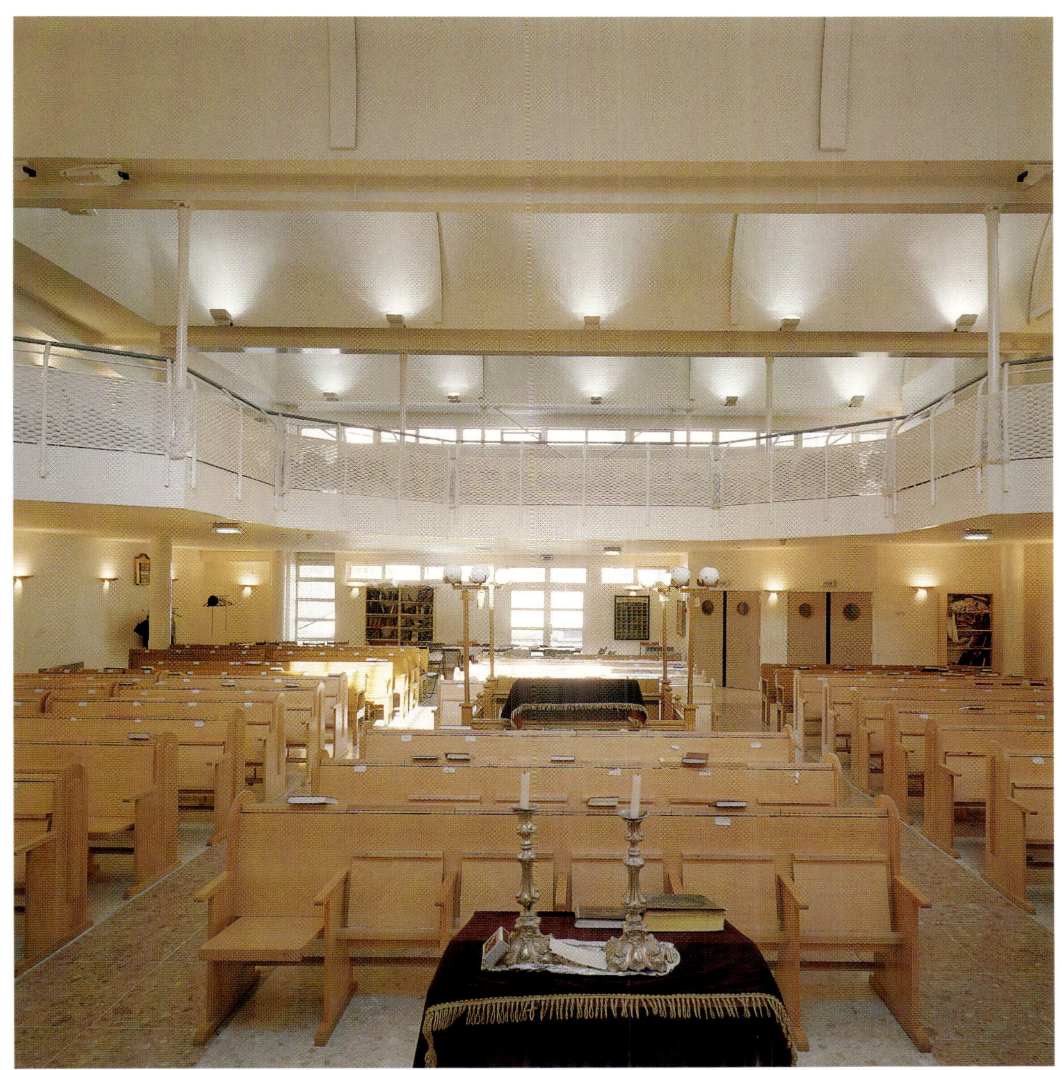

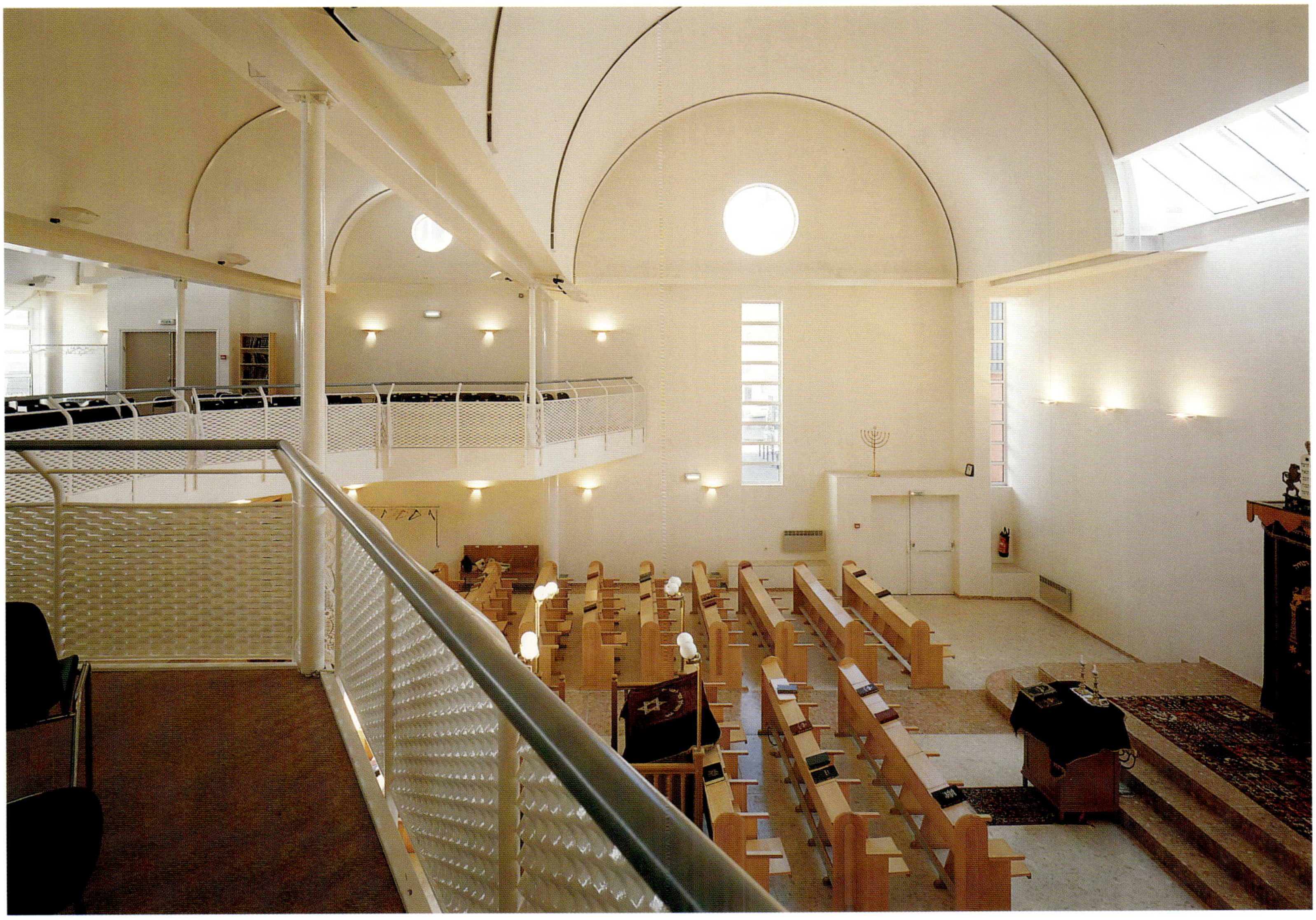

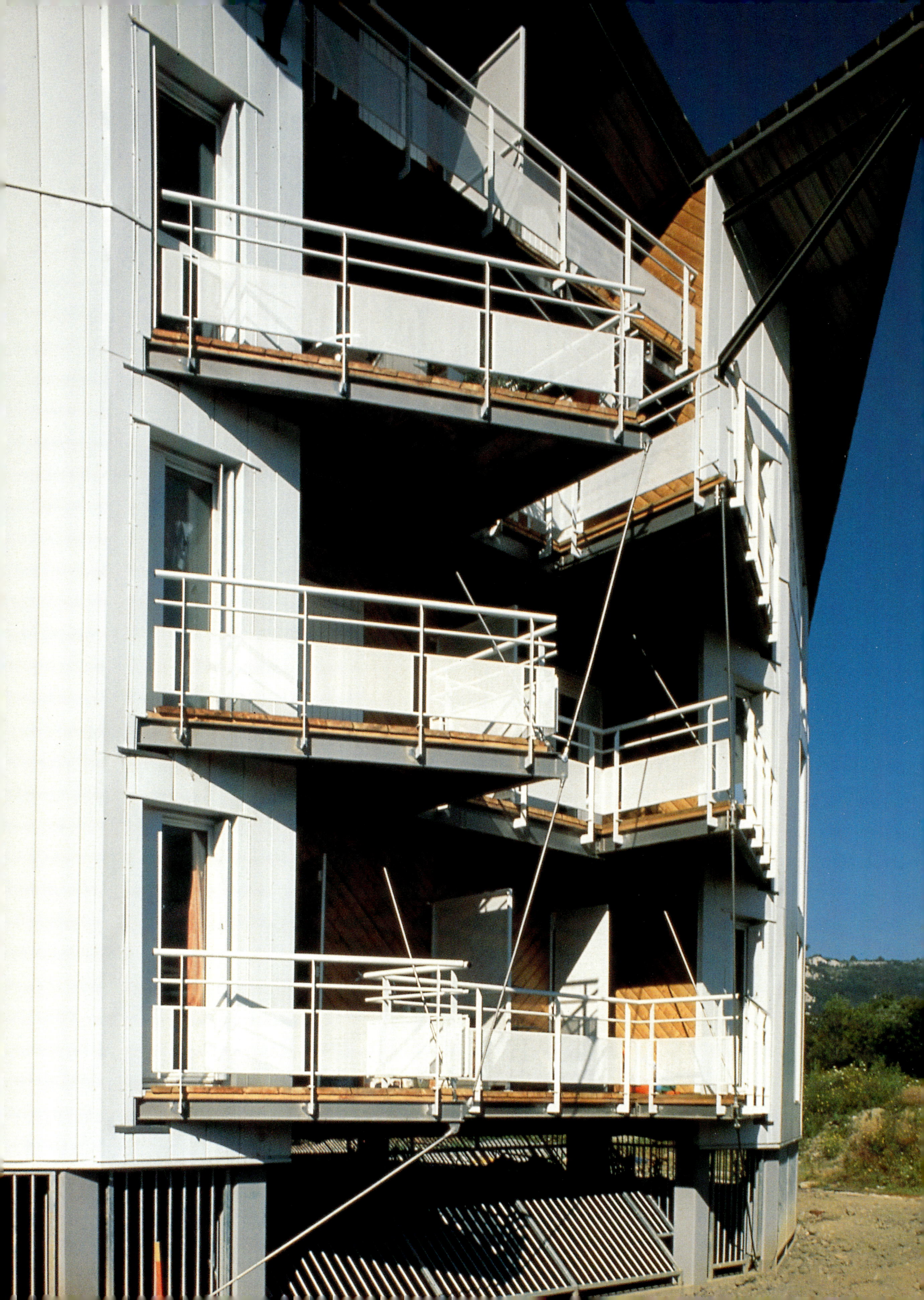

Parc des Taillées Housing Complex
Saint Martin d'Hères, 1996

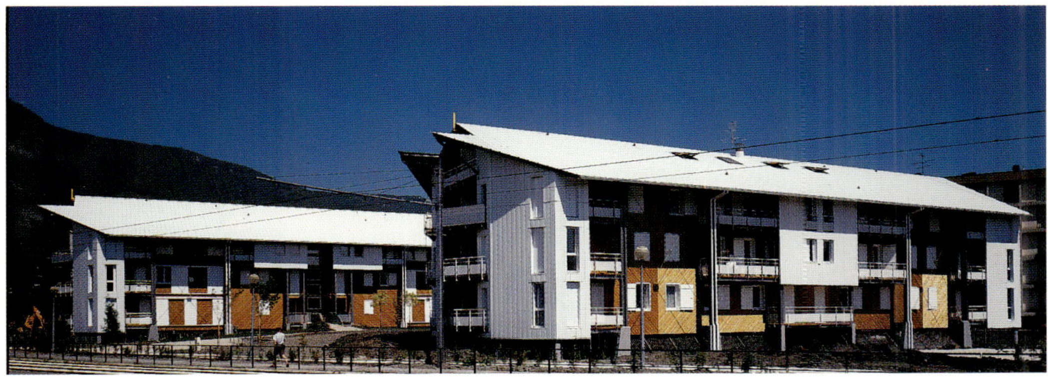

This project is part of a Zac (Concerted Redevelopment Area) near the edge of Isère, offering picturesque views across the surrounding mountainside.

This particular ZAC is located on the border of a university campus and is served by a modern tramway line.

The site plan is designed around two identical buildings, facing each other on opposite sides of an internal garden, as part of a plan to landscape the wide open spaces of the university complex.

Car traffic is confined to a minimum by parking the vehicles beneath the buildings in a special naturally lit and ventilated semi-underground parking lot.

The ground floor is slightly raised and the car park forms a predominantly open-type basement level. Two walkways link the garden to the halls to allow access for the disabled.

The decision to focus on communal family housing resulted in the construction of two long low-level buildings designed to enhance the residential nature of the site. The lowness of the buildings means that the stairs do not need to be closed in and can be treated like a structuring architectural feature, around which the halls and inside corridors are constructed.

The centrality and transparency of the complex visually divides the buildings into two houses connected by a central space.

The exposed metal structure and regular pattern of the smooth slightly set-back facade frame give the entire building a highly up-to-date architectural design.

The buildings are covered by a wide overhanging roof held up by an exposed metal structure interacting with the facade. The partly central entrance is marked by a porch leading from the outside walkways through to the glass stairwell. This transition area, where people mix together, is located between the basement and main entrance, the garden and hall, exterior and interior.

Most flats have a corner angle or watchtower in the lounge area offering panoramic views of the surrounding mountains.

The top two floors are designed on a duplex basis to recreate the kind of private space associated with houses. All the flats have at least one balcony.

The spaciousness of the overall building scheme fosters the kind of neighborly, family-like relations associated with pleasant housing estates.

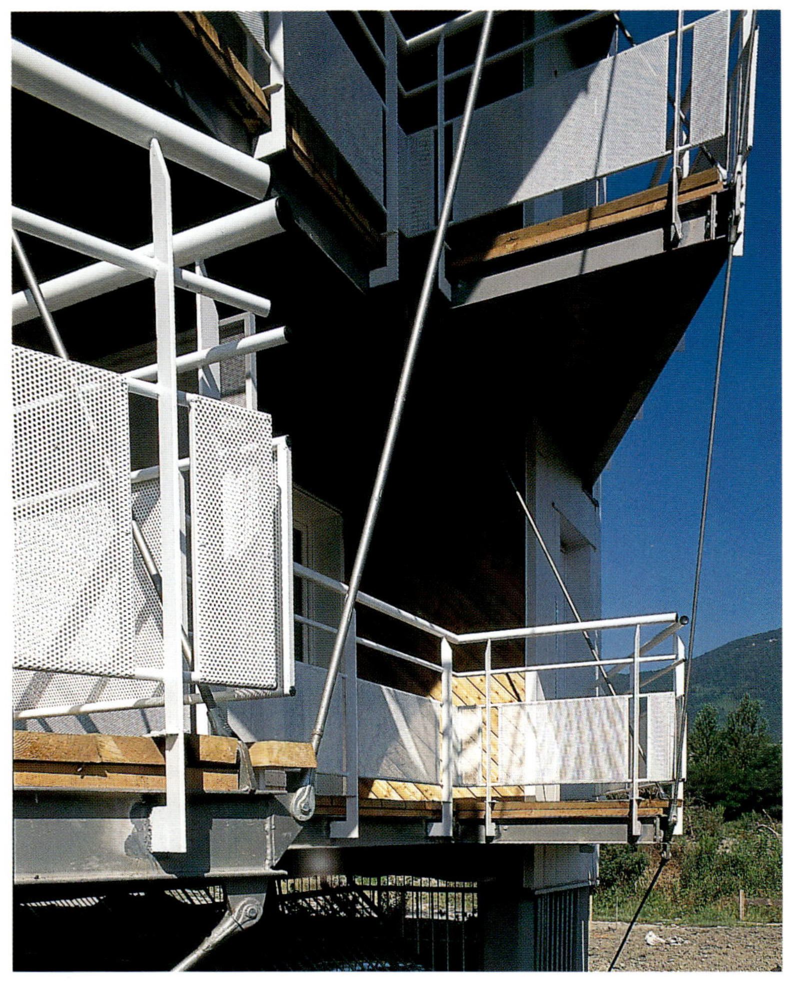

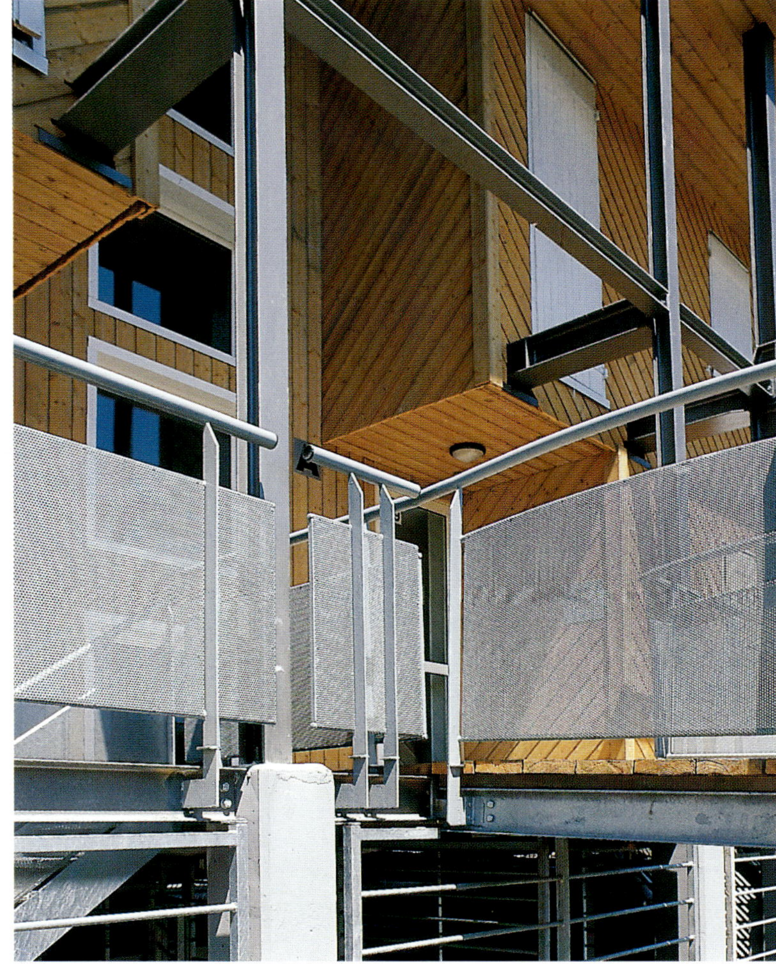

Details of the front facade and entrance marked by a portico connected to a walkway and glass atrium. Below, constructive details of the P.C.I.S. (Plancher Composite Interfactive Sec) slab system elaborated by Dubosc and Landowski and used for the first time in this project. This totally dry slab system offers certain advantages over its concrete counterpart: it fits in perfectly with the overall construction system while retaining mechanical resistance, horizontal-vertical stability, sound proofing and fire proofing.

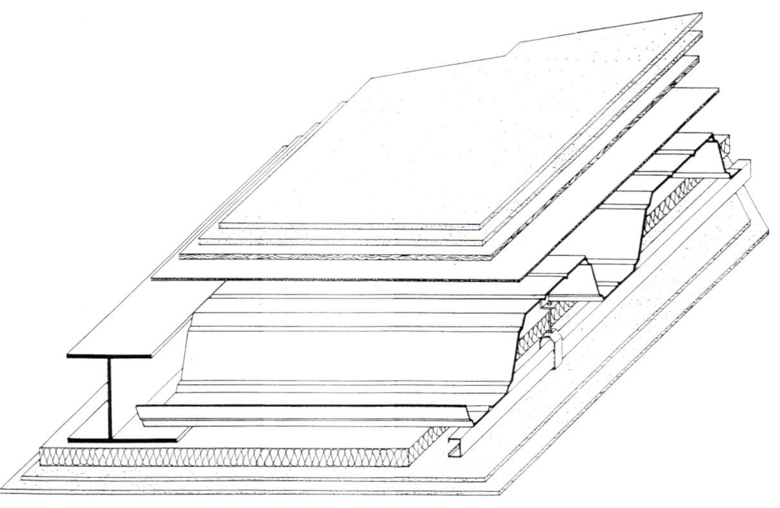

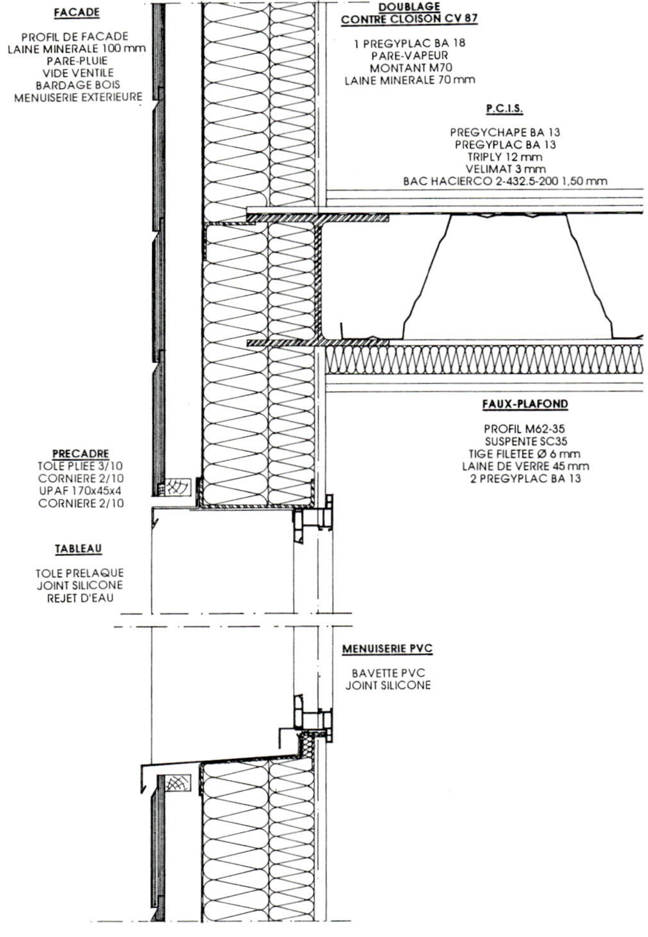

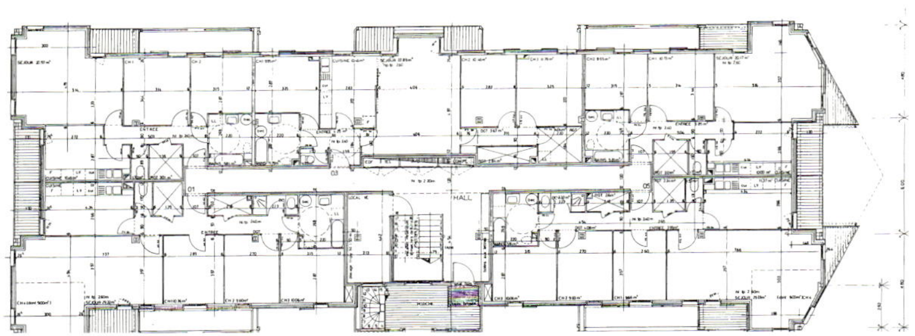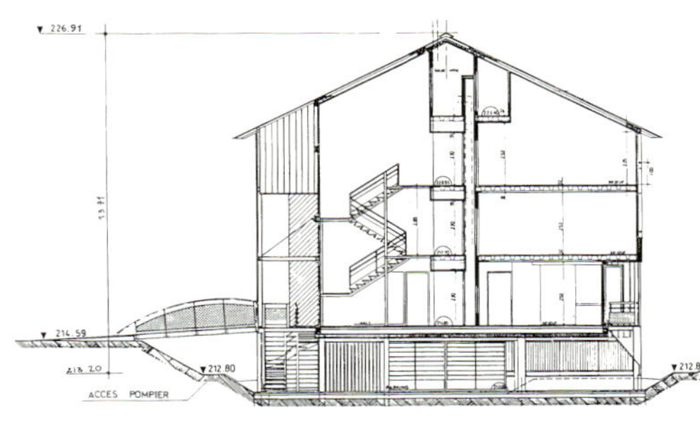

Ground floor plan and cross section. Below, the rear facade.

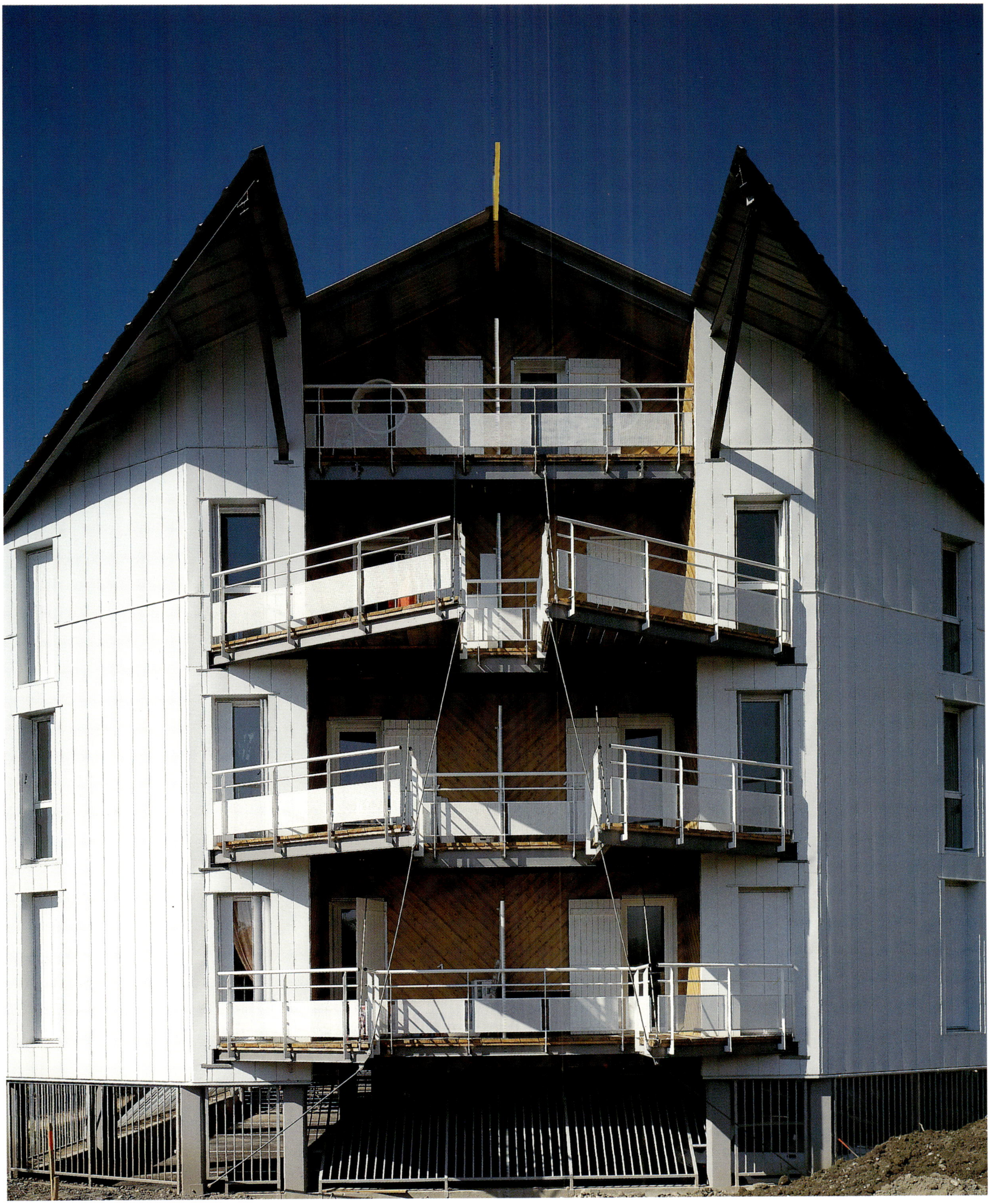

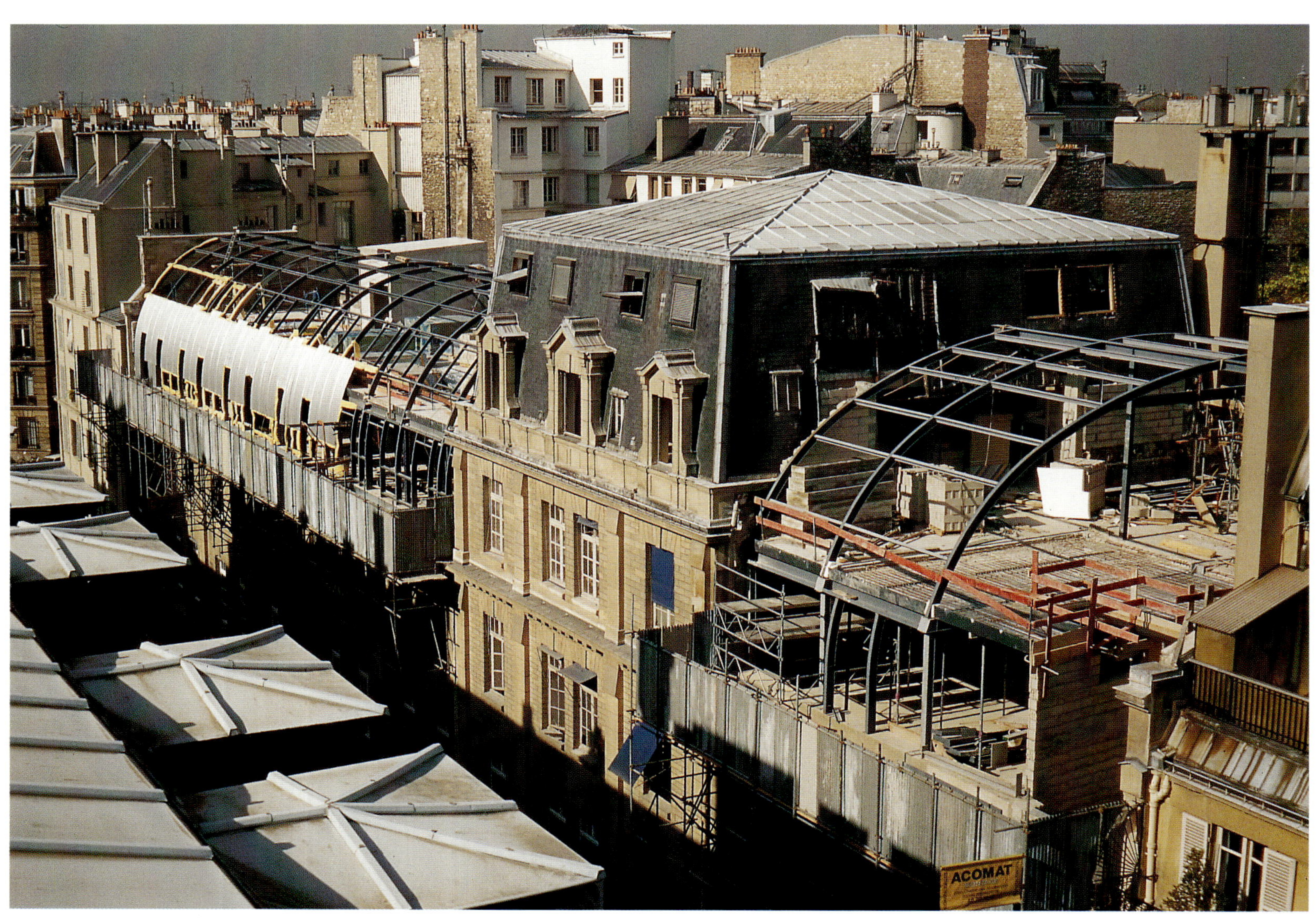
ACOMAT

Academy of Music
Paris, 1996

The Paris City Council bought this historical old building to house the Academy of Music.

It soon realised that radical restructuring work needed to be carried out, which, without interfering with the facade, allowed the main building to be reinforced and modernised to cater for new teaching requirements thanks to the construction of extra facilities.

The competition organised to meet these demands specified the need to raise the top floor on either side of the central core.

Dubosc and Landowski decided to design one of their favourite large barrel vaults projecting up from the original gutters level to recreate the original facade of the top-floor dormer windows before continuing on to the new level. In this case, the design was intended to underline the difference between this new addition and the original structure, as part of a deliberate attempt to highlight the fact that this classically styled building was going through a new phase of life.

Deep excavations were also carried out at the base of the structure, alongside the foundations, to create two underground levels holding both the main concert hall and other facilities for certain specific instruments (organ, percussion instruments etc.). The main section has been opened up slightly through carefully gauged demolition work through the facade to "open up" the building even more towards the outside and make it look older. The glass windows will allow even more light to flow into the inside corridors.

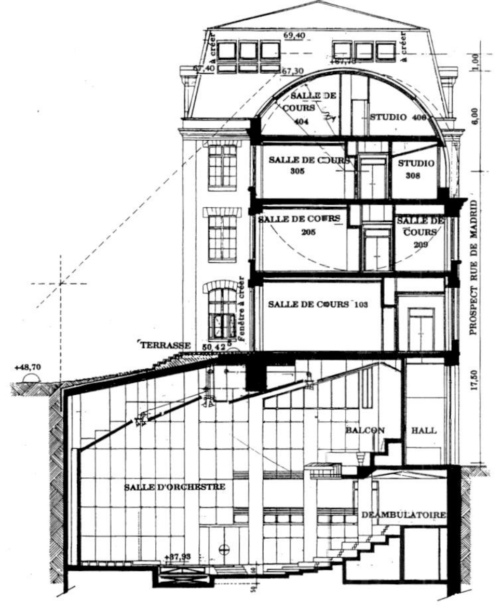
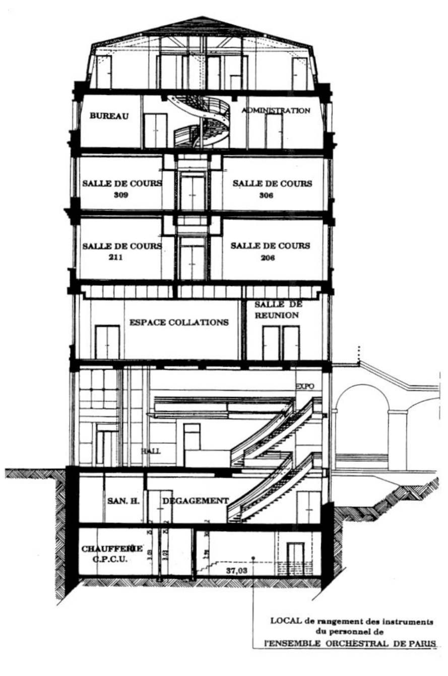

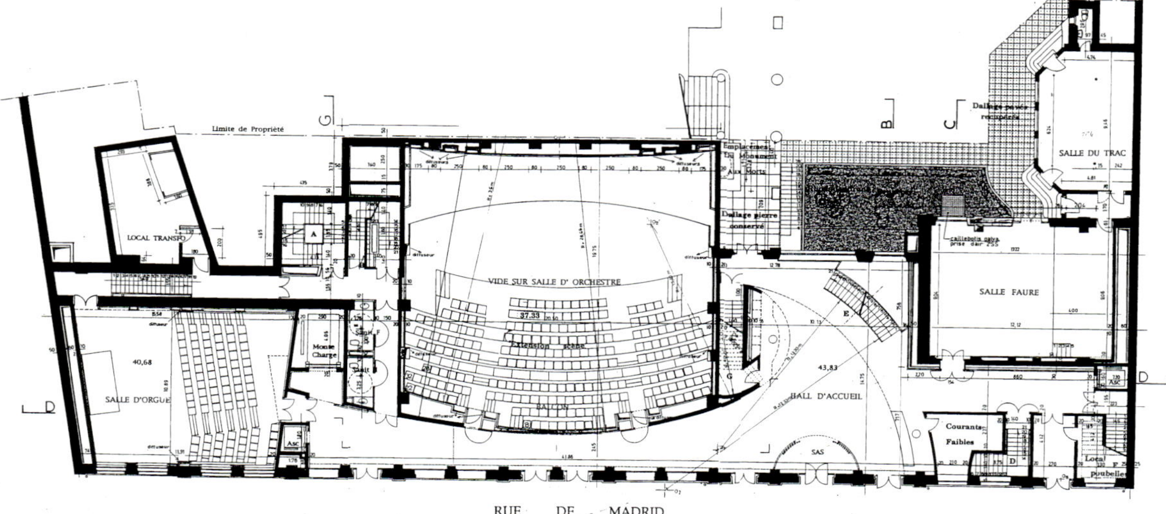

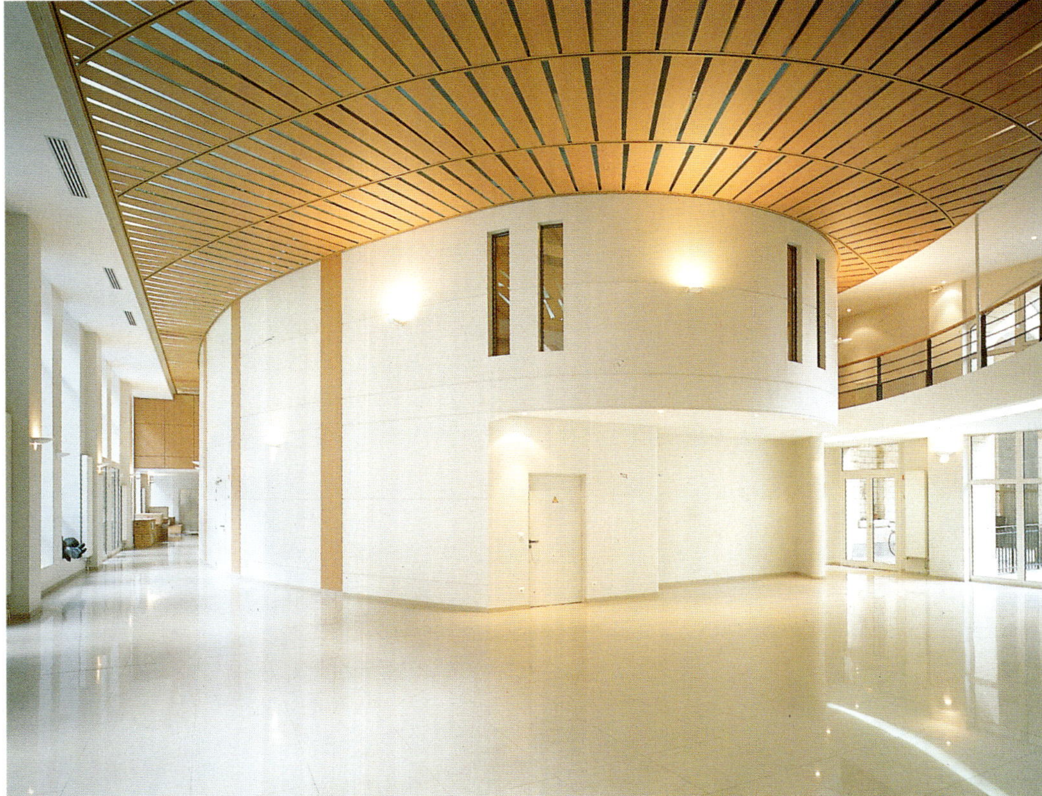

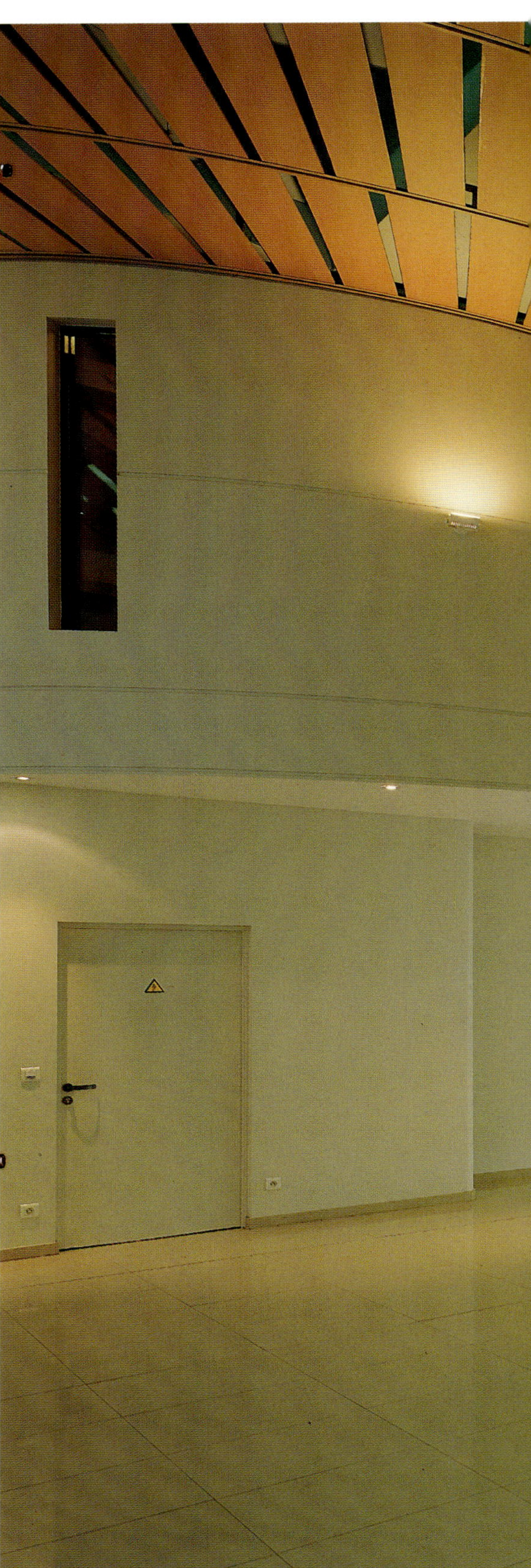

Top of page, plan
of the ground floor
and, opposite page,
plan of the mezzanine.
Above and right, the
entrance lobby.

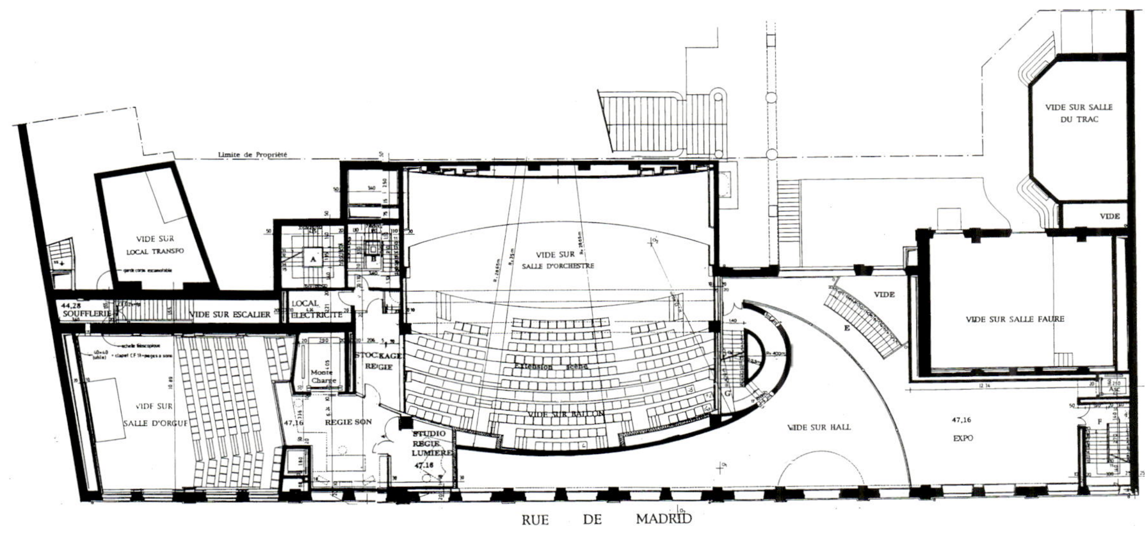

VIDE SUR SALLE DU TRAC
VIDE
Limite de Propriété
VIDE SUR LOCAL TRANSFO
VIDE SUR SALLE D'ORCHESTRE
VIDE
VIDE SUR SALLE FAURE
SOUFFLERIE
VIDE SUR ESCALIER
LOCAL ELECTRICITE
STOCKAGE REGIE
VIDE SUR SALLE D'ORGUE
REGIE SON
VIDE SUR BALCON
VIDE SUR HALL
EXPO
STUDIO REGIE LUMIERE
RUE DE MADRID

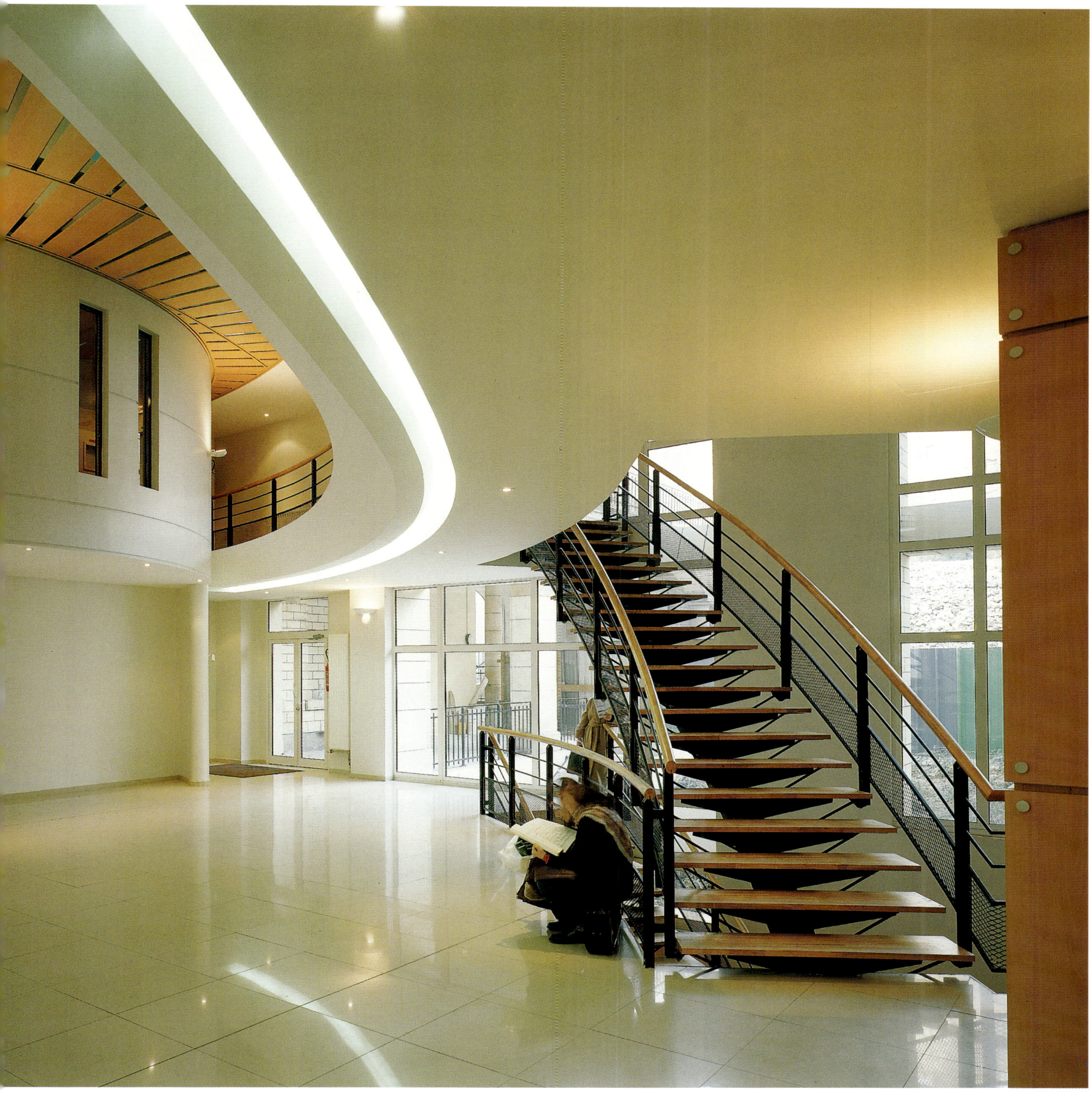

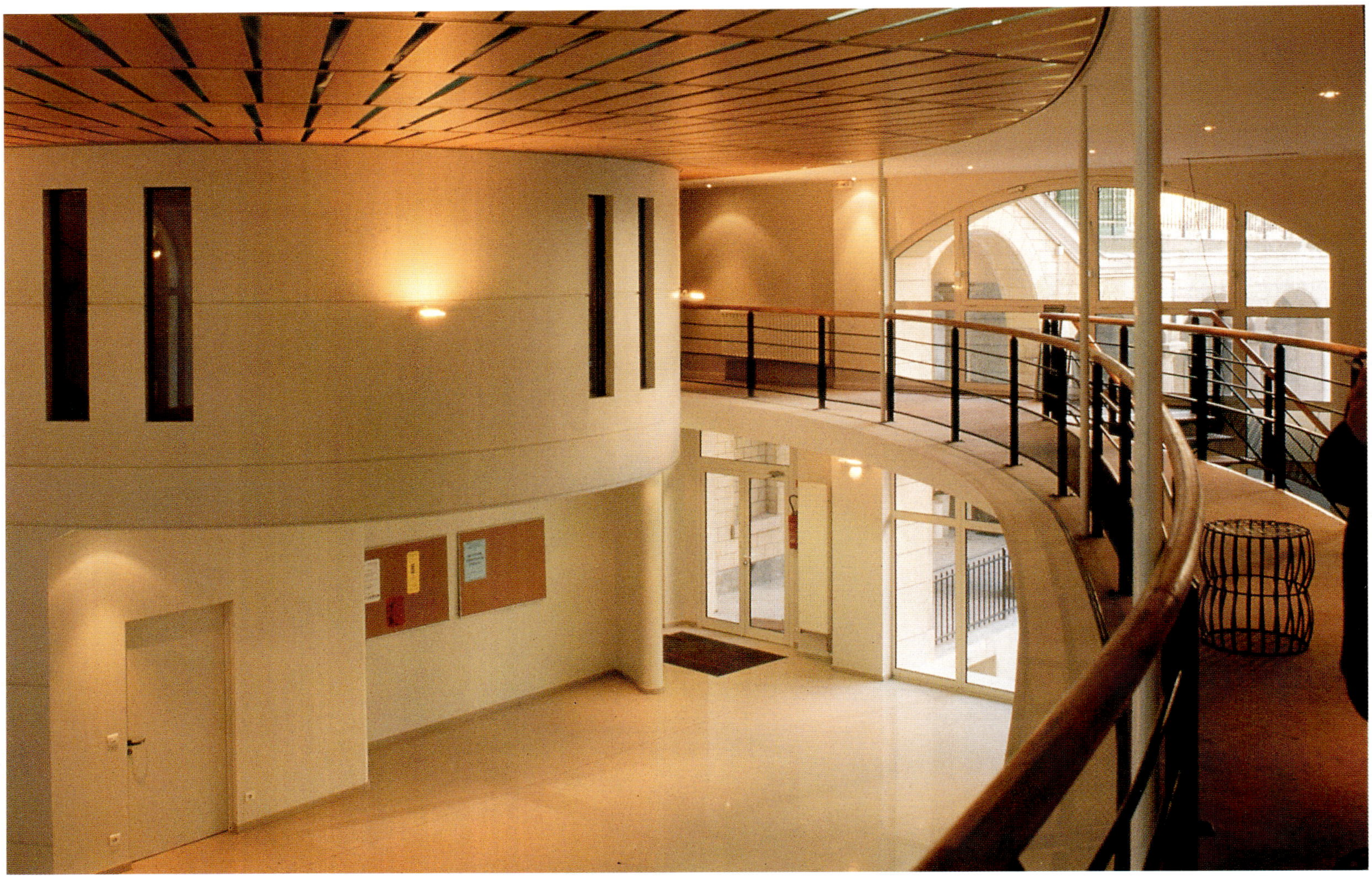

Above and opposite page, details of the mezzanine overlooking the double-height lobby. Right, the auditorium room.

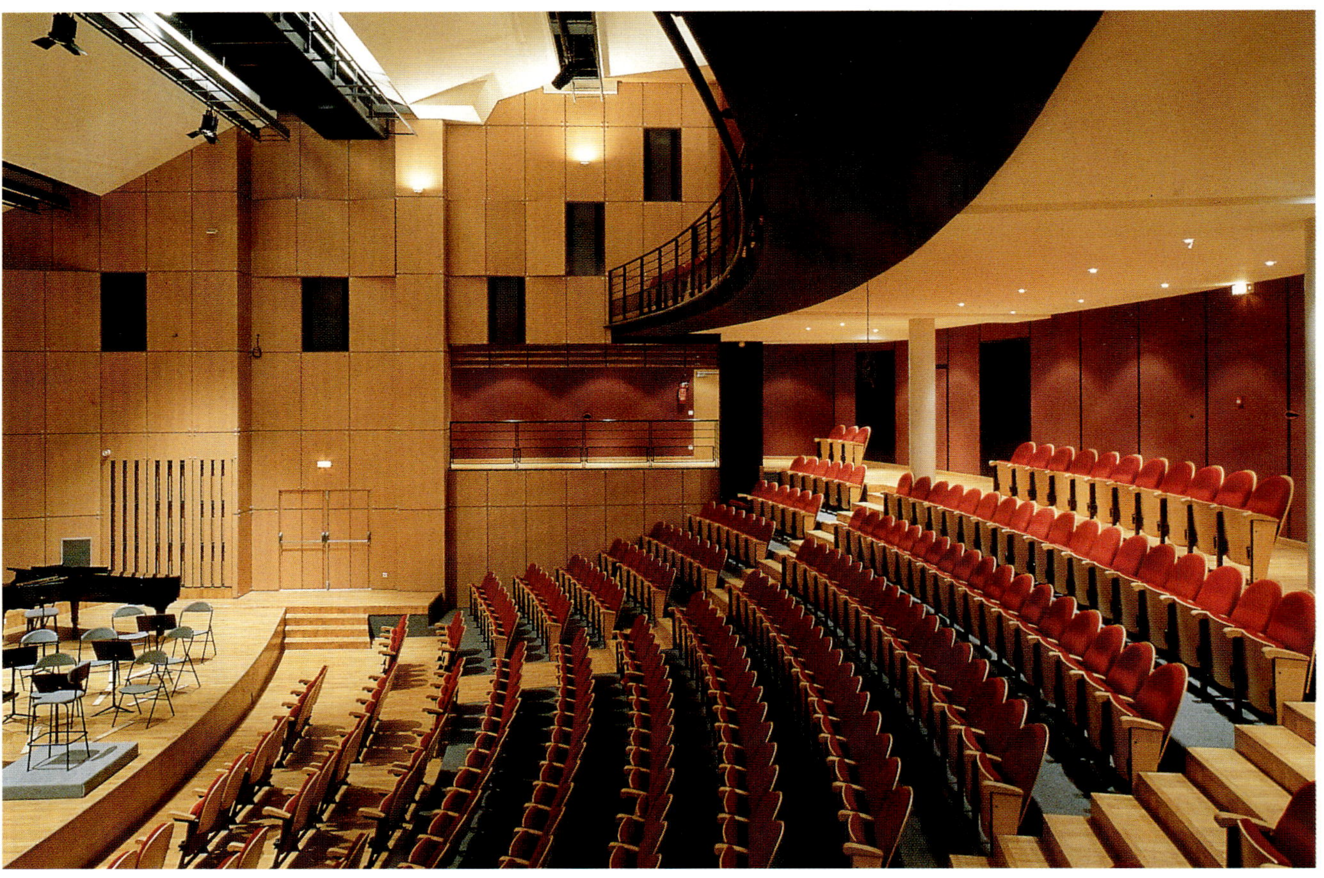

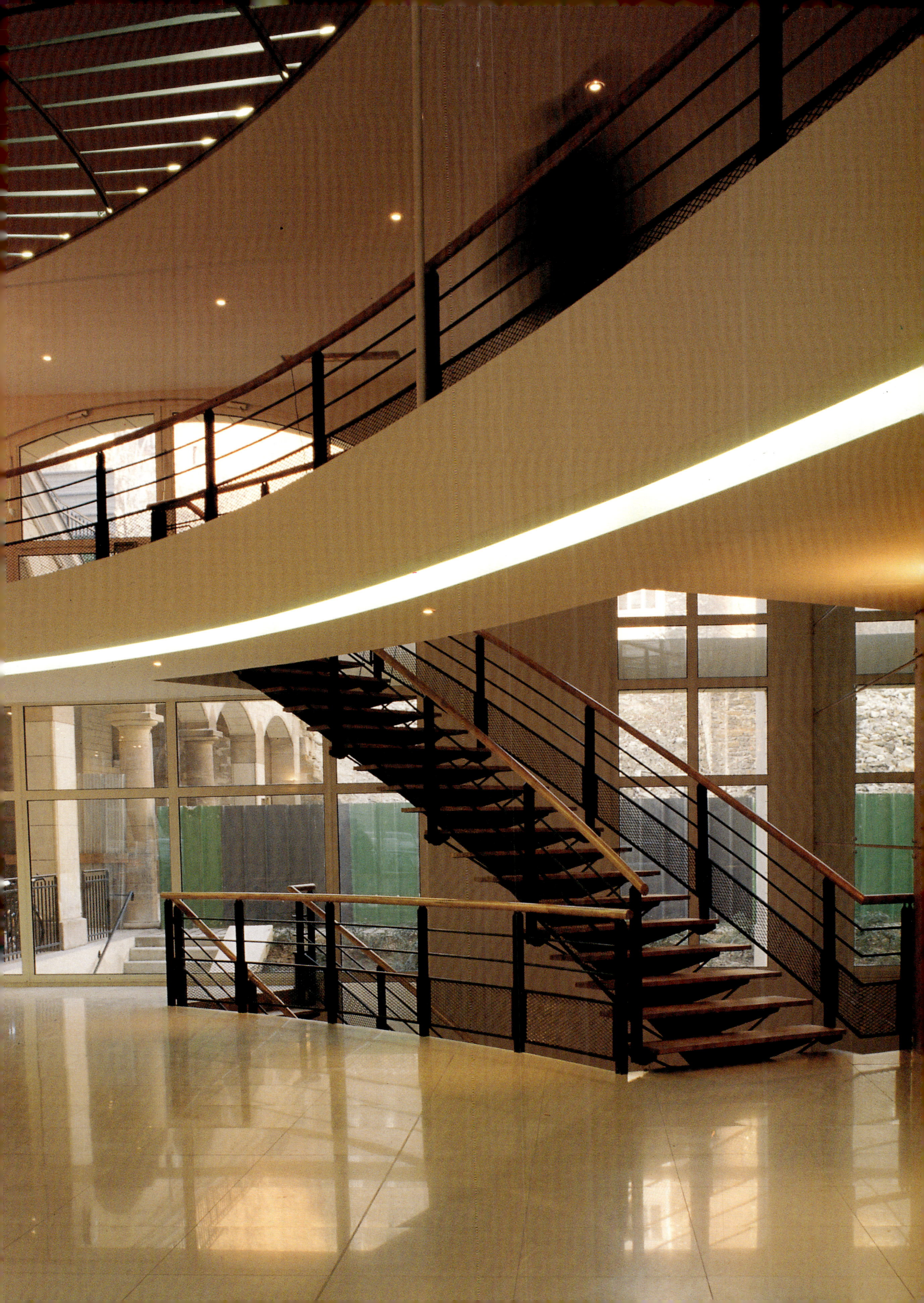

Projects in Progress

François Clouet High School, Tours

This vocational high school to the north of Tours was extended and restructured without interfering with or jeopardising the existing state of affairs. The entire complex is constructed around a series of low-level buildings spread across a park, which anyone would instinctively like to see extended due to how pleasant it is to wander through its grounds. This is the kind of situation we find on many university campuses.

The new administration building is an extension of the old facility, to which it is connected by a new hall.
The three buildings (two for ordinary day pupils and one for half-boarders) are designed to interact to create interesting external spaces in the form of a small sub-urban village.
The key points of the project may be summed up as a quality urban redevelopment program, which exalts the

natural qualities of the site on a rational basis without resorting to outmodish forms of Romantic landscaping, and an extremely modern new architectural design for the school backed up by an economically viable construction program.

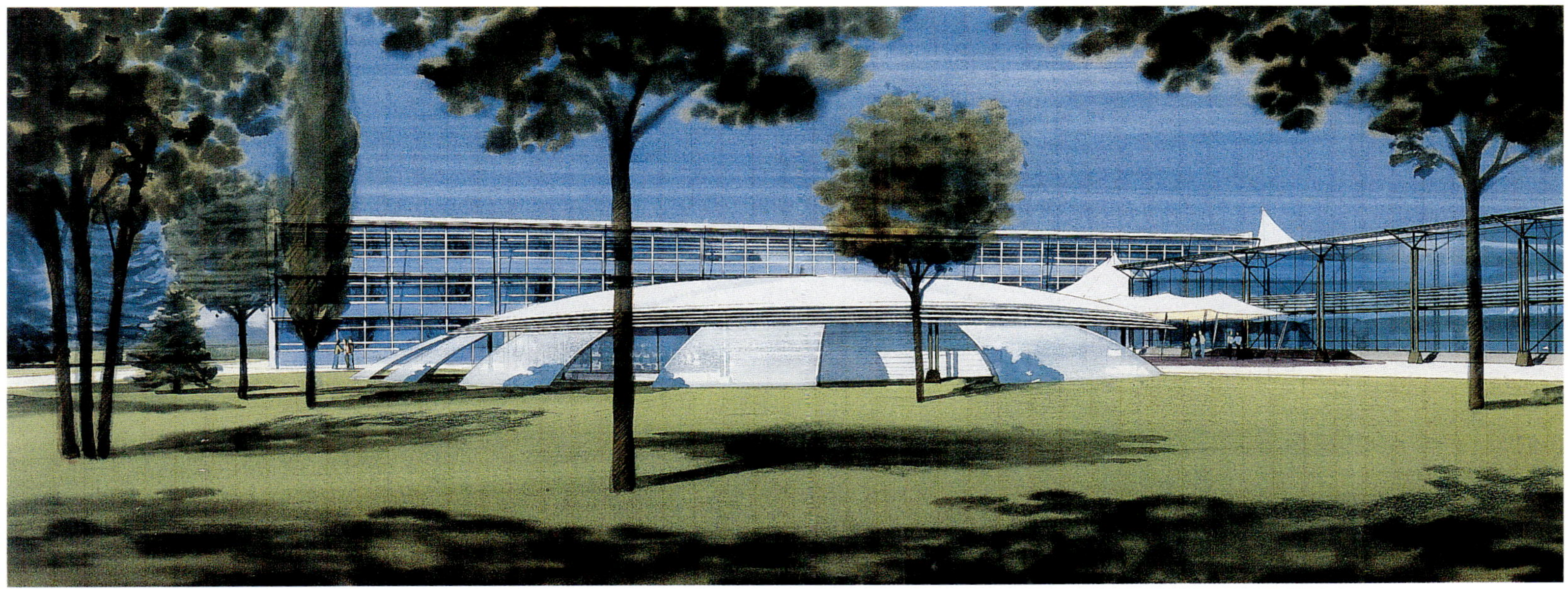

Perspective view of the school's entrance facade. Below, right, plan of the first floor and, left, plan of the second floor. The round building and the one on the right are new.

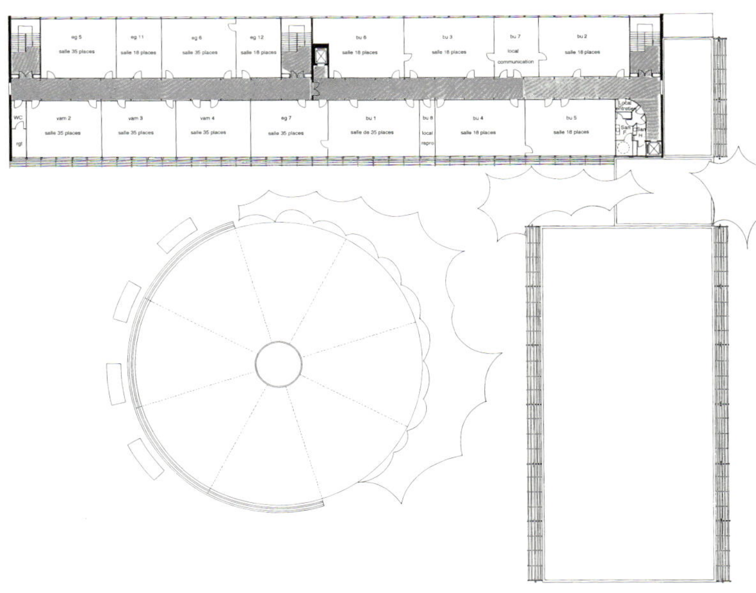

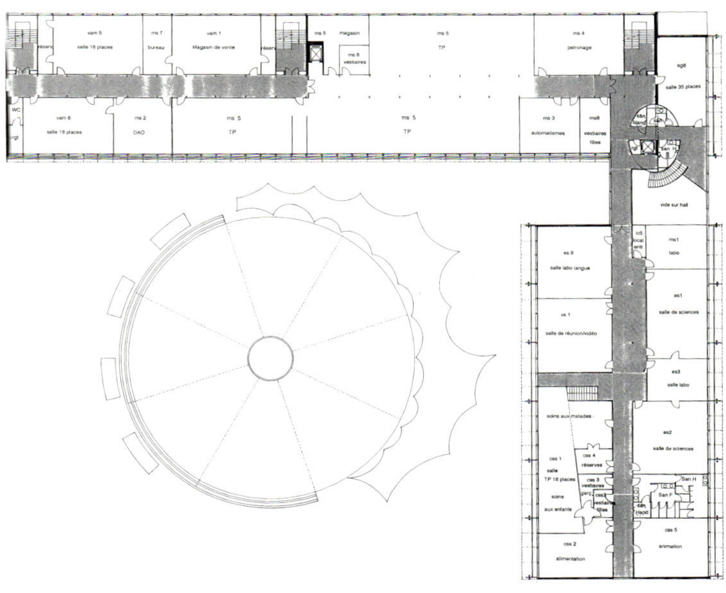

Hall of Finance, Evry

The new Hall of Finance will be a gateway to the Administration and Business district of the New Town. The building should structure the urban area by its striking presence. It should visually impose its own image on the surroundings. The site is not exciting: only a high unbroken line of buildings on one side and low black roofs on the other. The program included four departments in two building phases. The client pushed for autonomy throughout the various phases. It was also important to plan technical systems that would allow the financial services to evolve with time: flexibility and reserved free space were to be key factors in making efficient use of the building.

The project is designed in the form of two towers that rise up face-to-face across a pedestrian square. They will cause sufficient impact, through their form alone, on the existing environment. These two towers emerge from a socle that houses the public parts of the building. The different administration facilities occupy the towers themselves. The last level is occupied by official housing. The structure is supported by steel posts, not concrete shells, and has a large span to eliminate bearing points within the towers. Double ceilings distribute utilities. An open level allows for future extensions if necessary. A steel macro structure supports the towers. Wind bracing is guaranteed by the central circulation core. The outdoor elements of the structure are protected by paint guaranteed for twenty years without maintenance (hopefully). The envelope, facades and roofing, are durable and require little maintenance: lacquered aluminium, stainless steel, granite enamelled glass, clear glass.

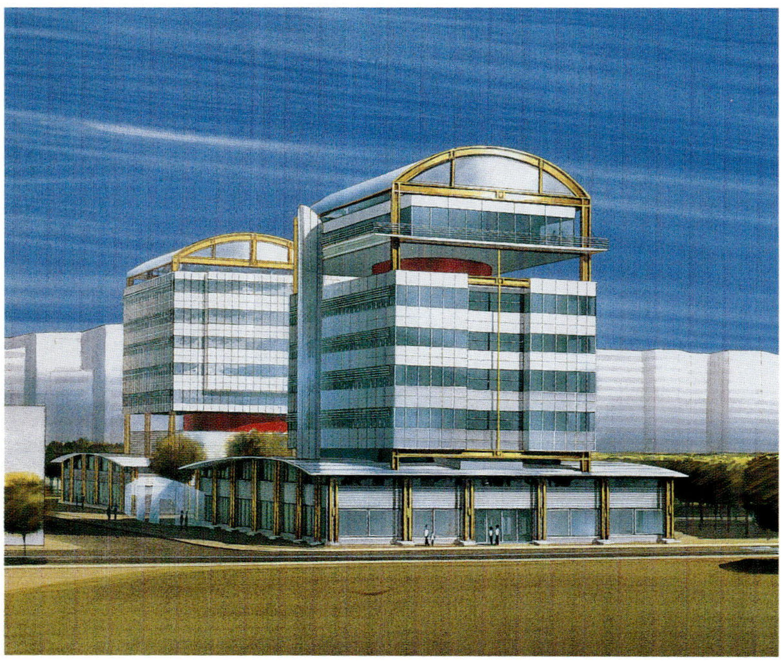

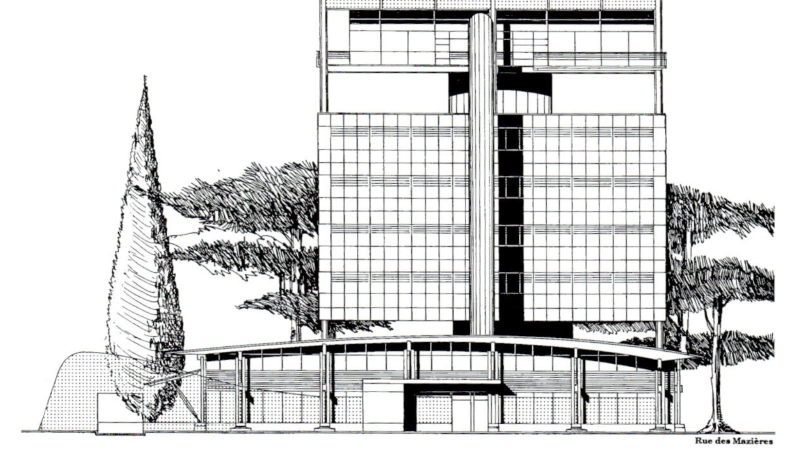

Above, perspective view and longitudinal section of the preliminary project for the Hall of Finance in Evry.

Building work began in October 1997. Belowe, plan of the first floor.

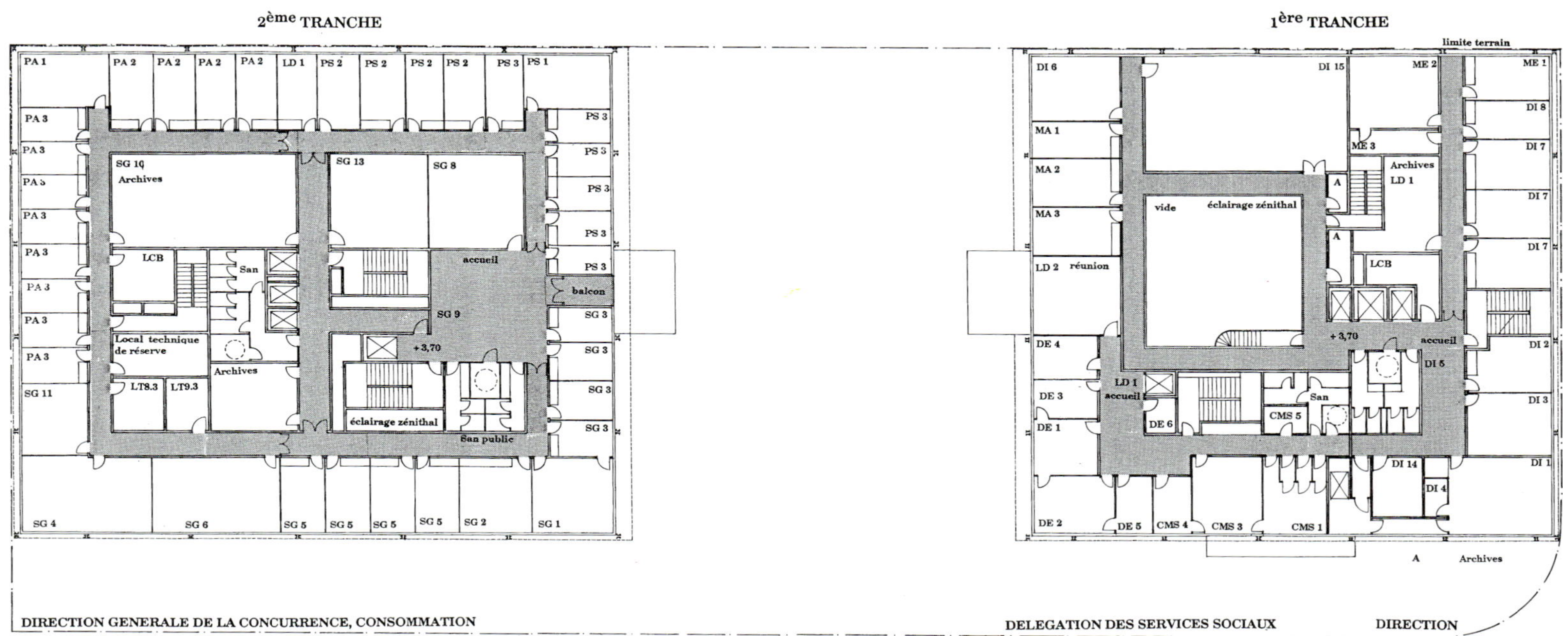

Sports Arena, Andrezieux-Bouthéon

The arena's three basic facilities - a basketball court, gymnastics hall and reception centre - could have been accommodated in three separate buildings. But the designers decided that this would not really have fitted in with the project's ambitious pretensions to create a powerful landmark in the surrounding neighborhood offering a variety of urban socio-cultural opportunities for the local community.

Despite the presence of a few quality buildings, the neighborhood has grown up on a rather random, interrupted basis, featuring an alternating combination of rather casual solid structures and empty voids which do not really define urban spaces or set up dialectical relations with the built environment. Finally, there are no real symbolic landmarks capable of drawing together the neighborhood in a comprehensible way for all its inhabitants.

These factors eventually led to the construction of one large imposing building, whose majestic forms are designed to powerfully embody the re-birth of this neighborhood and its projection into the future.

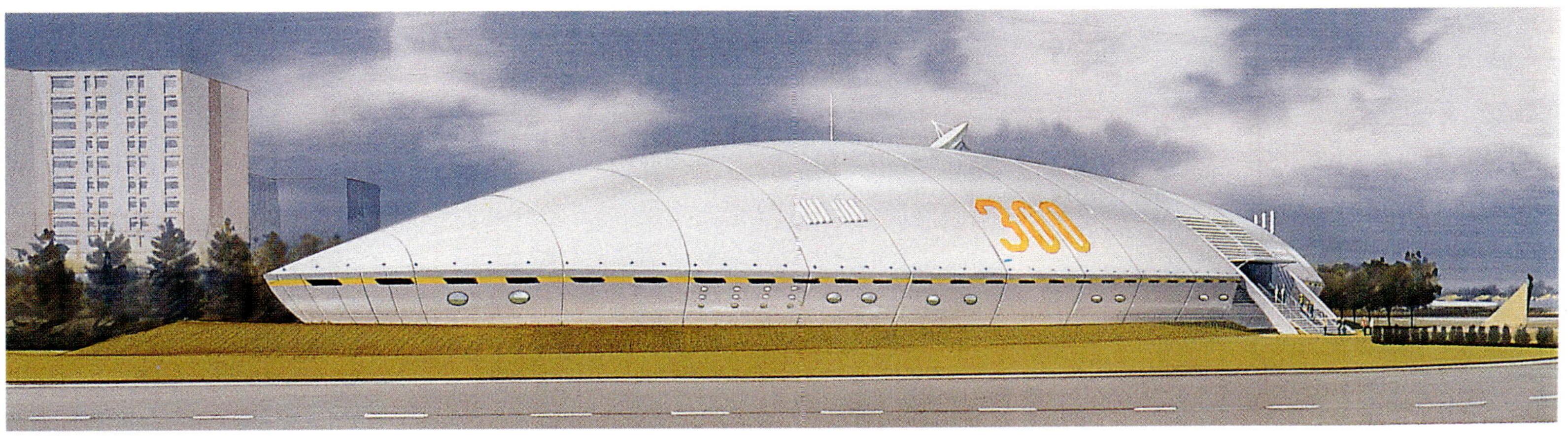

Rendering of the Sports Arena. Below, left, plan of the ground floor and, right, plan of the first floor.

Bottom of page, south-west elevation.

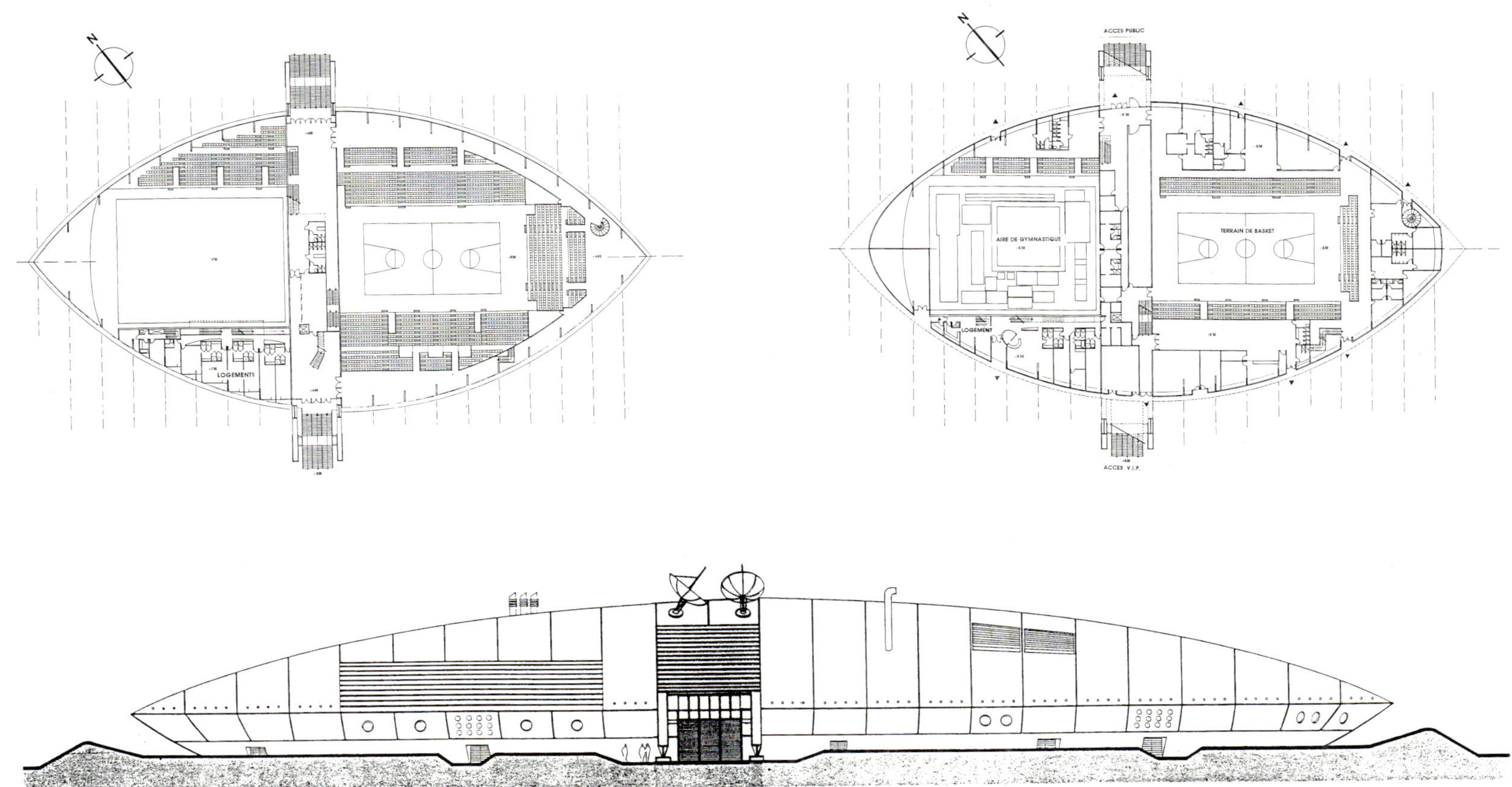

Toll Area, Boulogne-sur-Mer

This station is designed to shelter up to twenty-one different spots, although only thirteen will be built right away.
Its main structure is made of a series of metal arches placed parallel to the roadway; these arches are interconnected by light-weight reticular girders anchoring down the signals. A walkway runs along the entire length of the platform from the slope on the west side to the man-made embankment to the east of the station. This walkway will be reserved exclusively for staff.

The shelter is constructed out of two different types of roof: the roof over the motorway lanes is made of two translucent polyester/PVC membranes resting on two intermediate arches and running from one end of the walkway to the other; the walkway roof itself is also made of a canvas membrane, but the design is quite different.

Rain water is collected in two longitudinal gutters running along the edge of the roof and then down special pipes fitted in the arches.

The white-colored membranes, allowing a 16 percent diffusion of sunlight, are constructed out of a white mother-of-pearl structure.

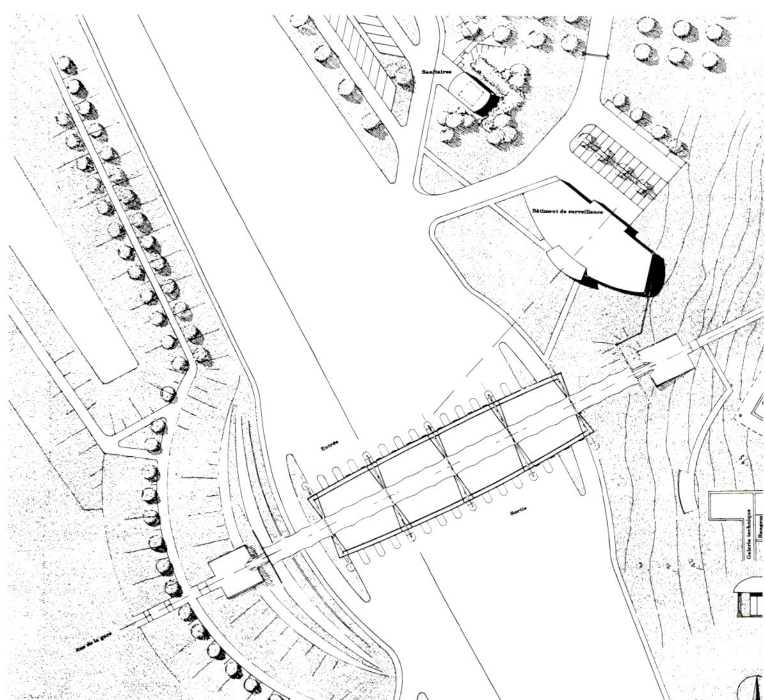

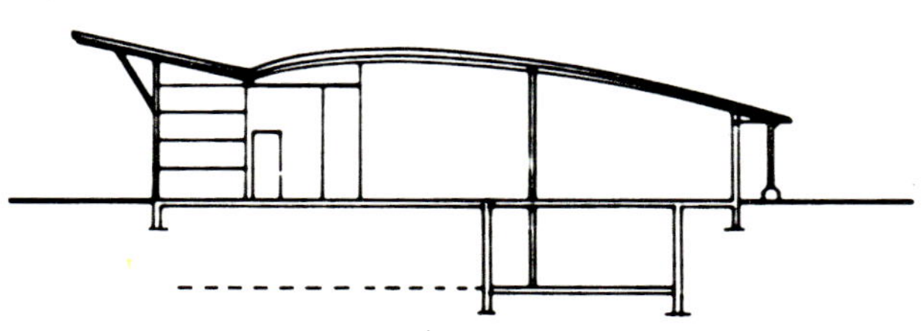

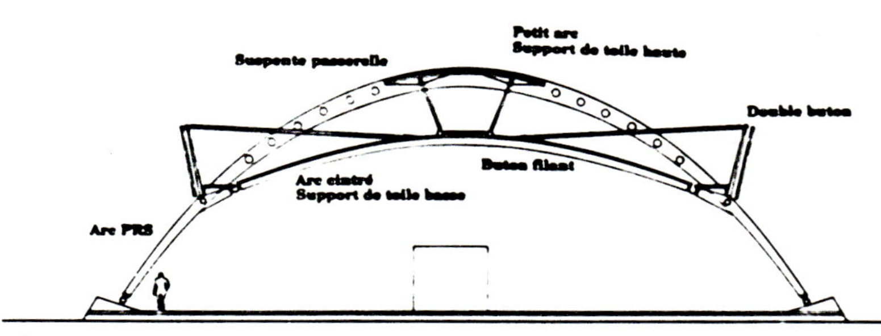

Above, site plan and sections of the control building and toll station.
Left and below, two views of the area.

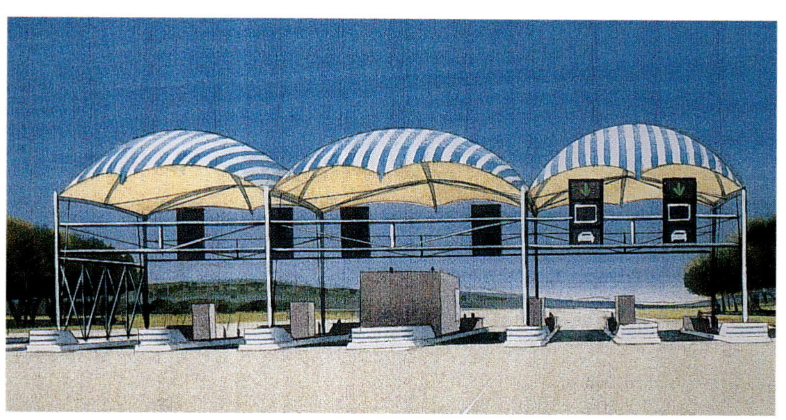

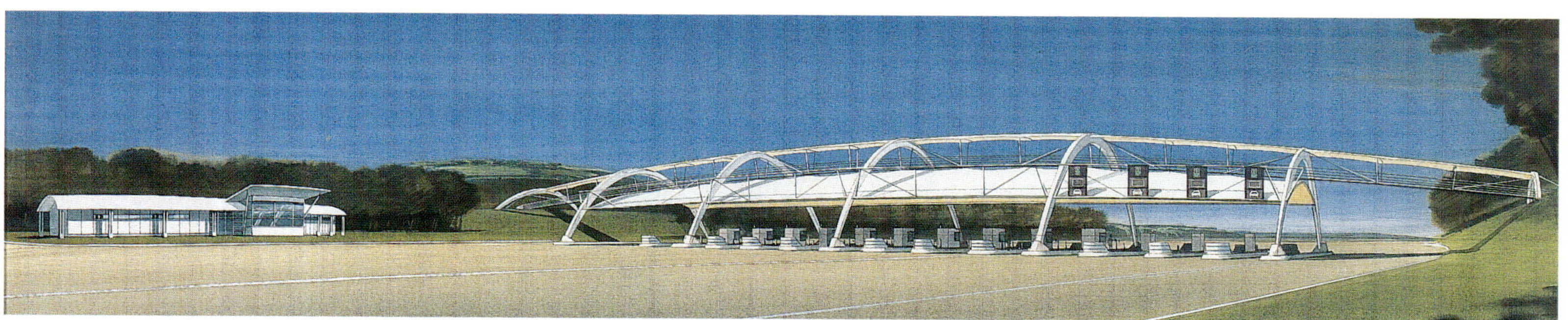

Toll Area, Souppe-sur-Loing

Two streamlined poles and two white-lacquered steel arches project across the motorway to attract motorists' attention to the toll area. Despite its function, this is, nevertheless, a quietly discrete design that does not detract from either the surrounding landscape or road signs; this is thanks mainly to the great finesse of the main structure and the transparency of the roof, smoothly designed out of translucent units that blend in unobtrusively with the surroundings.

Every section of the structure is ideally designed to enhance overall stability, drawing heavily on high-tech elements; the project is actually designed to be as flexible as possible, allowing the station to grow or change form in the future under the same basic roof.
The curved facade beneath the sloping pitch provides the surveillance building with a perfect view of the surroundings, while a large metal roof shelters the reception area.

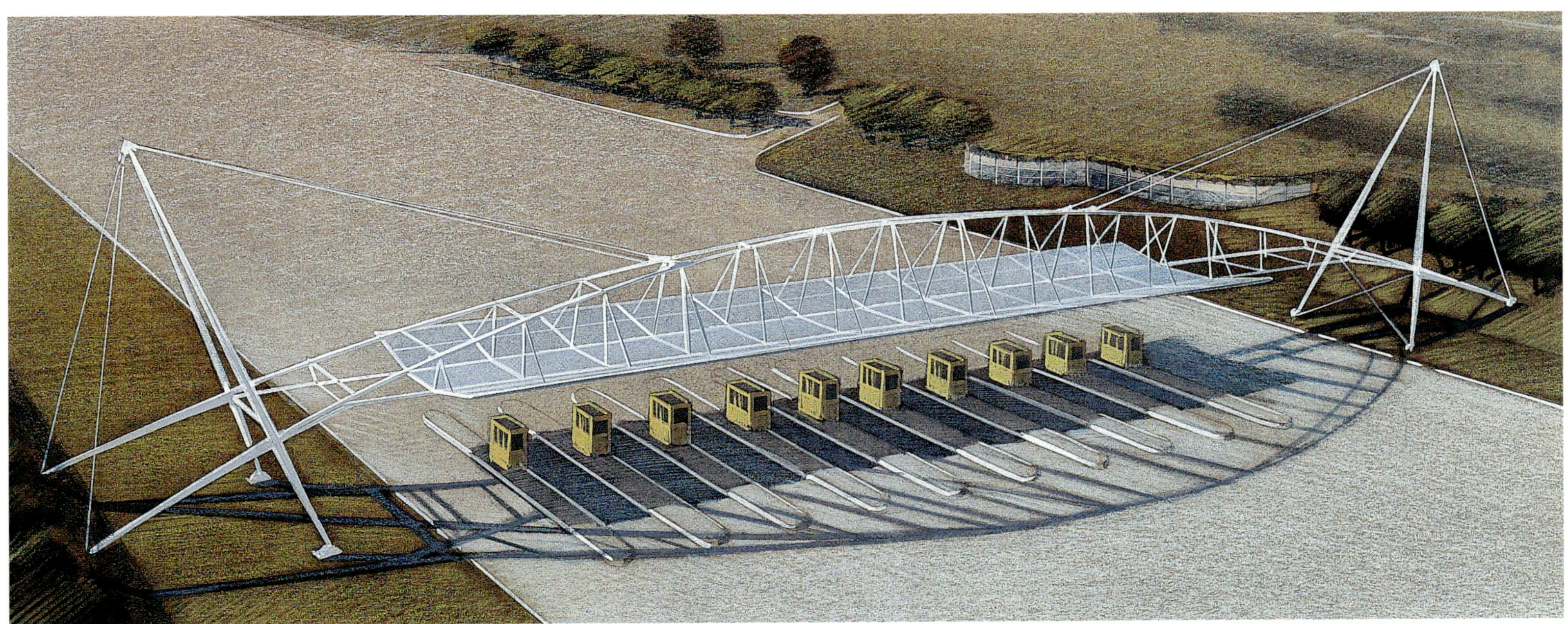

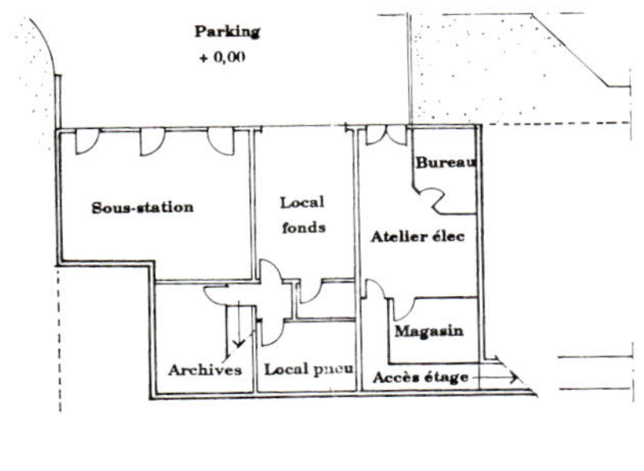

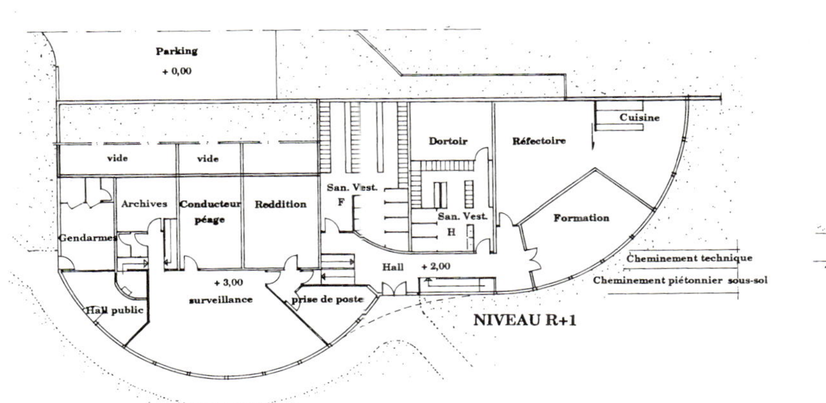

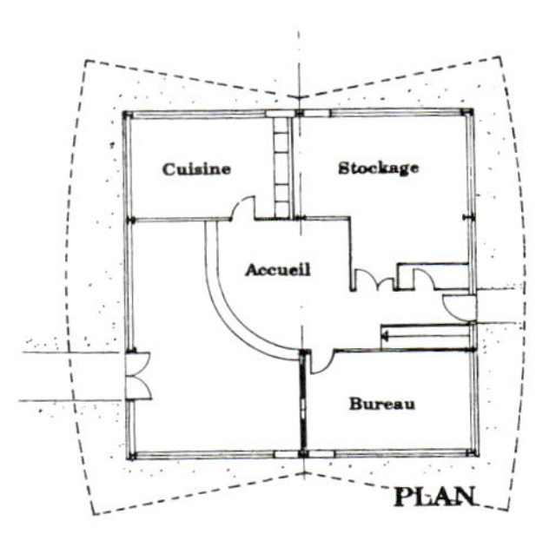

Top of page, perspective
view of the toll area.
Above plans of the
reception center
and control building.

André Maurois Boarding School, Limoges

First a path snaking through the countryside, then a spaceship ready to transport the pupils into the next century; these are the two key features of this highly stylised project designed to meet a brief aimed at transforming the old institute into a showcase for relaunching both the local neighborhood and its dull old school.

The path picks up the children from the roadside and leads them safely through to the school, at the same time providing a sort of signpost for the teaching facility. The path cleverly exploits the natural slope of the land. Architecturally speaking, the old building is drawn into the new construction which, in turn, blends in perfectly with the nearby avenue, simultaneously conjuring up the idea of a huge vessel.

The designers have explained why they opted for this design: "we wanted this building to be more than just a carefully gauged work of architecture that is nice to look at: it is also designed to embrace the year 2000 through futurist (in the broadest sense of the expression) morphological forms more reminiscent of a spaceship than a building. We expect the pupils to welcome this new school (their very own) with great pride and joy".

Rhetoric aside, there certainly has been a real attempt to break with the usual style of school buildings, as if to indicate that we must go beyond the present if we are to build a bright future (which actually lies in children's hands).

The important thing is that this should not be just a question of style but a radical re-thinking of the school as an institution and not just a building.

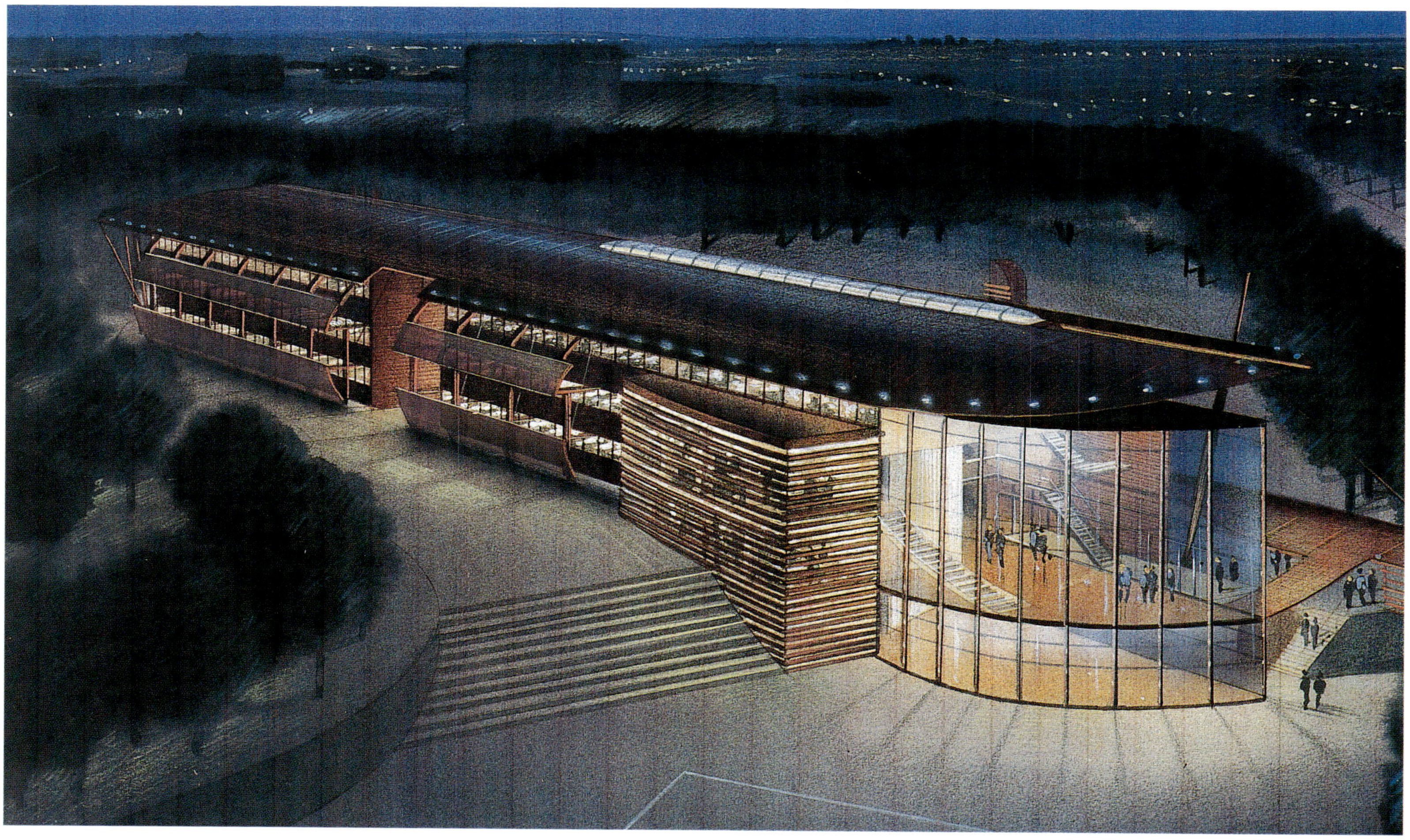

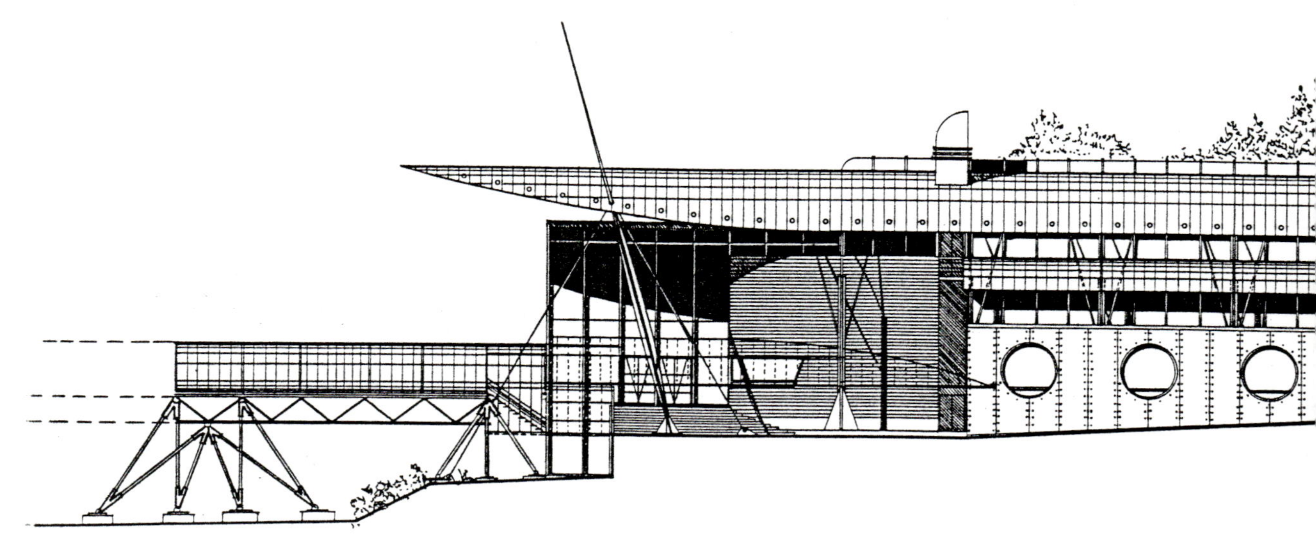

Opposite page, perspective view of the building used for teaching purposes and, below, south elevation.

This page, perspective view from the side of the school building and detail of the pedestrian path connected to the school entrance. Below, plans of the ground floor, first floor and second floor.

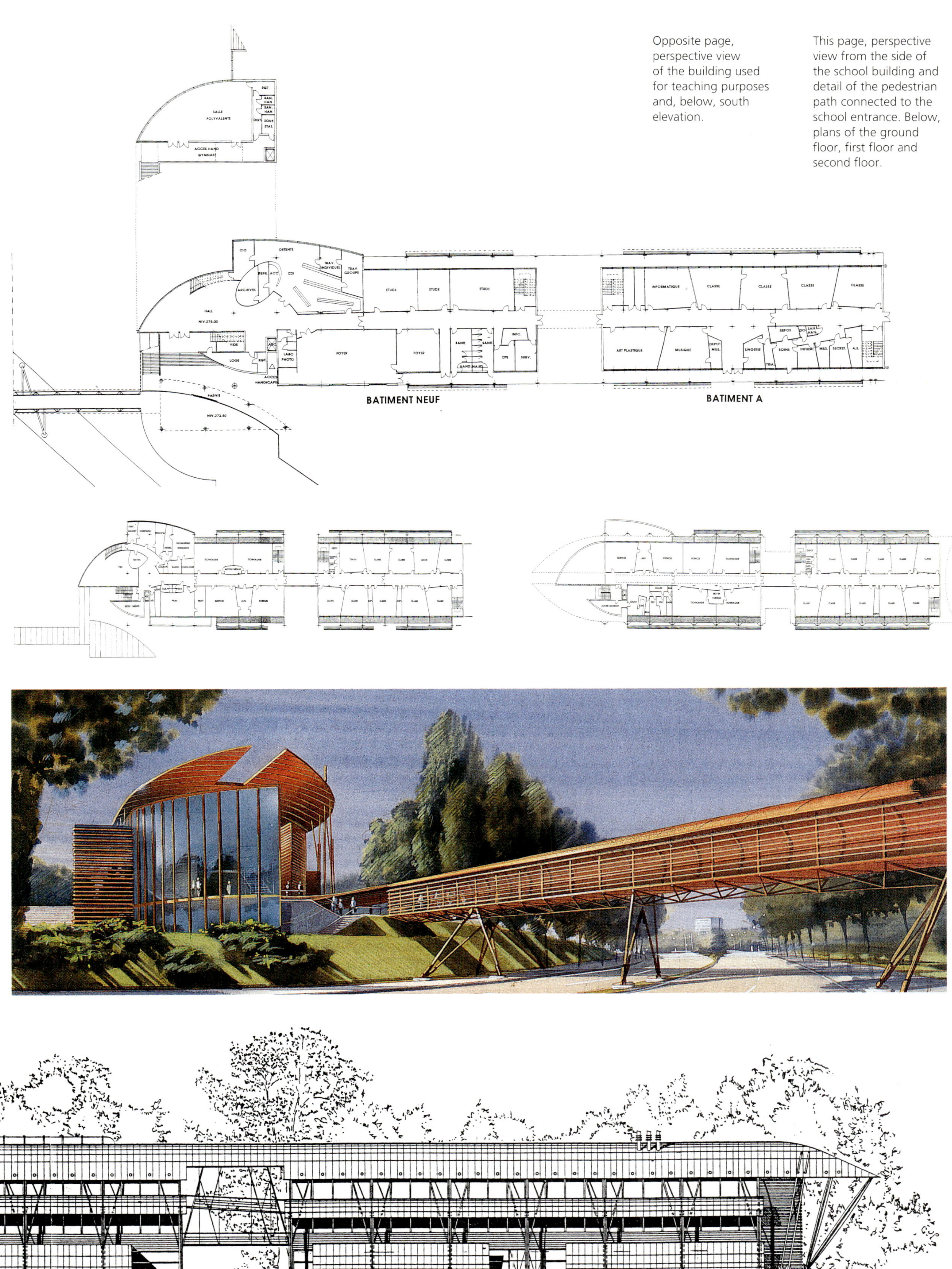
BATIMENT NEUF
BATIMENT A

List of works

Realisations

Hôtel de Finances, Evry
in progress

Lycée Franoçois Clouet, Tours
in progress

Lycée d'Enseignement Professionnel, Pleyben
in progress

Gares de Péage, Dordives/Cosne sul Loire
in progress

Gares de Péage, Amiens/Boulogne
in progress

Logements et Commerce, Orléan
in progress

Passerelles en KIT, Viêtnam
in progress

Logements, Evreux
in progress

Collège André Maurois, Limoges
in progress

Enveloppe de 200 Logements, Le Havre
1996

Logements, Saint Martin d'Hères
1996

Conservatoire Supérieur de Musique, Paris
1996

Remise à neuf Centre Régional
d'Informatique, Nemours
1996

Façade de la Résidence Universitarie,
Nanterre
1995

Logements la Vénérie, Montargis
1994

Cornservatoire de Musique, Sèvres
1994

Synagogue, Paris
1994

West Side, Suresnes
1994

Trois Immeubles Boulevard de Sébastopol,
Paris
1994

Extension/Réhabilitation Collège Henri
Durant, Meaux
1994

Extension/Réhabilitation Collège Albert
Camus, Meaux

1994
Extension/Réhabilitation Collège, Parc Frot
1994

Extension/Réhabilitation Collège, Montcornet
1994

Extension/Réhabilitation Collège 1200 "Les
Champs", Saint Etienne
1994

Logements "Amitié", Montreuil
1993

Atelier d'Architecture et de Style,
Issy les Moulineaux
1993

Hôtel de Ville, Gauchy
1992

Salle de Gymnastique de Compétitions,
Montargis
1992

Etude de Faisaisabilité Rehabilitation Air
France, Paris
1992

Logements "Kronos", Nantes
1991

Les Jardins de l'Amérique Latine, Paris
1991

Centre d'Etude et de Développement
de Sollac, Montataire
1991

Hotel Primevère, Givors
1991

Siége Häagen Dazs, Boulogne Billancourt
1991

Logements Marcel Dassault,
Boulogne Billancourt
1990

Centre Technique Municipal, Sèvres
1990

Hôtel de la Poste, Montargis
1990

Logements "Saturne III", Givors
1989

Siège Dow Chemical, Boulogne Billancourt
1989

Logements Grande Rue, Sèvres
1988

Logements "Le Castel Eiffel", Dijon
1987

Palais de Justice, Bobigny
1986

Gymnase, Voisin le Bretonneux
1985

Centre d'Activités / Passerelle, Saint Herblain
1985

Projects
Logements à Qualité et coûts maîtrisés
LQCM, Montargis / Suresnes / Boulogne
1996

Bureau des Syndicats Renault, Aubevoye
1996

UFR-STAPS, Orléan
1996

Palais des Sports, Andrezieux-Bouthéon
1997

Maison de l'Avocat, Bobigny
1996

Ecole de Musique, Carrières sur Seine
1996

Centre d'Entretien Souillac,
Autoroute du Sud de la France
1996

Gymnase et Salle de Danse, Puteaux
1996

Cogénération, Chevilly Larue/L'Hay les Roses
1996

Réhabilitation/Extension Lycée Hauptmann,
Saint Etienne
1995

Gymnase, Le Bouscat
1995

Eglise Paul IV, Sophia Antipolis
1995

Conservatoire Municipal de Musique
et de Dans, Colornbes
1995

Institut Universitaire et Technologique,
Tremblay
1995

Foyer/Salle d'Instruction Militaire/Salle
de Musique, Mont Valérien Suresnes
1995

ETAP Hôtel, Viry Chatillon
1995

Lycée Professionnel Paul Langevin, Waziers
1995

Collège Jean Maceé, Clichy
1995

Eglise, Rome
1994

Passerelle sous le Pont de Choisy
1994

Gymnase, Fontenay
1994

Musée de l'Espace, Les Mureaux
1994

Palais de Justice, Montreau
1994

Collège C. Pierne, Metz
1994

Collège, Aulnay
1994

Salle de Spectacles et de Loisirs, Romans
1993

Ecole Nationale Supérieur de la Statistique
et de l'Administration Economique,
Marne la Vallée
1993

Hôtel, La Foux d'Allos
1992

Gare du Val, Rennes
1992

Centre Technique Municipal, Valbonne
1992

Centre de Réalisation des Prototypes
et Batiment
1992

MEG-MA, LEE de Renault Guyancourt
1992

Conseil Général des Hauts de Seine, Nanterre
1992

Institut Universitaire et Technologique, Evry
1992

Collége la Clè de Saint Pierre, Elancourt
1992

Gymnase, Questembert
1992

Centre de Conditionnement Postal
International, Aéroport Charles de Gaulle
1991

Siège Social Europe, Kongsberg
1991

Lycée, Montargis
1991

Salle de Conférences Saturne-SOLLAC,
Dunkerque
1991

Maison de Retraite, Villemandeur
1991

49 Maisons, Dardilly
1990

Résidence Médicalisée pour Personnes Agée,
Saint Witz

Office Européen des Brevets
1989

Nouveau Quartier de la Faye, Fribourg
1989

Reestructuration d'un Quartier Existant,
Bruxelles
1989

Entrepôts Saint Pierre, Les Elboeuf
1988

Conservatoire de Musique du XIXème, Paris
1988

Biographies

Eric Dubosc

Born in Montargis, France
on September 13th, 1943.

1970 Bachelor of Architecture

1996 Consulting Architect - Ministry
of the Equipment, France President
of the Architecture Industry Club

President of the MARCH Commission -
EUROPEAN COILCOATING ASSOCIATION
(French Group)

Professor of Construction, Ecole
d'Architecture de Lille, France.

Marc Landowski

Born in Paris, France on March 23rd, 1944.

1969 Bachelor of Architecture

1974-1979 Consulting Architect - Var
Départment, France

1979-1981 Member of the Architecture
Director's Office in Paris

1994-1995 Visiting Professor, Ecole Spéciale
d'Architecture de Paris.

1996 Member of the C.S.T.B. Consulting
Committee

Consulting Architect - Issy Les Moulineaux,
France

Eric Dubosc, Marc Landowski, Jean Pierre Conqui, Jimmy Ratsimandresy,
Anna Kononowicz, Christophe Roy, Raquel Milagres, Nathalie Barbier, Elisabeth
Cambillard, Andrea Mueller, Scarlett Flegeo, Jacques Sanselme, Jacqueline Berger,
Karine Piaut, Monica Alexandrescu, Nicole Saikalis, Bertrand Bajart.

Principal Collaborators 1997

Architects
Monica Alexandrescu
Bertrand Bajart
Nathalie Barbier
Elisabeth Cambillard
Jean-Pierre Conqui
Scarlett Flegeo
Anna Kononowicz
Raquel Milagres
Andrea Mueller
Christophe Roy
Nicole Saikalis

Draughtsman
Jimmy Ratsimandresy

Photographer
Dalhiette Sucheyre

Designer
Jacques Sanselme

Architecture Student
Karine Piaut

Graphic Designer
Fabrice Alberti

Model Designer
Elisabeth Mathieu

Secretary
Jacqueline Berger